Family Connections

Family
Connections

An Introduction to Family Studies

DAVID H. J. MORGAN

Polity Press

First published in 1996 by Polity Press in association with
Blackwell Publishers Ltd.

2 4 6 8 10 9 7 5 3 1

Editorial office:
Polity Press
65 Bridge Street
Cambridge CB2 1UR, UK

Marketing and production:
Blackwell Publishers Ltd
108 Cowley Road
Oxford OX4 1JF, UK

Published in the USA by
Blackwell Publishers Inc.
238 Main Street
Cambridge, MA 02142, US

A CIP catalogue record for this book is available from the British Library.

Library of Congress Cataloging-in-Publication Data
Morgan, D. H. J.
    Family connections : an introduction to family
studies / David H.J. Morgan.
        p.   cm.
    Includes bibliographical references (p.) and index.
    ISBN 0–7456–1078–1 (hb : acid-free paper). --
ISBN 0–7456–1079–X (pb : acid-free paper)
    1. Family.   I. Title.
HQ728.M5729   1996
306.85--dc20   96–4124
                                                  CIP

This book is printed on acid-free paper.

Typeset in 10½/12pt Times by Photoprint, Torquay, Devon.
Printed in Great Britain by Hartnolls Ltd, Bodmin, Cornwall.

Contents

Acknowledgements

As with my previous two books, I owe a special debt to Janet Finch for her constant support and encouragement. In addition to this general support she also provided some detailed and helpful comments for the chapter on care. I am also grateful to Fiona Devine for reading and commenting upon the chapter dealing with stratification. A big thank-you also to Sandra Irving who tidied up and printed the final version of the typescript and to Gill Motley at Polity Press for her patience.

Early versions of some of these chapters were presented at seminars in various places. I am especially grateful to the gentle criticism and positive feedback that I received from colleagues in Manchester, Oslo and the British Sociological Association's 'Family Study Group'. I am also grateful to the BSA for allowing me, together with Liz Stanley, to edit *Sociology* for three years. This may have served to delay the completion of this book but it also put me in touch with a wide range of research and ideas within the British sociological community.

Unless otherwise stated, most of the references in this book deal with modern Britain.

Introduction

Fragments of Autobiography

During my two years of National Service I began to draw up a list of books that I intended to read once I returned to civilian life. I forgot about this list in the excitement of demobilization and becoming a student at Hull University. I began the B.Sc. (Economics) course, chosing, at the last minute, to take sociology as a special subject. Very rapidly, under the influence of Peter Worsley and Gordon Horobin, I realized that it was sociology, rather than economics, which excited me. Shortly after graduation, I rediscovered the list that I had compiled in the billet in Germany. It included such titles as *Family and Kinship in East London* and *Coal Is Our Life*, books that had been on my reading list during my first undergraduate year.

One way of reading this anecdote would be to claim that I 'always' had an interest in sociology in general and the sociology of the family in particular. More likely, however, this is a story of drift, into sociology at first and later into the sociology of the family and, later, into the sociology of gender. What needs to be remembered, however, is that the two sociology books on my list constituted key texts in the analysis of British society at that time. Such studies were 'community studies' and in such studies family and domestic relationships played a key part. Insofar as there were more specific references to 'family' on the sociology lists of that time it was in the context of such community studies together with one or two other pieces such as Titmuss's essay on the changing status of women and

McGregor's study of divorce in England. I was vaguely aware of Parsons at the time but felt reasonably satisfied that he had been demolished by C. Wright Mills.

Family matters entered into various pieces of my research, firstly a study of the social and educational backgrounds of Anglican bishops and, secondly, an observational study of women workers in a factory in northern England. But it was another near accident that brought about my more focused interest in family sociology. One side-effect of the devaluation of the pound sterling under one of the Wilson governments was the increase in the price of American textbooks. A group of colleagues, sitting around in a small common-room in Manchester, decided that we should write our own text. Peter Worsley took on the task of editing what became *Introducing Sociology*, with its various editions and associated readers. During this preliminary meeting, after a longish silence, I volunteered to have a go at the chapter on the family.

One of the aims of this particular text was to show the links between theoretical debates and substantive areas. Thus the chapter on 'the family' was designed to highlight some of the debates around functionalism. Hence, there was some attempt to think about the family in theoretical terms (I got to read Parsons at last!) rather than simply to provide a set of statements about domestic life in Britain at the time.

As a consequence of this rather haphazard decision, I began teaching courses on the sociology of the family first in the UK in my hometown of Manchester and then, for a year, in Canada. I became aware of the developing Women's Liberation Movement in North America and the radical psychoanalytical approaches associated with R.D. Laing and David Cooper. In reading these works I sensed a gulf between these accounts of family relationships and those which had, up to that point, appeared on my reading lists. My *Social Theory and the Family* (1975) was an attempt to explore this gap between mainstream sociological accounts and the more critical discussions. The book attracted a fair amount of comment and, insofar as I became identified with anything, it was with the sociology of the family.

However, things were not standing still. The feminist movement was gaining in influence within sociology and there were exciting developments within Marxism and structuralism. My course at Manchester on the sociology of the family was retitled 'Sex Roles and the Family'. It soon became clear that it was the former rather than the latter which attracted the attention of students and the course disappeared – to be replaced, shortly after, by a much more overtly feminist course taught by women. I continued to introduce family topics into a course entitled 'The Sociology of Modern Britain'. However, since then and until quite recently my teaching interests tended to diverge from my research and writing interests.

In discussing these experiences with colleagues from other universities, I found that they were not all that unusual. A study group within the British Sociological Association on family and kinship gradually came to focus upon issues of gender and women within the family and, eventually, gave way to a study group on sexual divisions. This study group has recently been revived as the Family Study Group. There was a feeling that the sociology of the family had become somewhat marginalized, at least in Britain. The coherent and wide-ranging theoretical frameworks of Parsonian, and later Marxist, functionalism gave way to more diffuse critical accounts focusing upon patterns of subordination, exploitation and oppression within and beyond the household. Developments in theory (apart from feminist theory) seemed to have little time for the apparent trivia of domestic life. Family sociology was certainly not sexy and might have been more than a little politically suspect.

It is likely that many sociological sub-areas flourish on a certain amount of paranoia and a claim that a particular area has been marginalized or ignored is a familiar first move in an attempt to shift that area more centre stage. Nevertheless, it is possible to find some evidence for this particular claim of marginalization, at least up to the early 1980s. For example, in 1980 the British Sociological Association celebrated thirty years in a special annual conference at the University of Lancaster. In all the retrospective and prospective discussions there was not a single paper dedicated to the sociology of the family, a fact borne out by the three-volume *Transactions* (Abrams and Lewthwaite, 1980) and the single volume that was commercially published (Abrams et al., 1981). In a paper on the neglect of Freud within British sociology we find the following statement: 'In this culture there is no room for a major theoretical analysis of the family' (Bocock, 1980: 487). The author went on to make a partial exception of feminist writings in general and the work of Juliet Mitchell in particular. The volume of transactions contained two or three papers dealing with feminist or gender issues, mainly in relation to the discipline of sociology as a whole. The commercially produced volume contained one of the most influential papers dealing with the feminist perspective and British sociology (M. Stacey, 1981).

Another indication of the status of family sociology at about the same time may be found in a survey entitled *Recent British Sociology* (Eldridge, 1980). There are some fleeting references to family studies but by far the largest section of the book is taken up with studies of work and industrial sociology. Other topics treated include stratification, urban sociology, deviance and religion. Eldridge does in fact refer to a sense of relative deprivation on the part of family sociologists and then goes on to quote Allen and Barker who are, in fact, making the point about *gender* relationships (1980: 32). Something of the same sort of muddle is to be found in the bibliography where family studies are to be found under the general heading 'sex, gender, generation'.

Superficially, the picture did not look all that different nearly ten years later when the *British Journal of Sociology* had a special issue attempting some kind of 'state of the art ' assessment for the profession and its specialist areas. Once again, we find no article dealing with the sociology of the family, although Oakley's contribution on women's studies deals quite extensively with issues of family relationships and households (Oakley, 1989). Gender issues also appear very much to the fore in Crompton's article on class theory and gender (Crompton, 1989). It would be tempting, therefore, to argue that these two landmarks suggest that nothing changed during the intervening period and that the sociology of the family remained at the margin of British sociology. This would be misleading. It is part of the argument of this book that, during the period roughly defined by the 1980s, family sociology developed partly as a subject in its own right but even more so as a crucial element in some of the key areas within British sociology as a whole.

Family and Community

In my early acquaintance with sociology, 'family and community' seemed to be yoked together like Siamese twins. The linkage was made explicit, of course, in the first, and probably the most famous, of the Bethnal Green studies (Young and Willmott, 1962) but the general usage was wider than that. If you wanted to refer a student to work on the British family you would cite community studies. In Frankenberg's overview of such studies (Frankenberg, 1966) you can find relatively few separate or explicit treatments of family relationships; rather they tend to be woven into the studies of communities as a whole.

Whilst the concept of community and the focus on community studies came to be subjected to detailed criticism from the 1960s onward, it is important to remember some of the merits of this close identification of family and community. First, the reader is encouraged to think about family relationships in a wider context of overlapping ties of family, kindred, friends and neighbours. In institutional terms this entailed a willingness to see continuities between work and non-work, home and workplace, the public and the private. In its purer form, these overlapping sets of ties and relationships were to be located at one end of Frankenberg's 'morphological continuum' (1966). In a more urbanized context, it became possible, as he reminded us, to write a study of Bethnal Green that focused largely on relationships of neighbourhood and family to the exclusion, say, of an equally detailed study of work or political relationships. In one sense, this might be seen as the beginnings of the 'eclipse of community', although it could also be seen as the solidifying of links between family and community, albeit within a narrower ambit. Family and kinship relations became the chief, if not the sole, carrier of the idea of community or of a sense of locality.

However, community studies came to be seen, in some quarters at least, as somewhat nostalgic recreations of a way of life that was about to be lost or as the inappropriate application of social anthropological techniques and concerns to more urbanized, more industrialized and more mobile societies. The study of family relationships became separate from other sets of relationships. There was a focus on marital relationships and on parenting and socialization. Class became a source of difference *within* family relationships rather than a continuing and changing set of experiences woven around ties of family and locality. A variety of terms were elaborated to explain or describe this separation of the family, and family studies, from other areas of social life: privatization, the development of loose-knit networks, the relatively isolated nuclear family and so on. While the concept of community appeared to lose ground, the way appeared open for a more systematic focus on family relationships.

However, in marked contrast to the United States, there was, in Britain, little sign of the development of family studies. Possibly the supposed unit of study, the household-based family, looked too small, perhaps too dull for detailed, theoretically rich study. Whatever the reason, it was this unit, detached from wider ties of kinship and community, that became the focus of critical attention from figures as diverse as the social anthropologist Edmund Leach to the radical psychoanalyst, David Cooper. However, there seemed to be little to attract the sociologist, especially given the intellectual excitement to be found in macro-theory, new versions of Marxism, debates around stratification, critical studies of deviance and so on. When more critical attention did come to be turned on to family relationships it was from the perspective of a developing feminist analysis.

The Impact of Marxism

During the period covered in the first section of this introduction, a variety of Marxisms made their impact within and outside sociology. My period at Hull University (1957–62) coincided with the development of journals such as *Universities and Left Review*, *The New Reasoner* and, eventually, the early issues of *New Left Review*. The later period of the 1970s was also one in which concerns were expressed about the supposed influence of Marxism on British sociology (Gould, 1977). It is worth stressing, however, that the impact of Marxism was never as direct or as pervasive as the more right-wing critics maintained and, indeed, the relationships between Marxisms and sociologies were more likely to be characterized by mutual suspicion and non-comprehension (Sklair, 1981).

Very simplistically, the theoretical impact of Marxist theory could be summarized under three or four overlapping headings.

1   'The domestic labour debate'. This entailed a recognition of the importance of domestic labour within capitalism and an attempt to assess its wider theoretical significance. The chief impact of this debate was, possibly, the beginnings of a recognition of the domestic sphere in the analysis of economic life and the sharper recognition of gender as a strand linking the public and the private. However, this latter influence was probably more the result of more explicitly feminist interventions into the debate.
2   A stress on the family as an 'ideological state apparatus'. A concern with the apparent failure of mature capitalist societies to develop revolutionary potential and the apparent incorporation of the working classes into these societies led to a focus on those structures and institutions that provided for ideological domination.

Althusser's original account showed how the 'education/family couple' replaced the earlier 'religion/family couple' as being central in this process of ideological domination through the shaping and creation of subjects (Althusser, 1971). Later refinements were to include psychoanalytical dimensions exploring the deeper structures of these systems of domination.

3   A focus on the processes whereby the public/private split developed and how family, marriage and domestic life became strongly linked to the core values of privacy and intimacy. In this version, the family under capitalism became a central life project serving both as a compensation for the deprivations of the growing impersonalities and alienations of an advanced capitalist society and a means whereby, by default, the public worlds of business and politics could continue unchallenged (Zaretsky, 1982).

4   A focus upon the interactions between the family and the state, this time not so much in terms of ideology but more in terms of the ways in which the welfare functions of the state depended upon and reinforced particular models of family living and the sexual divisions of domestic labour (Dickinson and Russell, 1986).

It can be seen that there is considerable potential here for the development of a theoretical perspective which could serve as a stimulus to more detailed work. With some exceptions (especially the more historically informed discussions), it cannot be said that this potential was realized. There were various possible reasons for this. First, the family was never the main focus of concern within Marxist analysis. The chief areas of concern were classes, the state and ideology; the family was a piece in this jigsaw but had little significance outside it. Second, the analysis tended to remain at a macro-level so that, in many accounts, the analysis stopped at the boundaries of the domestic unit. The family was a unit or an institution within a wider system. Indeed, the label 'Marxist-functionalism' came to be used to characterize this mode of analysis. Third, the concern was to map what families under capitalism shared or had in common. Sources of difference or variation were of less significance unless these corresponded to broad class-based categories. Finally, in most of these accounts the family was a dependent variable. Apart from those accounts which stressed the potential strengths in, particularly, working-class families, the emphasis was on the impact of wider structures and systems upon the family.

As with the mainstream or bourgeois sociologies, these various Marxist accounts were surpassed by or incorporated into feminist analyses. Patriarchy, even where the word might not be used, became the thread that linked issues of domestic labour, ideology and subjectivity, the privatization of the home and the various interplays between the family and the state. Unlike the more gender-neutral Marxist accounts, feminist analyses not only provided a critical understanding of domestic relations but also generated an impressive roll-call of empirical studies, sociological and historical.

At the same time, the credentials of Marxism became challenged and eroded, partly as a result of critiques within the wider scholarly community but more impressively and decisively following the collapse of states that had owed at least some formal allegiance to Marxism. Yet the issues identified above have not gone away. A sociology of family relations still requires accounts that are historically informed, that allow for the interplays between the macro- and the micro-levels, that explore linkages between a whole range of inequalities and that allow for the possibility of change through human agency. Whether such an approach, or set of approaches, will be called Marxist or not is perhaps not as significant as the identification of a continuing need for such an approach.

The Impact of Feminism

As already noted, the volume marking the thirtieth anniversary of the British Sociological Association included an influential article by Margaret Stacey (M. Stacey, 1981). In part, this was a brief critical overview of the history of sociological thought, tracing the way in which the discipline, reflecting the masculine gender of its originators and of the profession as a whole, emphasized production as against reproduction, the public as against the private and the worlds and preoccupations of men as against the experiences and interests of women. Stacey argued for a transcending and reintegration of these divisions and focused in particular on the idea of 'people work', a theme which cut across these divisions. 'People work' involved both the largely unpaid labour within the home and the largely paid labour in the professions and many service occupations. Such a programme would seem to argue for a renewed critical focus on family relationships and, indeed, it is likely that this article, together with a host of other feminist critiques, inspired a series of empirical studies on different aspects of marriage and parenthood and, in particular, on the structure of informal care within the household and family. However, it cannot be said that the study of the family was wholly subsumed under feminist scholarship and, indeed, it might be argued that there were limitations on the possibilities of using feminism to develop a comprehensive sociology of the family.

There are a variety of reasons for this. First, gender relationships are not simply confined to the family and the domestic sphere. Gender relations, as Stacey made clear, are components of all social situations; to argue otherwise would be to perpetuate notions of two separate spheres. The family was a site, often an important one, for the reproduction of sexual oppressions, but it did not stand alone.

In contrast, it may be argued that while gender is an important and major theme within domestic relationships it is not the only feature and a feminist approach might, by implication, tend to downgrade relationships and dimensions which were not of direct significance in understanding sexual oppression. Here we might include questions to do with age and generation, relations between siblings and wider relationships of kinship. More recent scholarship has shown that feminist analysis can deal with these, and other, dimensions of family life. However, during the period under consideration, the focus tended to be upon inequalities within marriage and parenting.

Further, the feminist critique inevitably focused upon divisions, specifically sexual divisions, within family life. However, this is not the whole story. Family relationships are also about unities and patterns of co-operation. To recognize this is not to return to some reified notion of marriage or family as undifferentiated wholes. However, it is also the case that family members do have some sense of solidarity and unity, for whatever reasons, and these identities do have wider consequences.

One further point here is that, as several have noted (for example Oakley, 1989), 'gender' has tended to be a code word for 'women'. Again, this emphasis was clearly consistent with a project that aimed to recover and give significance to the lives and work of women, for so long obscured in sociological analysis. It was generally the case that men, in feminist studies, did not have the sharpness of focus that characterized many studies of the lives of women. Family relations, on the other hand, necessarily include men as well as women, even if the conventional models tend to give less significance to their experiences.

All this is not to argue that the growth of feminist studies was in any way harmful to family studies; indeed the reverse is the case. However, they were addressing different issues and some measure of tension existed, and continues to exist, between them. During the period of the 1980s, feminist or gender studies were radical, innovatory and challenging. Family studies, on the other hand, seemed conservative and somewhat pedestrian. The earlier linking of family and community was replaced by a linking of family and gender with the emphasis being very much on the latter term.

A recent textbook provides a feminist re-reading of classic sociological topics (Abbott and Wallace, 1990a). While the book includes a chapter entitled 'Family and Household' it is also clear that issues to do with different facets of family and domestic life pervade the text as a whole. This reinforces the argument that while, in the short run, feminist critiques might be thought to exist in some kind of competition with, or opposition to, family studies, in the long run they opened the way for a more serious and wide-ranging understanding of the linkages between family, household and many other areas of modern social life.

Definitional Issues

In the preceding pages I have used 'family' both as an adjective and as a noun. In the course of this book I shall tend to the former usage, with only occasional references to 'the family'. Further, in later chapters I shall sometimes refer to 'household', sometimes to 'household/family' and sometimes to 'domestic life' or 'home'. These usages are not perfect synonyms although they are closely linked. However, a concern with definitions has been one of the main factors contributing to a sense of fluidity and flux in family studies. Further, this concern is itself multi-stranded. A critique of functional-isms, Marxist versions included, led to and arose out of a dissatisfaction with the watertight boxes which were the key elements of this mode of theorizing. Feminists shared in this unhappiness with preordained categories and with the consequences of fixed understandings of 'the family' for the lives and experiences of women. Uncritical usages of the term 'the family' could reinforce popular understandings with possible implications for public policy. Somewhat similarly, Bernardes argued that sociologists should take their responsibilities in this matter more seriously and that talk of 'the family' could have definite social and political consequences (Bernardes, 1988). Feeding into many of these debates and concerns were critiques from ethnomethodological and phenomenological approaches which noted, among other things, the ways in which sociologists routinely drew upon common sense and everyday understandings of the world and then deployed these understandings in order to structure that world. Terms such as 'family' should be seen as topics to be explored further, in all their usages and ramifications, rather than as resources to be drawn upon uncritically.

There are a variety of strategies that might be elaborated to deal with these problems associated with the term 'family'. In the present book, the most common one is to use 'family' as an adjective rather than as a noun, using the term to refer to sets of practices which deal in some way with ideas of parenthood, kinship and marriage and the expectations and obligations which are associated with these practices. If we talk about 'family practices' we are referring to certain practices which participants tend to think of as being in some way 'different' and which may colour other practices which might overlap with them. Thus 'family practices' might overlap with and interact with 'gendered practices'. This strategy should serve to underline the argument that 'family' is not a thing, without denying that notions of 'family' are important parts of the ways in which people understand and structure their lives.

Elsewhere in this book I shall deploy, while being critical of, the associated term 'household'. The terms 'family' and 'household' are sometimes distinguished and often confused and it seems appropriate at times to play one off against the other, to explore the different and overlapping sets of concerns that each term connotes. Elsewhere, again, I shall explore another overlapping term, that of 'home'.

Throughout the book I shall remind myself and the reader that 'family' is often contested, publicly available, and often very powerful. Since people routinely use notions of family in their daily lives (although not always in uniform ways) it would seem to be somewhat cavalier to dismiss the term altogether or to strive for some alternative, scientifically neutral, term. At all points, I hope, there will be reminders to signal the multiplicities of usages and the consequences of these usages. The terms that people use, including the terms that sociologists use, become part of the social reality in which we live. If we cannot avoid using or hinting at these terms we can at least try to be alert to the possible consequences of such usages.

Family Sociology: Implicit and Explicit

By the end of the 1980s, sociological family studies could notch up a fair number of interesting and important studies. Many of these studies had certain affinities which might almost justify the title of 'genre'. They were nearly all inspired by feminist debates or showed the influence of such debates. In addition to these feminist influences, the most likely theoretical influence would be some version of symbolic interactionism and, taking these two influences together, it seemed almost inevitable that the chosen methodology would be largely qualitative, using some form of extended or open-ended interview as the central research instrument.

This is not the whole story. We would need to add to this core of studies those which were based upon somewhat larger samples and which used some combination of qualitative and quantitative methods. We would also need to add demographical and statistical analyses of household structures and family processes, often using official records. In addition, we would wish to include several historically based studies. All these, taken together, could form a respectable basis for a British family sociology.

However, recognizing the importance of such studies clearly identified as contributing to 'family sociology', it is a main argument of this book that we should not confine our search to those works which are specifically labelled in these terms. What has taken place, largely during the 1980s, is a weakening of the boundaries between family/household studies and other kinds of sociological studies. The real strength of 'family studies', theoretically and empirically, has come, and is likely to come in the future, from this increasing fuzziness at the borders.

By way of illustration it may be useful to consider the works examined by Gordon Marshall in his spirited defence of British sociology (Marshall, 1990a). Of the ten studies considered in his discussion, only one (Bott, 1971) could be considered as being within the specific field of family studies. However, another four studies could be considered as having strong family connections: Goldthorpe, Llewellyn and Payne's study of social mobility; Jackson and Marsden's more qualitative study of education and the working class; the affluent worker studies; and Brown and Harris on women and depression. Further, Rex and Moore's study of Sparkbrook is not at too great a distance from family studies and the same could be said of Townsend's massive study of poverty. In Marshall's work, only three studies could be said to have minimal family connections, in treatment if not necessarily in potentiality.

This weakening of the boundaries between family sociology and other sub-areas is part of a more general trend reflected in the increasing deployment of the metaphor of the kaleidoscope (for example R.E. Pahl, 1984). The increasing critique of functional sociology, together with the growth of feminist scholarship also impatient with conventional divisions, boundaries and classifications, led to a desire to explore the ways in which areas such as work, family, gender and leisure were all mutually implicated in and affected each other. Thus when Pahl used the title *Divisions of Labour* he was pointing to continuities between the public and the private and between economic life and domestic life. Later, such an increasing sense of fluidity was clearly in keeping with postmodernist sensibilities, even where no avowedly postmodern programmes were being declared.

The point, therefore, is to look at the various ways in which family and domestic life become implicated in areas of sociology more conventionally kept apart from these topics. In the present book, I shall begin with the interplays between family matters and the study of work and economic life because it is here, in a sense, that the debate began. I shall then go on to consider class and social stratification, a key area in almost any version of sociological inquiry. Issues of family and household have not been absent from these concerns, although the main thrust of theory and research has been with the activities of men in the public sphere.

In a sense, the next topic to be considered, that of gender, could have come first since the linkages between family and gender are probably more obvious than elsewhere. However, it might also be argued that this over-identification of the two elements may have been to the detriment of both. Further, in terms of mainstream sociological discussions, gender arrived later on the scene than these other two themes of work and class. After this chapter I move on to a linked topic, namely that of care. These discussions also build upon and feed back into the earlier discussions of work.

The next two headings represent more recent developments in sociological thought and theory which would appear to be at some distance from family matters. Recent interest in the sociology of the body has emerged from feminist scholarship, from the sociology of health and illness, from cultural studies and from interests in postmodernity. However, once again family and domestic relationships may be found waiting in the wings. Similarly, interests in time and space have, on the whole, developed without a great deal of direct reference to domestic life. However, the growing interest in the life-course (to name one development) has led to a more focused attention on temporal matters within family sociology. Interests in time and space are scarcely new within social science but the full implications of these interests for family sociology have yet to be explored in depth.

Finally, I shall examine a couple of more specific areas, drawing upon many of the themes already mentioned. A focus upon food draws together aspects of gender, work, care and the body in the context of domestic relations. And finally, the study of the home, distinct from but also closely overlapping with family and household, also draws together many of the previous mentioned themes, especially gender and stratification.

This book, therefore, seeks to argue that family sociology still has much to contribute not simply in the more immediate terms of its own specialism but also, and perhaps increasingly, in terms of the way in which family themes are woven into other sociological concerns. The earlier bracketing of family and community emphasized the importance of going beyond a narrow focus on a limited range of marital and parental relationships. Yet the term 'community' was itself too limited to provide the basis for further development. The approach suggested here draws upon feminist and postmodernist discussions in order to argue that family practices have a key place in the analysis of a complex and fluid society.

1

Work, Employment and the Household

Introduction

Until fairly recently one of the most abiding orthodoxies in sociology was the separation of work and home in industrial society. Notions of rationality or rational capitalism, for example, explicitly depended upon the idea of such a separation. In writing this, I am conscious that I probably played some small part in perpetuating this orthodoxy. In the first edition of *Introducing Sociology* (Worsley, 1970), I was largely responsible for the chapters on work and the family. I saw the separation of home and work as being one of the key features of work in industrial society, the other two being the linked features of rationality and alienation. However, perhaps more than any overt statement, the location of these two chapters in different sections of the book underlined this central, and largely unexamined, set of assumptions.

My account was not significantly out of line from prevailing orthodoxies of the time. The argument about the separation of home and work (with all the qualifications that might be made) was supposedly based upon the historical impact of the industrial revolution and was reinforced through a range of theoretical models. Functionalist and most Marxist models, for example, depended upon this idea of separation. With the benefit of hindsight and feminist analysis it may also be argued that these widespread assumptions were also reinforced in constructions such as 'the family wage' and therefore had wider social and political implications.

Early feminist accounts highlighted the gendered nature of this division but did not necessarily criticize the theoretical status of the very idea of separation. Weaving around these gender distinctions between home and work were other critical divisions such as those between private and public. Having set up these more elaborated distinctions, it was often difficult to forget them, even when seeking to show how they necessarily affected each other. On the one hand was the economy, focusing upon waged labour and rationality; on the other was the home and the family, focusing upon primary interpersonal relationships between men and women and between parents and children. The links, frequently represented by arrows between boxes, emphasized their separateness.

The Redefinition of Work

The critical reassessment of the division between home and work was strongly encouraged by reconceptualizations of work and economic activity, one of the major themes within the British sociology of the 1980s. The most common assumption had been that work tended to equal paid employment. Paid employment represented the key point of anchorage around which other distinctions and understandings revolved. The related term 'the economy' was a little more difficult to define, perhaps easier to indicate by example than to define with precision. However, the focal point remained the production and distribution of goods and services insofar as these were mediated through the market or, in the case of command economies, through some series of state mechanisms that acted in place of the market.

It would be wrong to say that earlier writers were unaware of the complexities of these understandings and of the failure of real life and everyday experiences to match up to these theoretical divisions and models. Even in my somewhat conventional textbook account, I gave recognition to the fact that there was a range of understandings attached to the word 'work', lay as well as professional. However, there were some more specific influences that shaped and gave impetus to the redefinition of work.

Undoubtedly, the feminist critique was the major influence here. First, there was the recognition of the importance of women's employment outside the home. Too often the image of the 'worker' (in socialist iconography, for example) was of a male figure. Where the presence of women in the labour force was recognized, their presence was often seen as problematic: either as a potential source of tensions within marriage or difficulties for young children or, more theoretically, as a topic to be explained. Later work emphasized the deep historical roots of women's labour force participation (Tilly and Scott, 1978) as well as the continuing and growing significance of married women's employment. Theories sought not to explain why they were there but why women's position in the labour market tended to be a disadvantaged one (Yeandle, 1984: 20–1).

Such accounts stressed that the world of work and employment was far from being a masculine one. However, it could be said that this recognition alone did little for the reconceptualization of work or the critique of the home/work divide. However, groups such as the Resources Within Households group aimed to examine the issues around the economic activities that took place within the household. They aimed to look at the economic exchanges, activities and gendered inequalities that existed within households (Resources Within Households, 1985).

The work of the Resources Within Households group brought together a variety of streams of thought and analysis that were already taking place, stimulated by various influences. One of these was what was to become known as 'the domestic labour debate'. This initially took place within Marxist economic and social theory and while the complex details of this debate, dealing with distinctions between productive and unproductive labour and theories of surplus value, need not concern us here, the abiding significance was in the attempt to give recognition to the work performed by women outside the labour market. This was not simply a moral recognition; it was also an attempt to assess the economic and theoretical significance of this labour. At roughly the same time there were growing moves in the direction of establishing a perspective derived from the sociology of work as applied to the labour performed within the home (Lopata, 1971; Oakley, 1974). At the simplest level it could be said that such studies argued that housework really was *work*; women themselves tended to see it in these terms and sociology should aim to do likewise. These developments, woven into the general feminist critiques of sociological practices and assumptions, led to a whole host of studies which either explored these issues directly or which routinely gave recognition to the importance of domestic labour in the lives of women. To take just one example: Cornwell in her Bethnal Green study stressed the integral part played by the domestic division of labour in the lives of the working-class women she studied, how women clearly saw housework and child care as their job and, most important for the present discussion, how they invested their activities with all the moral significance normally attributed to paid employment (Cornwell, 1984).

However, there were also limitations in the attempt to study housework within existing paradigms, whether derived from Marxism or from the sociology of work. What was needed, and what developed in the course of the 1970s and 1980s, was a more finely nuanced appreciation of the nature of housework and of differences between various kinds of housework. There were differences, for example, between the kinds of household tasks – washing ironing, cooking etc., which could be readily quantified and analysed according to the gender of the person most likely to perform such tasks, and the less measurable tasks and responsibilities associated with caring and emotional labour (see chapter 4 for further developments of this theme). There was, therefore, a need to appreciate some of the specific characteristics of domestic labour as well as those characteristics which it shared with other forms of work. In a somewhat under-recognized article, Bernice Martin (1984: 21) argued for the ritual significance of some household activities:

> housework as the ritual creation of order also confers a form of domestic power on women which is so 'natural' and habitual that we have largely ceased to recognise its existence, though its consequences reverberate through the gender and generational tensions in the family.

While Oakley, Lopata and others certainly considered some of the ways in which housework might be positively evaluated, it is probably true to say that the overall impression of much of this research was the equation of housework and drudgery or, at the very least, the establishment of parallels between housework and other forms of relatively low status and alienating forms of manual labour.

However, it was clear that as a result of these developments, domestic labour could no longer be ignored. Its wider economic and moral significance was coming to be recognized and the uncritical equation of work and paid employment came to be more and more open to challenge. The ground was laid for a more detailed understanding of the household as a site for 'non-market economic activity' (Roberts, Finnegan and Gallie, 1985: 365) or the location of household activity within the somewhat broader framework of the informal economy (e.g. Handy, 1984).

While the recognition of the unpaid domestic labour of women was the most important impetus to an understanding of the household in economic terms, it was not the only one. Another major influence was the recognition of unemployment as a more or less permanent feature of the British, and other, economies. The focus, initially, was upon male unemployment and, like some of the classic studies of the inter-war period, this was seen as having an impact upon domestic relationships. Unemployment, more importantly, was also beginning to call into question the model of the single, usually male, breadwinner as the key link between home and work. Roberts, Finnegan and Galllie (1985: 1–2) concluded: '. . . the lifestyle and aspirations of a family may, in the future be less determined by the occupational status of the male head of household'. Another important consequence was an increasing recognition of forms of labour which took place outside the formal economy.

Further, increasingly writers were no longer content to focus simply upon *male* unemployment. The recognition of increasing proportions of married women in the labour market also entailed a recognition that unemployment was a feature of the lives of women as well (Martin and Roberts, 1984). Combining this recognition with the growing significance accorded to domestic labour set the stage for a much more complex set of interchanges between the traditional categories of home and work. We also find a more complex understanding of gender differences within and around the household.

Two other developments contributed to this broader understanding of work. In the first place, there was a growth of a more comparative approach, especially focused upon the lives and experiences of women (and men) in the Third World. For example, the argument that female-headed households formed between a quarter and a third of households world-wide inevitably called into question assumptions that had been derived from a relatively short period of Western history and confined to certain classes as well (Redclift, 1985). Increasing numbers of studies of the work of women in many parts of the world heightened the ethnocentricism of Western models but also asked questions that Western sociologists might ask of their own societies. By expanding the range of activities and sites which might signify 'work', comparative analysis brought about a much richer understanding of work back home. For example, attention was paid to 'home-working' within Britain (Allen and Wolkowitz, 1987; Pennington and Westover, 1989). Such developments, by no means confined to working-class women or women in ethnic niches, clearly reinforced questions about the boundaries between home and work and strengthened the impetus to see the household as a site for economic activity.

Finally, the reconceptualization of work and the focus upon the household, although originally developing from a broadly feminist perspective and although focusing upon the paid and unpaid activities of women, could also be seen as having implications for men as well. A growing number of studies of men in the home and as fathers came to be critical of the idea that, for men, work was the sole or even the central basis of personal identity. For example, looking at family-based roles, Cohen distinguished between those men who had broad or narrow conceptions of such roles, cross-cutting these distinctions with another between high or low opportunities for such domestic or family involvements. He argued, on the basis of a small sample, that most men tended to have relatively broad and positive understandings of their domestic or parental roles but relatively low opportunities for their realization (Cohen, 1987). Such a study can begin to point to different expectations and experiences of the household for men as well as for women and may, therefore, complicate the traditional homework separation still further.

These influences merged and converged on a variety of studies carried out or published during the 1980s. Perhaps the most prominent was the initiative set up by the Economic and Social Research Council on Economic Life and Social Change (SCELI). An early statement and marking out the territory was made in a volume based upon the proceedings of a conference held in 1983 (Roberts, Finnegan and Gallie, 1985). Here we see that 'new approaches to economic life' entailed a much sharper focus on issues of gender and ethnicity and upon the household as a locus for economic activity. Although not directly connected with this initiative, a volume entitled *Employment in Britain* included articles on gender, ethnicity and the household (Gallie, 1988). Also during the 1980s, there was a conference on work and employment (S. Allen et al., 1986; K. Purcell et al., 1986) and the establishment of the journal *Work, Employment and Society*, both of which reflected these new perspectives to some degree. The SCELI projects began to see the light of day in the 1990s (Anderson, Bechofer and Gershuny, 1994; Gallie, Marsh and Vogler, 1994). But perhaps the most influential and most discussed work reflecting these new trends was Ray Pahl's *Divisions of Labour* (1984).

l clearly stated his dissatisfaction with the orthodox view
ting work with paid employment and used the household
is basic unit for exploring a variety of divisions in terms of
ss and gender. He was concerned with divisions within and
between households. The study, based on the Isle of Sheppey,
clearly showed the influence of feminist scholarship, of the need to
consider the impact of long-term unemployment and the need to
draw upon historical and anthropological or comparative work in
order to understand social and economic change in contemporary
Britain.

From Family to Household?

Thus a variety of trends contributed to the development of a more
complex understanding of work and economic life and, as part of this
process, an increasing focus upon the household as a site for
economic activity. While it would not be true to say that the term
'household' replaced the term 'family' during the 1980s it is certainly
the case that there was a shift of emphasis from the latter to the
former. Sociologists who, in the past, had had relatively little to say
about the family appeared to be much more comfortable in dealing
with the idea of the household, approaching this from a broader
interest in the sociology of economic life rather than the domestic
sphere.

What were the implications of this shift in emphasis? First, there
was a recognition that the household should be treated as a unit in
the analysis of all aspects of economic activity, production as well as
consumption. This implied not simply the erosion of conventional
boundaries between home and work but also a shift from a focus on
the individual (conventionally the male breadwinner) to the collective
unit of the household.

If the household were to be treated as the unit of economic
analysis, what might this mean in practice? The implication was that
a set of activities could be attached to the unit of the household
which could then be used in the analysis of economic life. To this end
Wallerstein and Smith suggested the term 'householding': 'We shall
call the multiple processes by which they [households] pool income,
allocate tasks, and make collective decisions *householding*' (1990:
43; their emphasis). The use of this term clearly emphasized activity
and process rather than a thing.

The more popular term, however, appeared to be the growing one of 'strategy'. The use of the term has a long and complex history in social science and its use is by no means confined to sociology or to the study of the household. There is evidence that the usage first appeared in management studies while of course the origin of the metaphor was to do with the allocation of military resources (Crow, 1989; Knights and Morgan, 1990; Morgan, 1989; Wallace, 1993). The usage was especially influential in historical studies, especially of poorer or working-class families during the periods of proto-industrialization or industrialization. There was increasing talk of 'survival strategies', 'reproductive strategies' and 'housing strategies'. Feminist sociologists began to write of 'coping strategies', although others warned against too ready an acceptance of the term (Edwards and Ribbens, 1991). Such usages were by no means confined to British studies and more comparative work could, for example, write of the adaptive strategies undertaken by female-headed households under conditions where employment was irregular or scarce (Red-clift, 1985).

Whether talking about 'householding' or 'household strategies', the implications were similar: namely, that it was possible to write of the household as a unit in economic life. Further, this unit could be seen as a social agent, not simply reacting to wider economic, demographic or social processes but also actively affecting these processes. Put more strongly, the emphasis upon household strategies suggested less the idea of households responding to 'the economy' but more that of households as an integral part of economic life. The household was not simply to be treated as a whole but as an active whole.

The concept of 'strategy' implies an understanding of household resources. Wallman, for example, developed a complex elaboration of her idea of resources in an analysis of London households. There were features of structure, the familiar trinity of land, labour and capital and there were features of organization, time, information and identity (Wallman, 1984: 29). While not all discussions developed such a sophisticated analysis of the resources which might be deployed by and within households, there was a growing awareness that such resources were not simply or narrowly material in their character. Resources might include such matters as access to net-works of information, issues to do with status and position and so on. This could be seen as an expansion of the concept of the 'material', parallel perhaps to the conceptual shifts implied in the redefinitions of work and economic life.

Defining the Household

It is possible that a growing preference for the term 'household' over the term 'family' reflected the apparent simplicity of the former as opposed to the latter. Certainly it seemed more straightforward to provide operational definitions of the household:

> In 1991 a household was defined as:
> (i)   one person living alone; or
> (ii) a group of people (who may or may not be related) living, or staying temporarily, at the same address, with common house-keeping. (Dale and Marsh, 1993: 22)

This refers to the 1991 UK population census. As in 1981, enumerators were supposed to define a group as a household if they shared at least one daily meal together or 'if occupants shared a common living or sitting room' (1993: 23). Most other usages correspond closely to this census definition.

Such straightforwardness, however, might be more apparent than real. For example, the British census definition allows for single-person households; indeed, these currently account for over a quarter of all households (*Social Trends*, HMSO 1994: 33–4). Some more anthropologically inclined discussions, on the other hand, would not allow for single-person households. If, for example, you treat the household as 'the next biggest thing on a social map after an individual' (Netting, Wilk and Arnoud, 1984: xxii) this would seem to preclude such a possibility. However, the same volume does in fact include several accounts of such households. The apparent contradiction may be squared by distinguishing between the individual as individual and the individual as household or household member. However, even probing this one issue serves to highlight potential complexities which are sometimes smoothed over.

Other complexities revolve around the idea of 'residence' or 'co-residence' (La Fontaine, 1986: 25; Netting, Wilk and Arnoud, 1984: xxvi). A co-resident may be someone who spends most of his or her time at a particular location, or who spends most of his or her nights there, or who does not sleep there but spends a proportion of each day at that address or who happens to be defined as such according to the census enumerator's practices. Similar complexities arise when we consider sharing a meal, a living room or common facilities. How do we treat marginal cases such as a person who might eat regularly at a particular residence but sleep elsewhere? Within our own society the growing number of 'commuter marriages' where the partners work in different locations during the week and share a residence at the weekend point to some of these complexities.

However, it is likely that some of the firmer definitions of household are somewhat ethnocentric and have a limited applicability when attempts are made to develop comparative analysis (Saradamoni, 1992). This is partly because of the range of practices already indicated in the previous paragraph so that the notion of a stable and relatively fixed set of activities and practices 'under one roof' may be much more fluid in reality than in theory. It may also reflect the fact that the term 'household' and its range of usages may vary considerably between societies. My 'lay ethnographer's' understanding of modern British society is that the term is not much used outside professional discourse. People are more likely to use the term 'home', which carries many more complex meanings and associations. Anthropologists, however, sometimes claim that folk terms are routinely used and that these can be most appropriately translated as 'household'.

What is perhaps at the centre of the debate is an approach to households which focuses more or less on structure and one which focuses more on activities and processes. In the case of the British census definition, there appears to be a sliding back and forth between the two. Activities – taking meals, sharing facilities – are taken to be signifiers of households which are then used to define different household structures, one-person, single-parent and so on. Alternatively, we are invited to read off practices from structures. The more comparative approaches seem to focus much more on activities and processes. Thus Wilk and Netting describe households as 'groups in which there is a high density of activity' (Wilk and Netting, 1984: 5). Such an approach clearly allows for a much more fluid and protean understanding of household than would seem to be apparent from its usages in British sociology.

One implication of this fluidity is that the conventional distinction between household and family may not be as straightforward as might be supposed. Thus Netting, Wilk and Arnoud (1984: xx) describe the distinction in these terms:

> While both households and families are culturally defined, the former are task-oriented residence units and the latter are conceived of as kinship groupings that need not be localized.

Yet this clearly allows for overlaps. While households need not include people related by birth or by marriage they often do and this is often part of the rationale for co-residence in the first place. The more fluid our definition of household, the more likely it is to find overlaps between the ideas of family and household. The distinction, as we shall see, is an important one and one which needs to be preserved. But the recognition of this need should not obscure the considerable areas of overlap as well.

Opening Up the Black Box

One possible problem with the development of a focus upon households might be that the unit will be treated as an undifferentiated whole, a black box, which ignores or smooths over differences within it. Clearly this remains a problem if the analysis stops at the household walls. However, as the analysis developed, this danger seemed to be held in check. It was, indeed, probably the Resources Within Households group that first gave emphasis to the dangers of treating the household as a 'black box' and sought ways of opening it up (Brannen and Wilson, 1987). The concern, therefore, was not simply with the household as a unit receiving various inputs, deploying certain strategies and examining the possible outcomes of these strategies for both individual households and for society as a whole over time. There was a need to go beyond a holistic understanding of the household which seemingly reproduced the ideological norm of privacy that surrounds family and domestic life. This tacit understanding was perhaps most clearly seen in usages of the term 'strategies'. The notion of 'household strategies' seemed to assume that members of a household acted in unison in order to produce an identifiable outcome. Similarly, the idea of 'household resources' seemed to assume a set of resources, material and non-material, which were equally accessible to all household members.

Such an approach can be defended (for example Warde, 1990). Theoretically, the argument would recognize that real households do not necessarily behave in this way but that there is something to be gained, analytically, from treating the household as if it were a unit of this kind. In examining the role of the household in economic life, it might be necessary to adopt a stance of theoretical indifference to what actually took place within it. In the case of more historically based discussions or discussions based upon the use of large-scale data sets, the argument might be more one of practical necessity. Some modes of research deny the researcher the opportunity to

examine what actually takes place between individuals within household units. All we have are various inputs and assumed outcomes
and under such circumstance it might be quite legitimate to speak of
'household strategies', especially if the researcher be aware of the
limitations of adopting this approach.

Much, of course, depends upon the overall concerns of the
investigator. In the case of feminist scholars and those working
within the Resources Within Households group, priority was given
to gender as a major division within households that prevented or
inhibited more holistic treatments. In common with many other
scholars they were interested in departing from conventional models
of the nuclear family. They were also interested in widening the
concept of 'resources' beyond that of the material and to include
considerations of time and emotional caring. Inevitably, issues of
power were raised in these analyses.

It is important to underline the theoretical significance of this
concern with processes within households. In the first place, there
was the argument that gender continued to be a major division
within society and that sociological analysis should treat this as a
matter of course. However, there were other theoretical arguments.
If a central sociological concern was the relationship between an
individual and society, between agency and structure or between
micro- and macro-processes, then an analysis could not end at the
boundary of any particular unit selected as a theoretical whole,
whether this unit be an organization, a theoretical institution or a
household. It was important to see how particular outcomes were
produced, thus avoiding possible dangers of reification. Households
might well be seen, theoretically, as greater than the sum of their
parts but this did not mean that the parts were unimportant. Rather
it is important to see how the parts, gendered and aged individuals
or micro-processes, interacted in order to construct the whole,
the household, as an ongoing unit (for example, Thorogood, 1987:
20–1).

One of the important implications of the work of Brannen and
Wilson, Jan Pahl and Ray Pahl and several others concerned with
household processes was the realization that the study of women
could no longer be a specialist topic area, of interest to feminists or
others with a somewhat specialized concern with gender. Indeed,
studies of the sexual division of labour within households has been
an important part of family studies, in Britain and the United States,
for many years now. There was, for example, the questioning of
some of the more optimistic assumptions about symmetricality or

equality within family units. There was the desire to explain and to map the relatively slow shifts on the part of men in their participation in domestic tasks. The concerns with inequalities in households were building upon a well-established tradition of research and theorizing.

There was also another well-established concern within family sociology. American studies, in particular, had been concerned with the effect of the wife's employment on relationships within the home, on the sexual divisions of labour and on shifting power differentials between husbands and wives. (It should be noted that while this discussion dealt specifically with husbands and wives, much of the analysis could equally be applied to cohabiting couples.) More optimistic accounts suggested that the employment of women outside the home was a lever leading to greater gender equality within. Early feminist discussions criticized these more optimistic conclusions (for example the now classic article by Gillespie). The new emphasis upon the household both developed and inherited a somewhat more complex and finely nuanced set of understandings about the interconnections between paid employment and work and power within the household. It became clear that employment alone did not have a straightforward effect on the redistribution of tasks and power within the household. Similarly, the influences of male unemployment were more complex and more varied than might at first be supposed (Gallie, Marsh and Vogler, 1994; McKee and Bell, 1986).

One factor influencing the power and task allocation within the household continued to be the differential earning power of men and women, although again the effects were not always straightforward. A focus upon the economic life of households contributed to a reconsideration of some of the most basic economic resources, especially money. Again this was not simply treated as an input. There was also a growing concern with how such resources were managed, controlled and distributed within the household. Jan Pahl, in particular, explored the complexities of money management and control within the household and the way in which these patterns, while undergoing processes of change over time, continued to be strongly influenced by gender (J. Pahl, 1990). In the light of these considerations it was possible to provide new answers to the old question as to whether women in general benefited or lost out through marriage (G. Wilson, 1987: 139). It could also be seen that a focus on earnings and their distribution within the household could also be a way of exploring the interrelationships between class and gender at the level of the household.

Money, although a major focus of concern, was not the only resource to be examined in the context of the dynamics of intra-household processes. Another basic resource, food, was also being explored as a way into the understanding of family and household dynamics (see chapter 7). Similar considerations also apply to time and space (see chapter 6). Such an expanded understanding of the idea of resources went hand in hand with a desire to open up the black box of the household.

Although the chief focus, in opening up the black box, was upon gender differences within the household, there was also a growing concern with issues to do with age and generation. In part this reflects a growing concern with children and childhood, not necessarily confined to their positions within the household (James and Prout, 1990). Among the range of issues considered have been the distribution of food along lines of age as well as gender; the relatively unexplored areas of the child's contribution to economic activity and resources within the household (Hutson and Cheung, 1992; Jones, 1992) and the positions of young people, especially in conditions of youth unemployment, within the home (for example Morris, 1990: 147–84).

Differences Between Households

One of the rationales for using the household as the unit of analysis was to explore the ways in which social divisions and inequalities might be mediated through households. We have already looked at gender differences, differences that to some degree cut across households. We are now concerned more with differences between households. Some of these issues will be discussed further in chapter 3 but here we shall be considering patterns of economic inequality without exploring further issues of class. Thus, for example, when authors write about 'family poverty' they are concerned with the location of poverty in a unit rather than in a collection of atomized individuals. Quite how economic inequalities and disadvantages are mediated through domestic relations remains a controversial issue; that they are mediated is much less in contention.

One issue that developed during the 1980s was that of polarization between households. During some of the earlier speculations around the reformulation of the concept of work, some rather optimistic predictions suggested that the loss of one source of income through unemployment might be compensated for by a variety of household-based strategies. Thus the loss of a traditional male breadwinning role through unemployment might be compensated for by the female partner seeking paid employment. Alternatively, or in addition, household members may derive income or goods and services in kind through a greater involvement in the 'informal' economy. Further, and continuing to expand our understanding of economic activity, there might be an increasing range of 'self-provisionings' including forms of do-it-yourself, cooking at home, clothes making and growing vegetables. In part taking a cue from studies of Third World cities, these predictions suggested that households could develop strategies which might at least cushion against some of the worst effects of long-term unemployment.

While there was considerable value in exploring these hitherto unexplored forms of economic activity, it became apparent that these predictions tended to be too optimistic. Far from there being some kind of trade-off between the formal and the informal economies, studies tended to reveal a process of polarization (Morris, 1990: 30; R. Pahl, 1984; Roberts, Finnegan and Gallie, 1985: 366). Those households which had relatively secure positions in the formal labour market were also better positioned in less formal systems of employment and exchange. Thus a recent study suggests that unemployed people, both men and women, were more likely to find a job if they already had a partner in employment (Gallie and Vogler, 1994). Relevant considerations included the fact that most forms of self-provisioning or do-it-yourself require some existing resources; that employed people were more likely to have access to informal networks of information about employment or other economic opportunities; and the fact that informal norms of reciprocity tended to inhibit individuals' participation in informal exchanges. At the other end of the scale, dual-earner households tended to multiply their advantages and to have access to a wider range of strategies than was available to less advantaged households. Thus the use of waged domestic labour amongst middle-class households not only might have some impact on domestic divisions of labour but might also be a strategy for maintaining a middle-class life style (Gregson and Lowe, 1994). Clearly we would expect to find national and regional variations; however, the new focus on households and their relationship with the economy has highlighted processes where-by those who have are able to increase their relatively secure hold within the wider system while those who have not tend to lose out. It is, in a sense, an old and familiar story, given a new perspective through a focus upon households as potential mechanisms or conduits of polarization.

Of particular importance, perhaps, is the way in which these processes interact with gender differences within households. The more optimistic accounts argued for a kind of trade-off, with the unemployed man, for example, taking a greater share in domestic tasks. This can happen (Wheelock, 1990) but it is by no means inevitable nor, as far as one can see from the available evidence, the most likely effect. On the contrary, the more likely pattern would seem to be one where better off couples tend to have both partners working, with some, albeit modest, effect upon the domestic division of labour. As in many other issues to do with households, gender and class interact.

The analysis so far considers the way in which households may be said to mediate, to amplify or to moderate, the effects of external economic changes. To this extent, households are seen as intervening or possibly dependent variables. But one of the rationales for the use of households in economic analysis was to consider the ways in which they might be seen as independent variables or, at the least, more active agents in the processes of social and economic change.

There are two ways in which such an analysis might progress. More historically based analysis of household strategies might seek to develop the cumulative effect over time of a whole range of broadly similar household strategies. Thus the adoption of certain reproductive strategies, affecting the number and timing of births, might have an effect upon women's availability for paid employment outside the home and the overall economic status of the households concerned. Such strategies might be part of a broader, long-term transition from a household-based economy to one based on wage-labour and factory production. The actual chains of cause and effect are inevitably difficult to disentangle using the limited resources available to demographic historians; nevertheless such research at the very least allows for a much more active role on the part of households as historic agents.

A second and increasingly controversial area where households might be seen as more active agents in economic life is in seeking to differentiate between types of household. Thus demographic analyses of households are often based upon distinctions between household types reflecting their size and structure. Of particular concern in recent years has been lone-parent households. Throughout the world such households have more often than not been headed by women and have been associated with some degree of poverty (Graham, 1985: 57). Does this mean, therefore, that lone-parent households are, as some have argued, key elements in the construction of an underclass? The question is a difficult one to answer and part of the reason for this is the need to consider both individual and household strategies, resources and outcomes. A household as a whole with an employed man present may be better off than a household headed by a lone-mother. However, the individuals within this former household may not share equally in the increased resources available. Further, and expanding the idea of resources, a mother may prefer the limited control that she might have over the deployment of resources within the household as compared to the situation where she is dependent upon a man.

This example illustrates both the potentialities and difficulties in developing a household analysis. On the one hand, there could be a much more detailed analysis focusing upon a whole range of different types of household and considering their role in wider patterns of economic life. Such an approach would be a valuable counter to models based upon assumptions about a normal, nuclear-family based household. On the other hand, such an approach could not be at the expense of a more individual analysis, focusing upon outcomes for individuals in the contexts of different kinds and structures of households.

Links Between Households

As the household analysis developed, some commentators expressed the concern that it might replace more traditional concerns with family and kinship altogether (Wilson and Pahl, 1988). For the present, family and kinship relations can be taken as referring to part of a wider set of relationships, namely those that exist between households. Thus, for example, family businesses are now rarely confined to a single household but may involve complex connections between several such households. Hence a modified version of the model which sees the household as mediating between the economy and the individual would be concerned less with isolated households and more with their interconnections.

Sociology contains a variety of terms that have been designed to capture the idea of interconnections between and across households. 'Family' itself may be one such term and 'kinship' may be another although it may be felt that the use of such terms might exclude other kinds of connections and relationships that might be considered important. A long-established term in British sociology was that of 'community' although, as we have seen, the theoretical usefulness of such a term has been increasingly questioned. Yet it clearly did deal with some aspects of inter-household relationships and sociologists continue to be interested in themes of locality even if the term 'community' is less likely to be used now than it was perhaps in the past.

Another well-established term has been that of 'network'. While the units in many forms of network analysis have tended to be individuals, there is no reason in principle why households should not replace individuals. In any event, network analysis pointed to relationships across and between households. Networks are best seen not as things but as sets of potentialities, to be used and mobilized when the occasion arises. The idea of network does seem to capture some of the features of everyday relationships, some relatively weak, temporary or fleeting and some more solid or permanent, which might tend to get obscured in the more traditional ideas of 'community'. The part of Manchester where I have lived for almost thirty years would not conventionally be described as 'a community'. Yet it would be a rare day when one would not see people talking at street corners, outside front doors, at shops or bus-stops or while waiting at the supermarket checkout. Networks, with all the possible variations in strength, solidity and duration can begin to capture this complex mosaic of inter- and extra-household relationships.

The third term is that of 'local labour market'. Use of the term in the plural serves to underline a shift away from macro-economic models towards examining the way in which the search for employment is located in and mediated through more immediate sets of relationships. While somewhat narrower than the previous terms, the emphasis upon the search for employment serves as a useful strand for tracing interconnections between individuals across households. Numerous studies have demonstrated the importance of local information and informal ties, kin and non-kin, in the process of seeking formal or informal modes of employment. These links are important for women as well as for men (see, for example, Gullestad, 1984: 184).

One focal issue in the analysis of relationships between households has been the mobilization of support in the event of a crisis such as unemployment. While more optimistic or sentimental models of traditional community ties have been replaced by discussions of processes of polarization, it is nevertheless the case that such events can potentially demonstrate the importance of links between households. McKee, for example, outlined three types of support that might be available for families facing unemployment: regular and sustained, back-up help in the face of an identifiable crisis and 'treats' on special occasions (McKee, 1987). It has often been noted how family members might use events such as birthdays as opportunities for providing support for relatives in a way that was least embarrassing to the recipient (Bell, 1968). While households in time of crisis might benefit from all three kinds of support, it could not be regarded as automatic. The detailed analysis of such patterns of support and the values surrounding such patterns have been explored in considerable detail by Janet Finch and others in their studies of family obligations (Finch, 1989; Finch and Mason, 1993). Here, as elsewhere in social life, norms of reciprocity were important, although composed of several complex interweaving strands. Acts of generosity could be seen both positively and negatively; much depends upon the meanings assigned to offers of help, financial or otherwise, and the existing frameworks of familial or interpersonal expectations.

It would seem, therefore, that a variety of studies indicate that a focus upon the household as a unit of analysis cannot replace other analyses in terms of family relationships. The emphasis in household studies not only tends to be upon relationships within households and the links between such units and the wider economy; it is also more economistic in tone, focusing upon divisions of labour, resources and strategies. Considerations of family and kinship inevitably raise other matters. These are, for example, to do with the very nature and deployment of family obligations in all their complexity. The metaphor of the kaleidoscope would seem to be especially apt. With one turn we see a blending of distinctions between home and work, family and economy, and the idea of the household moves into sharper focus. With another turn, the apparently solid boundaries of the household dissolve and we see family and kinship, and possibly other, relationships spreading out across these fainter boundaries. With each twist of the kaleidoscope we see that these patterns are differently coloured according to gender, age and generation and other social divisions.

Process and Change

At a first glance there is something rather static about the idea of a household. Even when these wider connections considered in the previous section are included the discussion is extended spatially rather than temporally. It is easy to slide from the concept of the household to the image of the home, physically located in a house or an apartment. However, this apparently static picture is misleading. Households are essentially dynamic entities. People enter and leave them as they themselves move through their individual life courses. In these processes of movement, ties are established between and across households. Households, as a result change in terms of size and composition (see, for example, Wallman, 1984: 20–6).

Life-course analysis suggests complex exchanges between individual change, household change and historical change (see Morgan, 1985; and chapter 6). As an example, let us take the familiar topic of the sexual division of labour within the household where we find a complicated mixture of stability and change:

> . . . none of the data seems to warrant any suggestion that the traditional female responsibility for household work has been substantially eroded or that male participation has substantially increased. This does not mean to say that it has not *significantly* increased. (Morris, 1990: 101–2; her emphasis)

This focuses upon patterns of historical change. But there may also be change, or lack of change, within individual or household life courses.

Theoretically, the importance of this kind of analysis is in terms of highlighting the links between household and economy over time. These changing divisions of labour within the household are not simply passive reflections of processes of social change taking place elsewhere; rather, they are to be seen as constituting these very processes. At the micro-level, these processes can be seen in terms of the multiple strategies and negotiations that take place between men and women (and between adults and children) within the household, using the whole range of resources, material and ideal, that are available to them individually and collectively. The degree of jointness is, of course, not to be assumed, but seen as a variable shaped through interaction with other institutions and individuals. These changes negotiated at the level of the household are not completely open-ended; they come up against structural limits such as the organization of the working day or the structure of the local labour market. The wider processes of social change are not simply built up through the aggregation of the 'work' of all the households in a given social context. Rather, it is individuals with gendered social identities operating in household contexts that provide the dynamic of change within the sexual division of labour. This is not simple methodological individualism. Gender, to take the most important theme, is not a matter of individual choice or strategies, although, as will be seen in chapter 3, it is a socially available resource as well as a socio-biological set of constraints.

At the most general level it can be argued that the analysis of economic change cannot simply begin and end with the formally constituted workplace. Households, as important mediators, are implicated in these processes of change. For example, there has been considerable discussion in recent years of post-Fordism and of the development of flexible working arrangements. More critical analysis has seen these trends in terms of the development of new managerial strategies and new patterns of control over workers' time. Once such issues of time enter into the calculation we are necessarily considering the connections between the formal workplace and the household and differential uses of time as a resource. Changes in working arrangements affecting work times are bound to have an impact upon households and, especially, upon women within households. Given the persisting stabilities of sexual divisions of labour within the household, it is likely that the development of flexible working hours, affecting both men and women, will put new demands upon women within households as they attempt to juggle family responsibilities. However, it can also be argued that changing practices within the household, or changing beliefs about such practices, may also lead to a demand for changing, more flexible, working practices. The notion of strategies reminds us of the possibilities of new patterns developing which may provide opportunities as well as constraints.

It should also be noted that the concept of household itself has not developed in an historical vacuum. In other words it is not simply households which are located in historical time; the study and focus upon households is similarly located. Many of these wider changes have been discussed in terms of privatization and domestication. Some argue that such processes, entailing a greater focus upon the home and marriage as central life interests, represent a truncation of the concept of citizenship. Others may see it as the basis of a new model of individualism and citizenship, a blend of personal responsibilities for others in the context of the home coupled with the realization of more individualized projects. Domesticity, constructed in terms of links between as well as within households, may possibly be viewed as keeping alive the spark of social obligation that is implied in the idea of citizenship.

Such debates, between optimists and pessimists and between conservatives and radicals, will continue for some time. Certainly, Pahl and Wallace suggest a more pessimistic interpretation of the patterns of domesticity that have emerged in many parts of the UK and elsewhere: 'Our analysis suggests a tragic precariousness at the centre of people's lives . . . We feel that we are describing a *dependent* domesticity . . .' (1985: 383; their emphasis).

The realization of domestic projects is often in the context of increasingly uncertain employment prospects with, for example, the inevitable impact upon abilities to keep up mortgage repayments. I have suggested here that the increasing focus upon the household was not simply a theoretical development taking place in a vacuum but was in some ways influenced by these wider shifts in the direction of privatization and domesticity, certainly in terms of the wider political and ideological debates about the balance between society, the family and the individual. Hence, a critique of the overemphasis on the idea of the household as a unit might also be part of a wider critique of trends within the social order.

Conclusion

Perhaps the most important aspect of the shift to a focus on households is, as Roberts et al. noted, that it entailed a shift from a concern with economic models to one for economic life (Roberts, Finnegan and Gallie, 1985: 18). From a sociological point of view this clearly has its attractions. Moreover, as has been suggested, households are 'good to think with'. In focusing upon the household and in pulling at the various skeins that mingle within the context of the household, we are readily led to other areas of concern and interest: gender, class, issues of time and process, space and locality, the idea of the home and so on. All these will be discussed in subsequent chapters and these discussions will, in some measure, bring us back to households.

However, difficulties have been noted. In the first place, there were the dangers of reification, of treating the household as a thing or an undifferentiated black box that engaged in strategies and exchanges with other areas of the economy. However, given the feminist origin of much recent discussion of households, this is probably less significant than it might have been, since feminist scholarship was essentially concerned with deconstructing established theoretical units along gender lines.

The other difficulty, already hinted at, is the danger of overstressing household relationships at the expense of family relationships and a loss of a sense of what makes the latter distinctive. In stressing the importance of the difference between the household and the family there was the danger that the latter might take a back seat. This may be because of the ideological baggage that the term 'family' seems to carry around with it and perhaps because the family, shorn of these economic considerations, would seem to be dealing with issues on the margins of sociology, namely matters to do with emotions and, possibly, biology. A focus upon households might be part of a new realism which is happier with rational quasi-economic models than with accounts which take seriously the complexities of emotional life. However, it is doubtful whether we can make clear distinctions between the emotional and the economic: 'The very ideas of "the housewife" and "the husband" are fusions of emotional relations, power and the divisions of labour' (Connell, 1987: 125).

In the enthusiasm to stress the family/household distinction and to pursue detailed analyses of the model, there may be a lack of consideration of the areas of overlap between the two and the extent to which this overlap makes a difference in the kinds of analysis that we will be required to carry out.

In terms of the degrees of overlap or otherwise, the following kinds of distinctions may be made:

1 Single-person households. As we have seen, these constitute an increasingly significant proportion of all households. Clearly such households do not involve family relationships in the strictest sense of the word. However, we may need to distinguish between those single-person households which are formed out of previous two or more person households, for example surviving spouses or persons divorced or separated from their former spouses, and those single-person households which are deliberately set up as such and where there are no 'ghosts' or former partners or family members to contend with.

2   Households which consist of two or more persons unrelated by birth or by marriage. Here there may be some negotiation of meanings involved in deciding whether or not such groups constitute 'families' or whether the members wish to be so described. Further, it is a matter for further investigation whether relationships between unrelated persons who deny the label 'family' nevertheless develop emotional ties which have some affinities with family processes.

3   Households which consist of people who are related by birth or by marriage or who wish to be so regarded. While consideration of such relationships within households does not exhaust the possibilities of family analysis, since family relationships cut across households, the overlap between household and family is probably not a trivial matter. It should also be stressed that the range of domestic relationships within this category is very large: single-parent households, childless or childfree couples, three or more generation households and so on.

4   Compound households consisting of (3) plus one or more persons unrelated, such as lodgers, houseguests, servants etc. Again the extent to which such individuals become or are considered as 'one of the family' is a matter for further investigation.

The point of this list is to demonstrate that, even ruling out of consideration questions of relationships between households, household analysis can rarely be completely separated from family analysis.

We need, therefore, to ask further questions about what makes households distinctive as units. While it makes sense to consider them as economic units they are not simply that, and family analysis, as opposed to economic analysis, needs to recognize this fact. Part of the reason for this distinctiveness, it has been argued, is that households often constitute important sites for the interweaving of family themes even if they are not coterminous with families.

There are perhaps further, wider, issues at stake. We have talked about the blurring of distinctions between work and non-work and of the introduction of terminologies to do with strategies and rational choice within the context of household analysis. But are there losses as well as gains here? Put another way, are there possible gains, theoretically and humanly, in maintaining some kinds of boundaries between work and non-work?

It would seem to be the case that individuals do routinely make some kinds of distinctions between work and non-work, although the ability to do so is almost certainly a reflection of gendered power differentials. Further, such distinctions are not always clearly mapped on to distinctions between employment and non-employment. Roughly speaking, we may identify three possible overlapping usages:

1 Work as 'paid employment', often entailing 'going to work';
2 Work as the expenditure of effort. This could include some activities carried out within leisure contexts as the term 'workout' suggests; and
3 Work as 'obligated labour'. This is the most general and the most abstract usage. This overlaps with although is not identical to the other two meanings. It points to elements of compulsion or obligation and would certainly include housework and emotional labour.

In each case there are usually some demarcations implied between work and non-work. This is usually fairly straightforward in the case of paid employment, although is blurred when individuals literally or metaphorically 'bring work home'. In the case of effort, especially physical effort, there are clear distinctions again to be made, the transitions often symbolized by a shower or a change of clothes. Even in the case of 'obligated labour' where such work may never be completed, there may be recognized breaks, however short, for a cup of coffee, a cigarette or to put one's feet up.

Many of these complexities may be lost in the focus upon the household. Yet it is important that people understand work in several different ways and often make distinctions between work and non-work. If we are to continue in the direction of exploring the household as a site for economic life, it would seem to be important to go beyond simple accounts of what goes on within such units to consider how such activities are described and evaluated by the participants themselves. What do household members define as work or non-work? How do they draw the boundaries, cognitively and in terms of everyday strategies? How do lines of power and authority within households shape not only what work is done by whom but also the strategies which might be devised to resist work demands or to set up demarcations between work and non-work?

Discussions of 'emotional labour' have possibly focused more upon the labour than on the emotional (Duncombe and Marsden, 1993). We know, and shall be exploring further, how work under-taken between and for family members becomes transmuted into a 'labour of love'. Family work, within households, includes the drawing up of boundaries between work and non-work and their evaluation. Such family work may perhaps have something to do with ethical notions about the limits of rationality.

One suggestive way of taking the argument further has been outlined by David Cheal in his discussion of 'moral economy' (Cheal, 1988a; 1988b). He firstly makes a distinction between moral economy and political economy, noting that the two are not mutually exclusive. He gives particular emphasis to the exchange of gifts between and within households. Such gifts are often, but not exclusively, made between individuals related by family ties. An analysis of such gift exchange in terms of rationality or political economy is clearly limited. In his terms: '. . . the gift economy is a ritual order of the social reproduction of small social worlds' (1988a: 104).

We may extend this analysis to all aspects of family work located within and between households. Such work clearly does have significance in terms of mainstream political economy and there is much to be gained from considering households as units within these wider macro-processes. But households do not simply function on behalf of the wider economy and it is important to consider the ways in which the moral economy meets and interacts with the political economy in the business of family life located in and between households.

2

Family and Stratification

Introduction

Issues to do with work, employment and the economy are also clearly linked to issues to do with social class and stratification. This in part reflects the Marxist, or at least broadly materialist, origins of many of the British debates about social class. Further, the fact that it is almost impossible to isolate discussions of work and employment focused upon the household from issues to do with class divisions is yet another reflection of the increasingly kaleidoscopic understanding of current social processes and categories.

In this chapter I aim to bring issues of class and stratification into sharper focus and to explore ways in which these have been or might be linked to family and household processes. I shall treat the term 'stratification' as the more general term dealing with the various ways in which hierarchical social divisions within society might be recognized or signified. Class I shall treat as an important form of stratification clustering around, although not always in an unproblematic fashion, forms of economic differentiation.

To some it might appear that the themes of this chapter have a somewhat old-fashioned air about them. Politically, there might appear to be a wide measure of agreement that 'class' is a thing of the past, with John Major aiming to move Britain further in the direction of a classless society, Baroness Thatcher claiming that the language of class is a relic of outmoded Marxism (Thatcher, 1992) and the British Labour Party apparently also keen to expunge the rhetoric of class from its vocabulary. In sociological discussion, the usefulness of the concept of class is being discussed and questioned more and more and the theoretical models, especially those which derive in some measure from Marxism and which focus upon the relationships between structure, consciousness and action, are increasingly found wanting (Crompton, 1993). It is almost as if the theoretical and methodological usefulness of class crumbled with the collapse of the Berlin Wall.

Putting these wider debates to one side for the present, I shall accept that modern societies such as Britain continue to be characterized by considerable inequalities which are broadly economic in nature and origin and that these inequalities have a structural character. By this I mean that their origins do not lie chiefly in individual characteristics and that they have some measure of persistence over time. Class remains one of the ways in which people other than sociologists talk about and understand their world, although these understandings may not always be congruent with those of sociologists. To be aware of major differences and discontinuities in lives and experiences I have only, as Engels did almost 150 years ago, to move out from the centre of Manchester to the affluent suburbs of Bramhall or Bowden. The question at issue is not the existence of such differentiations. It is more a question of whether the traditional theories and methodologies associated with the concept of class are adequate to describe and to account for these differences.

Class as a Key Variable

Perhaps one of the most obvious ways in which class enters into analyses of family processes is where it appears as a key variable. Thus we might have an array of attitudes or behaviour patterns associated with family living and an attempt may be made to see whether these are affected by social class. Class may be used as a test variable; for example it might be asked how much of the variance in conjugal relationships may be attributed to class as opposed to, say, social networks. Or it may be treated as an independent variable. Here class is hypothesized as being able to explain or account for variations in family practices or attitudes. In some cases it might appear that data may be analysed according to social class simply because previous researchers have always done so.

One straightforward example may be provided by Haskey's discussion of divorce and its association with class and occupation. At the outset, one problem is recognized. The majority of petitions for divorce are initiated by women but the measure of class is based upon the occupations of husbands, in this case provided by the wives initiating divorce (Haskey, 1984: 420). Haskey also notes the uncertainties involved in the classification of occupations, especially those which fall into Social Class V, the unskilled manual. In class terms, the three highest categories for divorce are the unskilled, the unemployed and members of the armed services; the three lowest are professionals, intermediate and skilled manual. In terms of more occupationally based socio-economic groups, the three highest groups are the unskilled manual, the armed services and personal service workers. The lowest groups are those who work on their own account, manual workers in the supervisory or foreman grades and professional workers.

Such findings are broadly consistent with findings elsewhere. However, there are clear problems at all stages of the analysis, from the very processes of classification through to the more theoretical understanding of the nature and significance of the discovered relationships. This is not to criticize Haskey or other scholars working within a broadly demographic framework. It is, rather, to point out that such findings not only need to be treated with the usual caution but that, more importantly, they have to be treated as the beginning rather than the conclusion of any analysis of the relationships between divorce and class or occupational status.

One well-known and important example of this usage of class is provided by the Newsons' various studies of child-rearing practices in Britain. These studies lay great emphasis upon the importance of the class factor in distinguishing child-rearing patterns. They also, explicitly and implicitly, raise questions about the logic and implications of this mode of analysis. Although focusing largely upon mothers and their relationships with and understandings of their children, the measure of class used is derived from the occupation of the male partner. In common with many other studies, they derive their classifications from the UK Registrar General, combining categories I and II (professional and managerial) and dividing category III into two, namely between the white-collar and the skilled manual. The combined categories I and II together with the white-collar workers in category III represent the middle class; the rest are taken as working class. The Newsons recognize the complexities of these operations noting, for example, that the working class category IV is something of a 'rag-bag of occupations' (J. Newson and E. Newson, 1965: 230). They also recognize, more generally, the potentially arbitrary nature of the categories and try to take this into account in their analysis: '. . . we have concentrated mainly on class differences which are comparatively clear-cut, and upon trends which remain consistent as one ascends the class scale' (1965: 154).

The Newson's account of the strategies adopted in handling classificatory anomalies and difficulties are particularly revealing. While the main basis of classification was the father's occupation, there were occasions where the mother's occupation, or former occupation, might be used in order to upgrade the status of the household. Thus, where a father was a shop assistant (III – white collar) and the mother a teacher (II), the class of the mother was adopted (1965: 153). Again, there were occasions where the classification might be difficult as a result of the vagueness of the occupational title: 'representative' or 'salesman', for example. Here, the Newsons argued that it might be necessary to take other factors into account such as the kind of house or '. . . the extent to which the wife appears to be an educated or cultured person' (1965: 153–4). Clearly, they took this business of classification very seriously and, perhaps more than other researchers, were prepared to spell out some of the considerations entering their routine decisions. However, such explicitness also provides insight into relatively un-examined ideas about the interrelationships between class and gender in the context of family relationships.

Other issues are to do with the fact that, in many cases, there were substantial overlaps between the classes. Thus, if we take their use of a compounded measure of 'child-centredness' we find that 25 per cent of middle-class respondents were classified as 'low scorers' while 32 per cent of working-class mothers were classified as 'high scorers'. (J. Newson and E. Newson, 1970: 532). Thus, while the overall trends were in the expected direction, with the middle class being classified as being more child-centred than the working class, in both classes there were minorities whose experiences might be worth exploring further.

Again, the complexities of analysis begin when one tries to account for these associations. Take, for example, the clear class divisions revealed around issues of sexual and bodily modesty (1970: 408–10). The differences are clear and consistent along the gradient, with the working-class mothers showing greater degrees of modesty than their middle-class counterparts. The intriguing question here is to do with explaining the connections between these beliefs and practices and class. Given that class is a complex and compound measure, what particular aspects either singly or in interaction contribute to these particular outcomes?

In more general terms, the Newsons certainly recognize the complexity of the operation of seeking '. . . to analyse the interconnections between two such complexities as child-rearing behaviour and social class' (J. Newson and E. Newson, 1965: 160). There are difficulties in controlling for variables and in assessing causation. They recognize that class is a multi-faceted phenomenon and the need for middle-class researchers to avoid class stereotypes (1965: 159). Stronger on description than on analysis, the Newsons approach questions of causation with understandable and exemplary caution.

With all these cautions, the explanations appear to be of two kinds. In the first place, there are broadly materialist understandings of class, often of a very simple and straightforward kind. Thus, the absence of spare rooms would be enough to account for children sharing a bedroom with siblings or parents. Similarly, hours of work and the structure of the working day might well limit a father's opportunities to interact with his children and these factors may be linked to other dimensions of class.

Elsewhere, however, the Newsons offer a more complex cultural understanding of class. They recognize that class is to do with social and cultural values as well as 'material achievements and expectations' and state, perhaps slightly provocatively: 'Indeed, if we knew enough about it, the way in which parents bring up their children might well provide a safer guide to social categorization than can the father's occupation alone' (J. Newson and E. Newson, 1965: 152). The language of dependent and independent variables becomes inappropriate. Class is not something outside child-rearing practices; these practices are part of how class is lived and understood. There is a mutual or circular causality, with the beliefs and practices contributing to the reproduction of class identities as much as class shaping these attitudes and practices. It would seem reasonable to argue that this more cultural understanding of class is the one which dominates in the Newsons' study.

The Newsons' study is a particularly rich and detailed example of the use of class as a key variable but it clearly does not stand alone. A more recent and more modest study, although dealing with related matters, is Mary Boulton's study of the experience of mothering (Boulton, 1983). Again there is reluctant use of the husband's occupation and an analysis in terms of middle-class and working-class responses. But she is also more concerned with issues of gender and the way in which this may sometimes establish commonalities both across and within class categories. In attempting to explore the class differences further, she suggests that crucial factors in the response to motherhood were education and previous work experience. Also important was the extent to which there was a community of mothers to serve as a kind of reference group. What we have here is the beginning of a more experiential and processual account of class.

The Unit Debate

John Goldthorpe, in his defence of the 'conventional view' of class analysis against those who criticized the apparent neglect of women in social mobility studies, argued that: '. . . it is the family rather than the individual which forms the basic unit of stratification' (Goldthorpe, 1983: 465). Such an argument is a well-established one in discussions of social class: 'The family, not the physical person, is the true unit of class and class theory' (Schumpeter, 1955: 113), or 'The failure of some writers to recognise that the family, not the individual, is the appropriate social unit of the class system has led to certain confusions in their analysis' (Parkin, 1972: 14). In the debates around Goldthorpe's defence, the formula 'the family not the individual' was repeated as a kind of mantra; the implication was that this was a self-evident statement about the world.

Yet there are certainly some unexplored ambiguities in the formulation. McRae amplifies her support for this argument in these terms: '. . . the primary means whereby advantage and rewards are transmitted from one generation to the next, with the major class divisions in society running *between* but not *through* families' (McRae, 1990: 119; her emphasis).

Marshall, on the other hand, when he comes to present Goldthorpe's restatement, refers to links between women's employment experiences, the class positions and mobilities of their husbands and voting patterns and continues: 'These and similar data confirm that the conjugal family remains the unit of class fate, class formation and class action' (Marshall, 1990b: 60).

While both these arguments might be true they are not necessarily referring to the same unit. Such ambiguities are also found in critics of the conventional view. Walby, for example, makes the point that 'a substantial minority of people do not live in family units' (Walby, 1986: 13). This is a perfectly reasonable point but it does not necessarily address the family-as-unit issue since while a substantial minority might not live in family-based households, the number of people without family relationships of any kind are very few indeed. When it comes to matters such as inheritance, an important mechanism for the transmission of class advantages, it may well be family connections rather than family units which are the important considerations.

Yet the logic behind treating the family rather than the individual as a unit seems clear enough. In the first place, the emphasis underlines the fact that the focus is upon class and class relationships rather than upon systems of, occupationally based, prestige. Further, the stress on family would seem to underline the structured nature of such class relationships.

In this context, class is seen as some combination of market situation and work situation, a reflection of differing mixes of Marxian and Weberian perspectives. This stress, however, implies a difficulty, namely how to account for those individuals who are weakly attached to or even detached from market or work situations, including some women and most children. The logic would seem to suggest that these individuals are either outside class altogether or connected to the class structure through others, mostly adult men, who are more centrally involved in the market.

This would seem to be the main argument, although there is an important subsidiary one to do with the reproduction of class relationships over time. Thus while, in a modern society, family relationships are not the basis for social stratification, they do constitute a major mechanism whereby such differences are reproduced. This argument, although an important one, is not one which emerged strongly in the debate about women and stratification and Goldthorpe's defence of the conventional view.

The difficulty which has received most emphasis has been that to do with the position of women in the class system. Children are only beginning to receive the same kind of consideration. It is pointed out that women increasingly have involvements in market and work situations in their own right and while these involvements may be different from those of men they are not necessarily of any less significance. Following a slightly different tack, it is further argued that gender is an important source of stratification itself and not one to be subsumed under discussions of class; divisions within families/ households may be at least as important as those between such units.

The argument is not simply one of sexism or intellectual justice. It is also that gender makes a difference, theoretically and empirically. Much of the debate here has focused upon the incidence and importance or otherwise of 'cross-class families', that is households where the class position of the husband differs from that of his wife. More generally, debate has focused upon the methodological difficulties that might arise where there is more than one earner within a household.

More complex issues arise if we ask what is meant by the idea of 'unit' in this case. Units may be simple wholes such that they would cease to be units were they to be broken down into their constituent parts or they may be complex or compound wholes where parts may be detached without seriously weakening the overall integrity of the unit as a whole. Further, units may be strongly or weakly bounded, clearly distinct from other units or overlapping or merging with other units. For the most part it may be said that, in a modern society, families tend to be complex units which are moderately bounded. This clearly has implications when we consider their position in some wider entity such as the class system.

But perhaps the most important difficulty is to do with terminology. In most cases the word 'family' is used, although 'household' is sometimes preferred. In some cases, both terms may be used in the context of a single argument. Often the referent seems to be even narrower, namely 'marriage'. Even Leiulfsrud and Woodward, while presenting some forceful criticisms of the treatment of the family as an undifferentiated unit still, in their actual analysis, concentrate upon marriage (1988). Such differences are important. If we are implicitly or explicitly referring to marriage we are raising questions to do with 'cross-class families', dual-earner couples, the determination of party political preferences and so on. To refer, implicitly or explicitly, to household raises all these issues but also issues to do with socialization and the status of children. Yet again, to use the term 'family' is to refer to ties based upon marriage and parenthood and issues to do with inheritance and the reproduction of class divisions over time. The failure to identify what is meant by 'family' represents one of the main weaknesses of this 'unit' argument.

One possible compromise has been suggested by Marshall where he argues that it is not a question of chosing between individuals or families but one of seeing individuals *in* families (Marshall et al., 1990: 61). This approach certainly does allow for a fuller recognition of gender differences and for an analysis of the interplay between class and gender differences, although it does not fully address the problem of the fluidity of familial boundaries.

Marriage, Family and Household

I have suggested that one of the major difficulties associated with the 'unit' debate is the failure to distinguish between marriage, family and household. Each term raises slightly different issues to do with the relationship between class and family practices. In the case of marriage, the focus has often been upon 'cross-class families' or couples. Here there have been debates over the actual incidence of such marriages, their particular structure, whether their identification is more an artifact of classification schemes rather than a 'real' source of divergence in class experience, and whether, if identified, they make any real difference (Britten and Heath, 1983; Goldthorpe, 1983; Leiulfsrud and Woodward, 1988; McRae, 1986). This last question is not simply a matter of voting behaviour. Leiulfsrud and Woodward consider class differences in terms of which partner looks after a sick child where both are working, issues of the control and management of money and differential access to symbolic property or cultural capital (1988). It may be important that the non-working-class partner has greater access to or control over those skills required in dealing with officialdom. The possession of such skills may well affect the well-being of the household as a whole. If it be recognized that most marriages consist of partners who, over the course of their whole individual life courses, have differing labour market and work situation experiences, then it should also be recognized that such differences are important in considering marital relationships:

> That unit is the meeting place for men and women, filtering relations of gender and power . . . The family unit may either moderate or amplify experiences gained in the relations of production. (Leiulfsrud and Woodward, 1988: 395)

Marriage may be seen as a context where class experiences are shared or clash. Halle's study of American blue-collar households, for example, found wives sometimes resenting the lower social status of their husbands and complaining about their language and presentation of self (Halle, 1984: 60).

Classically, marriage and discussions of marriage strategies (for example Segalen, 1986: 123–8) have been seen as crucial to discussions of class mobility and the cementing of class solidarities. Generally, the assumption would seem to be that such strategies belong more to pre-industrial than to modern societies. While the different class background of marital partners may be taken into account, in the analysis of divorce-proneness, for example, discussions of class and discussions of marriage would increasingly seem to belong to different areas of discourse. Yet it is by no means certain that such considerations belong to worlds we have lost or to the marriage strategies of members of royal families. Class considerations may still be of significance in the selection of a marriage partner just as marriage may be seen as one of the sites where class identities are constructed or reshaped.

Considerations of marriage clearly overlap with discussions of the household, although it should be remembered that significant numbers of households do not contain or consist of married couples. In discussions of households in general, as with the more special case of couple-based households, we are considering the different resources that members bring to the household, the processes by which these are shared or distributed and the consequences of these processes for individual life styles and life chances. With some modification this analysis could also apply to the growing numbers of single-person households in modern Britain and elsewhere. In terms of more compound households we may be considering what children (or other dependents) may derive from the household and also what they may contribute to that household and its overall class position.

Households, in so far as they are family-based households, raise further issues in the analysis of class. These are to do with socialization and the reproduction of class differences over time. In classical discussions it was often argued that one of the 'functions' of the family was the 'placing' of individuals within a class structure. Clearly such placing was not so passive or as straightforward as this way of describing the process might suggest. However, since most children are not born directly into work or market situations but into some form of family-based household, it becomes crucial to explore the processes whereby class identifications as well as life chances are transmitted to immature individuals.

Turning from households to families, we are turning from units which may or may not consist of family members to relationships within and between households, across or within generations. Again, the wider networks of family and kin are often important in considering processes of economic polarization and the strategies which individuals or households adopt in dealing with economic problems (see, for example, Payne, 1987). We also have considerations of the ways in which family members, located in different households, may be sources of overt or covert assistance regularly or at some crucial turning point in an individual life course (Bell, 1968; Finch, 1989; Finch and Mason, 1993). Such exchanges may sometimes be seen as mechanisms by which class positions are maintained or enhanced; conversely, the lack of access to such resources may be crucial in understanding downward mobility or processes of class polarization.

In considering intergenerational family relationships we are, of course, often considering inheritance in all its dimensions. Classically, such mechanisms were seen as crucial to the understanding of the transmission of privilege and disadvantage over time and therefore of the overall reproduction of class relationships. Some of the earlier statements about the family as a unit of class analysis (for example Schumpeter, 1955) had these considerations in mind rather than some of the more recently debated topics. More recent analysis has emphasized the continuing importance of inheritance, sometimes stressing the ways in which this might be gendered (for example Delphy and Leonard, 1992). Some sophisticated analysis could begin to unpick some of the complex interplays between family, private property, class and ideology (Abercombie, Hill and Turner, 1986; Savage et al., 1992).

These distinct, if interrelated, issues in class analysis may be summarized as follows:

Type of unit	Issue
Marriage	Cross-class marriages
	Marriage strategies
Household	Distribution of resources
	Polarization
	Socialization
	Reproduction
Family	Patterns of support
	Inheritance

Limits of Occupationally Based Measures

> . . . all class schemas are social constructs or, rather, the constructs of
> sociologists. (Crompton, 1993: 50)

Most models of social stratification, certainly most models of class,
use occupations as the basis for beginning classification. This
dominant orientation has implications for family studies.

As Goldthorpe and others have argued, the aim is to build up a
model of class which is a combination of market and work situation.
The work situation looks at hierarchies of skill and authority within
the workplace, while the market looks at the disposing of such skills
on the labour market and the differential rewards attached to their
disposal. Insofar as such scales seek to combine elements of Marxian
and Weberian approaches and claim to be broader than simple
measures of occupational status, it could be argued that they
encompass a lot of what, in the European context, is conventionally
understood by class. Problems exist as to where to draw the line
between different classes and around the descriptions of particular
occupations but nevertheless a case can be made out for the use of
such scales. Not only do occupationally based scales link market and
work situation they are also relatively simple, once constructed, they
have links with wider theoretical debates and, with some limitations,
they enable comparative research to be conducted.

In the context of family studies, however, and especially in the
context of the 'unit' debate, such classifications present problems.
The main one is in providing for the linkage between market and
work situations and domestic life. In conventional theory, Marxist or
functionalist, the link is usually seen as a financial one: the breadwinner or breadwinners bring in incomes for the support of the
family/household as a whole. It may also be suggested that certain
aspects of the work situation carry over into the home. A contrast
between a weekly pay packet and a monthly salary may have
implications for patterns of money management within the home
and, possibly, for the relationships between partners. Similarly,
contrasts between working with machines and working with people
might also influence domestic relationships:

> I'm involved with machines, my wife with people. You don't just turn
> off when you are involved with people. I turn off the machine and turn
> me off as well. Work, I leave at work. (MacRae, 1900: 80).

Community studies such as *Coal Is Our Life*, of course, showed how a predominantly male culture at work spilled over into domestic relations (Dennis, Henriques and Slaughter, 1956; see also Morgan, 1992). Hence it can be seen that occupationally based understandings of social class can point to important links between work and home, although the family tends to become a dependent variable in this mode of analysis.

Apart from the problem of establishing the nature of the linkages, theoretical and experiential, between home and work there are other difficulties with this occupational emphasis. Feminist scholars, for example, have pointed to difficulties when it comes to analysing the position of women within the class structure. Where these are taken account of at all, it is by no means certain that classifications developed on the basis of occupations will necessarily be a firm basis for the analysis of the class position of women. This is in part a function of the high proportion of part-time jobs within the British female labour market and the considerable bunching in certain semi-skilled or unskilled manual or non-manual occupations. Harris and Morris argue here for taking account of the distinction between positions in the occupational structure and positions in the labour market (Harris and Morris, 1986: 86–7). Women may always be seen as having a position, potential or actual, on the labour market even if they do not always have a position in the occupational structure. It may also be suggested that such conventional measures do not always accord with how women experience or understand the class structure. Abbott and Sapsford, for example, suggested that style of life might be more important than the job in shaping a woman's perceptions of class (Abbott and Sapsford, 1987: 128–9).

Certainly there are alternative ways of understanding social class: 'Individuals act within the class structure from a variety of starting platforms' (Leiulfsrud and Woodward, 1988: 395). As noted before, individuals are not born into occupations or, except very loosely, into market situations. They are born, as a rule, into households and into networks of familial and other relationships. Experientially, if not theoretically or methodologically, class begins at home and in the neighbourhood. Family relations do not simply function on behalf of class relationships: in a deep sense they *are* class relationships. This is not to substitute a family or a domestic model of class for an occupational one but simply to note that they both constitute major sites whereupon class understandings are shaped. If we wish to maintain the idea of 'the family' as a unit in wider systems of stratification then it is important to shift the emphasis away from work situations and labour markets.

Patterns of Class and Family Relations

In this section I aim both to illustrate some of the points already made and to take the argument further through drawing upon the work of sociologists and social historians. I shall look at some particular studies of working-class and middle-class family life in order to explore how it might be argued that 'the family' is a unit in these analyses.

The interplays between class and family relationships and the more subtle investigations into the ways in which the family might be said to be a unit of analysis have emerged most fully in some historical discussions. While earlier Marxist accounts might have given the impression that the family was at the receiving end of economic and historical processes, more detailed historical analyses, by no means unsympathetic to Marxism, allowed for a more complex analysis. This is marked, for example, in some discussions about 'proto-industrialization'. While the use and the meaning of the term is still open to debate, it can be said that the term developed out of a dissatisfaction with the conventional divide between pre-industrial and industrial societies and from the tendency, in the analyses of the transitions from the former to the latter, to view family and domestic relationships as merely responding to external forces. The analysis of 'proto-industrialization' did not simply aim to insert a new term between the familiar opposition but also to restore some sense of agency to ordinary households in a period of social and economic change and to allow for the exploration of diverse modes of transition. Key concepts included the analysis of household-based strategies in relation to demography, the deployment of household labour and household composition (for example Levine, 1977).

The classifications that follow refer to broad class classifications as they emerge in a variety of studies, historical and sociological. The purpose is largely illustrative, designed to show some of the ways in which the interplays between class, family and (often) gender emerge from and are analysed within these accounts. I look at three such broad headings: working class, middle class and the under-class.

Working-class families

Many of the insights and perspectives adopted in the analysis of proto-industrialization also appear in the analyses of processes of proletarianization and of working-class family life. Early accounts had tended either to see the working-class family as collapsing in the face of capitalism, industrialization and urbanization or as functioning, through the domestic division of labour within the home, to reproduce capitalist class relationships. Alternative accounts tended to stress the strengths of working-class family life and its ability to resist not only the potentially corrosive forces of modern capitalism but also state bureaucratic incursion into and attempts to control, the working class. Men and women, within these alternative accounts, could be seen as having some identities of interest and some ability to develop strategies or patterns of resistance and opposition (for example Humphries, 1982). Such revised accounts did not seek to sentimentalize the working-class family or to deny that there were indeed patterns of exploitation and domination between men and women within such households. However, they did seek to develop a greater sense of agency on the part of such households and to demonstrate the ways in which family relationships within and between households might contribute to the development of an oppositional working-class consciousness.

The cumulative effect of a whole range of socio-historical studies has been not only to provide for a more positive model of working-class family life but also to highlight variations within working-class experiences. In particular, attention was focused upon the lives of working-class women. Thus, Glucksmann stressed the importance of considering the ways in which women responded to the development of new industries and, in the inter-war years, in shaping working-class and gender consciousness (Glucksmann, 1986). These and other studies (for example Turbin, 1989) showed how class and gender each implicated the other and departed from conventional models which saw the working-class man as the chief bearer of class consciousness or class identity.

Yet this is not simply a question of gendering class analysis. If the origins of class differences might be said to lie in work and market situations, the day-to-day experiences of class lie across a number of intersecting sites with domestic relationships occupying a key place amongst these. A particularly apt example is provided by Jackson and Marsden's study of education and the working class (Jackson and Marsden, 1966). They consider the educational backgrounds and experiences of the parents, the importance of leadership in local organizations, the role of smaller families and of growing up in more or less heterogeneous neighbourhoods. Again, while focusing upon family influences, the family is not presented as a reified whole but as a set of relationships linked to wider locally based sets of relationships. Over twenty-five years later, Jordan et al., in their study of low-income households, were to show how members of their sample saw themselves in a local context, as members of an 'estate', as well as in a kinship context (Jordan et al., 1992: 254).

In looking at the socially mobile individuals themselves, Jackson and Marsden noted that husbands and wives tended to share very similar working-class and grammar-school experiences and this homogeneity extended to their intimate friends as well (Jackson and Marsden, 1966: 188). Despite their experience of mobility, many members of their sample continued to define class in terms of where they had come from rather than in terms of their present status. Their experiential accounts are expressed vividly:

> . . . a basic truth beyond the reach of our measuring tools was sometimes being affirmed. Class could be something in the blood, in the very fibre of a man or woman; a way of growing, feeling, judging, taken out of the resources of generations gone before. (1966: 192)

Yet to some, these working-class experiences were coming to be part of a world we had lost, part of a historically interesting but now superseded body of 'community studies'. In the decades following Jackson and Marsden's study there were increasing discussions of the 'new', the 'affluent' or the 'privatized' working class. It might be argued that here, indeed, the family was truly the unit of class analysis since nuclear family relationships embedded in the idea of the home became a central life interest, the major project which gave working, and the rewards attached to work, any meaning that might remain. Newby et al., suggested a useful contrast between the 'home-centredness' associated with the geographically mobile working class and the 'family-centredness' associated with the geographically mobile middle class (Newby et al., 1985: 96). Perhaps the contrast is never as sharp as this in reality but it serves as a useful reminder that class and domestic life may be combined in different ways, differently accented, and that these differences should be taken into account when locating family and household in discussions of the changing class structure.

Attempts to capture present day working-class experience seem to lack the certainties associated with both the 'traditional' working class and the 'affluent workers'. Their lives appear to be much more vulnerable, much more prone to the threat of unemployment as well as all kinds of environmental hazards from crime to air pollution. Yet Jordan et al.'s account of a low-income housing estate does have affinities with some of the earlier studies. The identity of male breadwinner still seems to be of significance and part of the way in which men present themselves as morally adequate individuals, both as workers and providers. Part of this self-identity, however, includes an understanding of government policy, income tax and the range of benefits and entitlements that might be available (Jordan et al., 1992: 131).

Somewhat more complex is Judith Stacey's detailed anthropological account of working-class families in America's 'Silicon Valley' (J. Stacey, 1991). Somewhat provocatively she argues that it is these families, rather than white middle-class families, that are 'the unrecognized pioneers of the postmodern family revolution' (1991: 26). Such household arrangements, prone to considerable flux and variation, seem to have little in common with the relative stability of traditional or affluent working-class families. Work and employment are uncertain just as marriage and parental relationships are uncertain. Yet, in common with some of the more historically based studies, Stacey seeks to go beyond images of such families as victims and explores the complex survival strategies that members of such families engage in. Further, again in common with other studies, it is women who are at the forefront of elaborating postmodern family practices (1991: 268).

Middle-class families

Again, historical studies seem to have relatively little difficulty in linking issues of class, gender and family life. Thus, in what must be seen as a major study of class formation, Davidoff and Hall show the importance of family-based projects in the making of the English middle class (Davidoff and Hall, 1987). They discuss the interplays between property, family relations and class formation; the interactions between religion, class, gender and family around notions of respectability; and the growing importance of domestic property and the idea of the home as a stable location of the self in growing contrast to the more impersonal worlds of commerce and business. A similar picture emerges from Dyhouse's account of mothers and daughters during the period 1870–1914 (Dyhouse, 1986). Here too, in a study using autobiographical material, we see a complex nexus linking gender, family, class, respectability and social and physical distance. While the basis of these middle-class homes was clearly the – often remote and distant – fathers' occupation, the day-to-day work of maintaining class boundaries and distance very much devolved upon the women within the home.

In North America, Blumin's account of the rise of the middle class emphasizes a variety of 'family strategies'. These involve limiting family size, socialization into values of achievement and respectability, keeping children at home for longer periods than had been the case previously, formal schooling and encouraging young men to delay marriage (Blumin, 1989: 187). Again, the vital role of women in the process of middle-class formation emerges clearly in this analysis.

Sociological studies of the middle classes, in contrast, have more often tended to emphasize features of the market and work situations. However, it is not entirely true to say that issues of gender and family have been absent from more recent discussions. In the case of gender, for example, Abercrombie and Urry lay considerable emphasis upon this as a factor in distinguishing what they see as a major fault-line within middle-class locations: that between the deskilled white-collar workers whose positions were becoming indistinguishable in many respects from those of manual workers and the 'service class' (Abercrombie and Urry, 1983). The former has become increasingly dominated by women workers, while the latter continues to be dominated by men, especially at the higher levels (see also Lockwood, 1958).

Issues of family are a little more difficult to recover from sociological discussions of the middle class, although these are becoming more numerous. It might certainly be seen as a submerged theme in the contrast between the 'service class' and the white-collar class. Crompton, for example, argues that the domestic responsibilities of middle-class wives may be seen as liberating their husbands to pursue a service-class career (Crompton, 1986: 124). She relates these possibilities to certain features of the service-class career: the unusual hours or demands upon time from workplace or colleagues, the irregular but sometimes frequent absences from home and the mixture of social and geographical mobility that such careers often require (see also Edgell, 1980). This kind of analysis can be developed to include dual-career households where both partners may be pursuing careers or further educational qualifications. In all cases it is not gender simply, but gender mediated through patterns of domestic arrangements that are important in the construction of a middle-class career.

In the period between Davidoff and Hall's study and more recent discussions of the deskilled white-collar classes, we are dealing with considerable varieties of middle-class experiences and it is possible that these experiences have become more, rather than less, various. However, even a brief overview must indicate how deeply the family is implicated in such class processes. Savage et al., outline the assets influencing middle-class formation as: property assets, organization assets and cultural assets (Savage et al., 1992: 17). It is not difficult to link these assets to household/family-based and gendered strategies. In the case of property assets we have issues to do with owner-occupation and social and geographical mobility. They argue that much modern middle-class migration is to do with changes in household circumstances rather than with work-based career demands (1992: 185). Such movements are also linked to cultural assets, associated with the character of a locality or its educational facilities. Other cultural assets are clearly home-based or home-linked, such as books, music and general style of life. Savage et al., also go on to distinguish a variety of household types relevant to middle-class men: single-male households, men with partners at home, men with partners in non-middle-class jobs and dual-career households. (1992: 156) Issues of family and household, again interweaving with gender, are central to their analysis.

Many other class/family themes may be isolated and explored. These include issues to do with inheritance, physical and cultural capital and the reproduction of class identities over generations. There are issues to do with patterns of support between households and generations which enable younger generations to develop or continue in a middle-class life style or occupation (Bell, 1968). There are issues to do with consumption and lifestyle which have complex relationships with occupation and market situation but which are also home-based to a very large extent. And there are a whole set of practices which might be described as 'class-work', that is domestically based practices which serve to preserve class and status boundaries and middle-class ways of being in the world. Again these practices are often highly gendered.

Certainly, family and marriage continue to be major themes in the lives of many middle-class individuals. Jordan, Redley and James, suggest that 'the family' may provide a major source of legitimation for some class-based strategies, such as seeking private education for children or taking out private health care insurance (Jordan, Redley and James, 1994). Themes of partnership and parenting are linked to more apparently individualistic ideologies of making something of oneself. (1994: 38). Contrary to earlier assumptions, family is not seen in opposition to individualistic striving; rather the two seem to be complementary.

The Underclass

Recent debates about the underclass raise further questions about the relationships between stratification and family relations. As Smith argues, the idea of the underclass is a 'counterpart to ideas of social classes' (Smith, 1992: 4). Members of the underclass: '. . . belong to family units having no stable relationship at all with the "mode of production"' (1992: 4). A straightforward way of identifying units is to see them as units which are more or less wholly dependent upon state benefits.

The idea of the underclass deals with a problem already identified in mainstream class analysis, namely one of how to treat those who have no stable relationships to work or market situations. While various attempts have been made to incorporate the experiences of women, children and the retired into conventional class analysis, the positions of those adults of either sex who belong to the long-term unemployed present deeper problems. The idea of the underclass would seem to identify those whose position, although defined in terms of the class system, are nevertheless outside that system.

Families would seem to be implicated in constructions of the underclass in a variety of ways. First, membership of the underclass is mediated through family or household units. Thus a person would not be defined as a member of the underclass simply because she or he had experienced long-term unemployment; the point would seem to revolve around membership of a domestic unit where no adult members had a regular relationship with the formal labour market. As Smith points out, such an understanding depends upon a fairly conventional construction of the nuclear-family-based household (Smith, 1992: 92). Second, considerable debate has focused upon those family structures or practices which are thought to be especially associated with membership of the underclass, in particular single-parent households. Not all such households can be defined as members of the underclass and not all members of the underclass can be identified as belonging to single-parent households. Nevertheless there are some associations between household structure, poverty and weak labour-market position in fact as well as in rhetoric. Whatever the realities of the situation, the single-parent household has been constructed as a key image in underclass debates.

The concept of the underclass has proved to be especially contro-versial partly because of its political implications and partly on theoretical or conceptual grounds. Thus it has been argued that the term has little conceptual power, that it is difficult to identify empirically, that there do not appear to be any major attitudinal differences between those so identified and the rest of the population and so on (Bagguley and Mann, 1992; Smith, 1992). Similarly, the supposed links between the underclass and particular household forms have been examined critically, showing the links to be weaker than is often supposed or calling into question the implied lines of causation from family forms to economic deprivation. Further, it might be maintained that the supposed underclass cannot be under-stood in isolation from wider processes of differentiation and polarization taking place within society. However, discussion of the underclass does throw into sharp light some of the problems with more traditional class analysis which is based upon relatively stable identifications with work or market situations.

Other Stratifications

Class is understood to be one example, often the major example, of a range of possible stratification systems. In all cases we are dealing with systems of structured inequalities, with class focusing upon economic inequalities. Many of the issues to do with class and family or household can also be applied to these other modes of stratification.

Issues of gender and age will be examined in more detail in later chapters. Both these have strong and apparently obvious connections with family structures and practices while also throwing up their own distinct set of theoretical issues. Issues of race and ethnicity have more obviously problematic relationships both with class, as the term has conventionally been understood, and with family.

The construction of ethnic boundaries and the assignment of individuals to racial or ethnic groups have clearly been of crucial political and theoretical significance in our own and recent times. It does not require too much effort to see both these processes as being concerned with real or imagined family connections. Bars on intermarriage, for example, constitute an important method of social closure for ethnic groups and the racialist identification of stigmatized or excluded groups depends upon a careful examination of family records and relationships. The rights and statuses of immigrants may depend upon familial identification.

Closer to home, family sociologists, including feminist sociologists, may be justifiably taken to task for adopting a too ethnocentric approach to their analyses, ignoring the varieties of ethnic traditions that exist within a modern society (Barrett and McIntosh, 1985). This becomes particularly relevant where 'the family' is identified as a major source of oppression. Is this true for all women? Or for all kinds of family?

These discussions do present analysts with a central dilemma. Clearly, all kinds of errors will be committed if we continue to talk of 'the British family', for example. Rates of divorce or remarriage, for instance, might be assumed to apply across the whole population. On the other hand, while seeking to recognize ethnic diversity in a multicultural society, ethnic boundaries may be too readily or too easily constructed by, say, white Western analysts. There may be oversimplified references to 'the Chinese family', 'the Muslim family' and so on just as, in the past, there have been over-simplified references to 'the Jewish family'. Popular white discourses, indeed, often identify different groups according to their supposed family practices: 'Asians' are considered to be more family orientated, more caring, have arranged marriages etc., while Afro-Carribean families are perceived as being more disorganized, more prone to breakdown. If we are to avoid the danger of reproducing widely held stereotypes we require more detailed analysis which, as in the case of Werbner's study of Pakistani families in Manchester, shows the interweavings of ethnicity, class and gender (Werbner, 1993).

Here, as elsewhere, one strategy might be to examine the dominant groups, that is, in this case, 'white families'. We have already noted, anecdotally, how members of white households might define 'others' in terms of their supposed family practices. In deploying these typifications, they are also engaged in the business of typifying their own family practices. To say that 'they' are more caring in relation to the elderly is also to highlight anxieties about our own groups and the treatment of the old or retired. More generally, we would be concerned with the strategies of closure or distance adopted by households around issues of racial or ethnic difference, housing strategies, marriage strategies and so on. There is little doubt that much of this material is already present but it does, perhaps, require being brought together in a framework which links family practices with constructions of whiteness, ethnic difference or ethnic superiority.

Perhaps one of the most interesting areas of social stratification from a family perspective is that to do with social status. Clearly this has links both with social class and, especially, ethnicity, although the study of social status has its own particular history. The term is taken to refer to the unequal distribution of prestige or esteem within a society, with the focus tending to be upon patterns of consumption and style of life rather than upon market relationships. The term conventionally applies to individuals, although it can also apply to families/households and to individuals within households or families.

In the classic American studies of status systems in small- to middle-sized towns – Middletown, Yankee City and so on – family relationships and family practices were found to be inextricably woven into everyday status assignments. There were wealthy or well-established families, dominant in power as well as prestige. These families will often be referred to by name. Other family groups may not be so individually identified but may be located in terms of some prized or stigmatized label: respectable folk, families who breed like rabbits, families on the wrong side of the tracks and so on. In the British context familiar distinctions between the 'rough' and the 'respectable' revolve, in part, around the status of households and the active ways in which they present themselves to the outside world: the way they look after their gardens or yards, how their children are sent to school and so on.

Perhaps a key concept here is that of 'reputation'. Reputation can, of course, be almost wholly detached from family considerations as when we talk of a person's reputation as a good worker, a good athlete, an unreliable individual and so on. Elsewhere, perhaps in smaller communities, whole families or households may gain prized or, more often perhaps, stigmatized reputations. In the case of the latter, interventions from various state agencies may play a major part in defining the negative reputations of particular families. Finally, there may be reputations within family networks; reputations as good or bad providers or as meeting or failing to meet what are understood to be appropriate family obligations (Finch, 1989; Finch and Mason, 1993).

Alternative Approaches

In considering the debate about whether it is the family rather than the individual that is the unit of class analysis, a variety of problems were identified. Nevertheless, as a brief consideration of some case studies illustrated, family and class can be seen as having a variety of interconnections. Considerations of other forms of stratification – gender, age, ethnicity and status – may complicate this analysis but may also suggest further lines of inquiry. In the light of these discussions I shall consider various strategies for taking family practices seriously in the analysis of class divisions.

It should not be forgotten that it was largely the feminist critique of the conventional approach to social class which revived some of these questions. In this connection, Abbott and Sapsford outline a range of possible solutions for the woman and class analysis problem. In the first place, the household is taken as the unit and the woman's occupational position is taken into account. This is commonly associated with analysis of 'cross-class families'. Second, and more simply, it is possible to locate women without any reference to household. This would, in effect, take the individual as the unit in the class system. Third, analysts may move away from occupation and work situations altogether and develop measures of class associated with consumption. Revised versions of 'housing classes' may be seen as one variation on this theme. Finally, there may be an attempt to locate women by taking account of both their paid labour and their positions in the domestic divisions of labour (Abbott and Sapsford, 1987: 18). For the sake of completeness we might also retain the 'head of household' approach with the modification that we take whoever is the chief or sole earner.

In much of this debate, the issue of cross-class families has attracted a great deal of attention. To date, probably the most sophisticated treatment of the problems associated with the analysis of such 'families' has been provided by Graetz (1991). He distinguishes between types of family class location. 'Families' (or, more properly, 'households') are first distinguished between single-earner and dual- earner. The latter are broken down into class homogeneous and class heterogeneous households, the latter being further broken down between traditional (where the man's status is higher) and non-traditional. Using a recent version of Eric Olin Wright's classification, Graetz distinguishes between degrees of class heterogeneity within marriage: households can be seen as class homogeneous, class compatible, class mixed or class opposing. In his analysis of Australian families, Graetz found that most households were most likely to be single earner, class homogeneous or class compatible (1991: 111). He also found that the degree of hetero-geneity mattered for an individual's class identification.

In these more complex models, the household becomes a kind of filter through which occupationally derived identities and experi-ences are filtered. An alternative approach is to develop a more composite model of class position which includes both domestic and occupational identities. Abbott and Sapsford, for example, suggest that a woman's 'style of life' was more important than job in determining a perception of class (Abbott and Sapsford, 1987: 128–9). Charles, while noting that a woman's subjective class appeared to be linked more closely to her partner's occupational status than her own occupational status, also pointed to a range of other influential factors (Charles, 1990). These included their own educational experiences, housing status and more qualitative and experiential accounts of their own backgrounds. In this more finely nuanced analysis, housewives did not necessarily feel marginal to the class system despite their relative lack of labour market status.

These more or less random suggestions have been given more solid status in various composite indices of class position. Thus Osborn (1987) combined father's occupation, the highest educational qualification of either parent, housing tenure, type of accommodation, number of persons per room and car and telephone ownership. Somewhat similarly, but with greater sensitivity to gender issues, Oakley and Rajan (1991) used six measures of social class: male and female occupations, tenure, woman's education, car ownership and telephone ownership. In these analyses, class remains a unity but it is a complex unity: the household becomes the unit in that it is the site where all these indices converge.

Such approaches are clearly important and, while introducing considerable complexity into the analysis, both take seriously the idea of the household as a unit while recognizing a variety of elements combining to make up class position. What is perhaps missing in these accounts is both a sense of the subjective meaning of these indicators, taken separately or in combination, and a sense of the processes by which these measures combine and influence each other over time.

Again, there are various suggestions in the literature as to how such experiential accounts might be constructed or developed. Thus autobiographical approaches to studies of social mobility recognize that such mobility is a matter of experiences combining over time, continuities with and breaks from the past or between generations (Bertaux and Thompson, 1994). Elliott argues for a recognition of the importance of the 'microclimates' of families, for example the shared experiences of siblings. Such understandings frequently get lost in more individualized surveys of social mobility or social class (Elliott, 1994). Jordan et al.'s lower income male breadwinners give a 'historical' account of their current employment situation, linking autobiography and history (Jordan et al., 1992: 90). In a different area again, Gill Jones's concept of 'class trajectories' (Jones, 1988) constitutes another suggestion as to how, in looking at young people, to structure father's class, age of leaving education, class of first job and current occupational class in order to culminate in a 'youth class'. Again this can be an analysis of some considerable complexity but it does provide what is missing in many other accounts, namely a sense of process based upon cumulative experiences. In terms of the present concerns, these analyses remind us that households consist of individuals who have histories just as the household itself has a history.

What we are moving towards here is the recognition of a variety of class sites, with occupation/workplace and household constituting two of the major ones. Halle, studying American blue-collar workers, argued that the image of class structure is based upon the following distinct identities: lives at work based on the identity of the working man or woman, lives outside work revolving around the middle-class/working-class distinction and a sense of 'Americanness' (Halle, 1984: 203). While lives at work may seem relatively re- stricted, lives outside work are identified with a 'certain fluidity' (1984: 77). In his historical analysis, Blumin (1989) writes of five 'categories of experience' relevant to constructing the middle-class way of life: work, consumption, residential location, formal and informal voluntary associations, and family organization and strategies (p. 11).

All these more pluralist analyses recognize the household as a major site for class identification. On other occasions, of course, workplace may constitute the major site. This point is argued directly by Coxon, Davies and Jones when they state that it is 'untenable' to argue 'that a single structure pervades the social consciousness' (1986: 13). They too stress the importance of the context in which class language is 'elicited and used' (1986: 161).

I would argue, therefore, for family and household relationships as constituting a major, but not an exclusive, site for the generation and regeneration of class identities. The extent to which such identities coalesce with identities generated from other sites remains a matter for empirical investigation, as does the extent or ways in which family/household generated identities become the basis for class action. Two other issues may be suggested for further investigation. The first is the question of class salience. We can no longer assume that class looms equally large for all individuals in society or that, where it does not occupy a large part in a person's social mapping, the person concerned is suffering from false class consciousness. Salience may therefore vary between individuals, within an individual's life course, and between different sites of class identification.

Linked to this is a theme which I call 'class embeddedness' which is also linked to questions to do with the experiences of class derived from various sites over a particular autobiography or career. Here I am talking about the ways in which different class sites reinforce or contradict one another. At one extreme, say the traditional working-class model, we see a cumulative and mutually reinforcing set of experiences through early family experiences, these embodied in a distinctive and homogeneous location, reinforced through subsequent experiences in education, work and the formation of new households. Clearly such embedded class trajectories may appear at all social levels. In contrast, we have the situation where the various sites are weakly connected or may, indeed, contradict one another. Over time there may be major discontinuities. Experiences of social and geographical mobility plus the effect of divergent class sites at any one time may lead to a more fragmented or pluralistic class identity. Using Parkin's analysis of social closure (Parkin, 1974), we may ask whether strategies based upon the workplace, such as monopolistic controls over the labour market, are paralleled by strategies within the neighbourhood. Patterns of work-based solidarity may not necessarily carry over into the family and neighbourhood. The links between different sites and different patterns of solidarity and exclusion would seem to be an interesting topic for further investigation.

In this connection, one factor of some importance would be the possible impact of family change upon class identification. Many models of family/class linkages seem to presuppose a conventional and relatively stable model of household structure. However, in a society characterized by high divorce rates and reconstitution of household units, stable class identifications on the part of growing children, or indeed their parents, cannot be assumed. Social and geographical mobility needs to be related to a sense of household mobility, the movement between and through differently constituted households. The consequences of such movements for class or status identification have yet to be systematically explored.

If, therefore, we wish to continue with the idea of the family or the household as the unit of class stratification it would seem important to depart, at least in some respects, from occupationally based measures of class. Simply combining the economic statuses of the adult household members, while clearly an advance, does not seem to answer all the problems associated with the original contradiction. Developing more composite indices answers more questions but raises further ones, especially in terms of the nature of class experience. Whatever strategies are adopted, it would seem likely that the requirement will be for more qualitatively based understandings of class and family living and a recognition of the diversity and range of sites through which class understandings might be generated.

Conclusion

It is clear that class analysis is in something of a crisis and that the one-time centrality of class in British sociology is no longer assured. There have been suggestions that class analysis has reached the end of its period of usefulness, either because of the overall decline of class salience and class understandings on the part of the population at large or because of the rising significance of other forms of inequality, notably those to do with ethnicity, gender and, possibly, age. Within social analysis, there may be suggestions that class is loosing its power as an explanatory variable.

Even those who argue that class analysis continues to have a promising future (Goldthorpe and Marshall, 1992) appear to do so in terms that suggest that such analysis no longer occupies the high theoretical ground that it was once supposed to occupy. There has been a growing recognition that the position has changed and that the centrality of class can no longer be assumed or taken for granted. Thus Newby et al. refer to the growing opaque character of the British class structure and class processes, arguing that this reflects the increasing social and geographical distance of the owners and controllers of capital, the increasingly complex occupational structure and the declining salience of the manual/non-manual division

(Newby et al., 1985: 92). Nevertheless, to point to these and to other difficulties is not the same as writing class analysis off altogether. It is likely that there will be a greater modesty in the claims made on behalf of class analysis, that the key issues will be to do with the interweaving of class, gender, ethnicity and other strands of inequality and that these accounts will be more rooted in qualitative, experiential approaches. It is also likely that the family/household will play an important part in these re-analyses and reassessments and that claims about the family as a unit will take on a more focused if more complex nature.

There is, after all, little doubt that marked inequalities exist within modern societies; that such inequalities are structured and have some degree of persistence over time. There is further little doubt that some of this inequality can be described in terms of differential life chances related to the disposal of skills and resources on the market. In such a Weberian analysis, family/household may be seen as entering the analysis in a couple of ways. In the first place, there is the question of inheritance, the physical and cultural capital that an individual has to dispose on the market; life chances, therefore, reach backwards as well as forwards. Second, the life chances are woven round the life course and the succession of households through which an individual may move (with the changing sets of relationships as this takes place) in the process of living out or through this life course. Such pathways or trajectories are not, of course, wholly a matter of a movement through different households nor are family relationships the sole set of significant others who might aid or frustrate the working out of life chances. But there is every indication that household and family relationships should be taken into account in considering the experiences of inequality and the strategies that may be adopted to maintain or to improve one's position in an unequal society.

3

Gender

Introduction

Looking at the previous two chapters it will be apparent that while an analysis might begin with a consideration of interrelationships between family and economic life or family and stratification it is not long before gender makes an appearance. This was not always the case and earlier discussions of work and employment or class were often conducted with gender as, at best, an optional extra. However, the recent reformulations of understandings of economic life and reconsiderations of the role of the household or the family in stratification were greatly stimulated through the development of feminist critique and scholarship. Such scholarship stressed that the study of women or gender could not be bounded and specialized topics within sociological analysis.

This chapter will examine the interconnections between developing analyses of family life and developing analyses of gender. The term 'gender', like the term 'family', is not an unproblematic one. We have moved away from considering gender as a simple 'face-sheet' variable according to which data could simply be ordered into categories labelled 'men' and 'women' (Morgan, 1986). The distinctions which were made between 'sex' and 'gender' were indeed attempts to recognize the problematic nature of sexual divisions and to highlight the fact that we were dealing with socially constructed distinctions rather than with fixed biologically based categories. However, such a distinction is itself problematic, partly because it tends to reproduce distinctions between biology and culture and other dualistic modes of thinking and partly because it still leaves the analysis with an apparently straightforward distinction between men and women. Going beyond this does not simply entail recognizing that some men will see themselves as being more 'feminine' and that some women will see themselves as more 'masculine'. It is also a question of overall gender salience, the degree to which gender is understood by self and others to be a socially relevant category as compared with or in relation to other potential bases of personal or social identity.

Gender may be understood in terms of *difference* or in terms of *inequality*. These different ways of understanding gender pervade scholarly and popular understandings. These approaches to gender can be combined in various ways (for further discussion, see Morgan, 1992: 190–9). In most studies there will be discussions framed in terms of both difference and inequality although the interrelationships between these two modes of analysis may not always be fully explored.

In the course of the discussion that follows I shall seek to analyse the interplays between inequalities and differences in the context of the study of family relationships. Four main sets of assumptions guide this discussion.

1 First, all social situations are gendered although few, if any, are purely a matter of gender. At the same time, I should wish to emphasize that gender is a necessary piece of information and should not be treated as something which is simply added on to the analysis of a particular institution or situation. Yet gender is rarely the only relevant piece of information and sometimes, although perhaps rarely, not the most important piece of information.

2 Second, gender is to do with men and women and not simply with women. This is not, it should be noted, a question of giving men 'equal time' in areas which may be seen as dominated by feminist or women's studies. It is, rather, part of a claim that the workings of systems of social inequality cannot be understood unless account is taken of the dominant as well as of the subordinate groups.

3 Gender has both a public and a private face. The distinction between public and private is itself a problematic one, the more so since it was conventionally understood to be mapped on to differences between men and women. It is more useful to see the

spheres of men and of women as each having their public and their private faces.

4   Gender is a process rather than a thing. We can be said to 'do' gender rather than to 'have' a gender. The increasing use of the word 'gendered' is a reminder of this processual understanding; the gendering may be done by social actors themselves, the institutions or organizations of which they form a part or by the observers examining their interactions in social institutions.

I seek here to explore the problematic relationships between 'family' and 'gender', recognizing throughout that gender is not wholly to be subsumed under or to be explained by or through family relationships. Connell notes that theories of gender tend to be either at the individual or the societal level and that if any intermediary institution enters into the consideration, that institution is 'the family'. One of the implications of this is that other social institutions may not be seen in gendered terms at all (Connell, 1987: 119). Thus it is, or ought to be, relatively easy to see gender at work in family relationships since so many of the key terms – mother, father, son, daughter etc. – are so clearly gender-marked. It might be less easy to see crime and punishment or the military in gender terms, although it is one of the achievements of feminist analysis that there remain few areas of life where there has not been some exploration of gender connotations.

A Simple Model

The model consists of two terms, 'family' and 'gender'. The relationships between these two terms may be *constructing*, of *obscuring* or of *modifying*:

FAMILY constructs GENDER
FAMILY obscures GENDER
FAMILY modifies GENDER

GENDER constructs FAMILY
GENDER obscures FAMILY
GENDER modifies FAMILY

A more detailed, comparative analysis might also explore the different patterns of relationships that might be assumed to exist between the theoretical objects, family and gender. Thus, in some cases, gender may be assumed to be largely subsumed within the wider ambit of family or kinship relationships. This is the case in those societies which have conventionally been described as 'traditional' societies. In other cases there may be close interconnections between family and gender, the one reinforcing the other in a series of feedback loops. Something of this kind is implied in various functional analyses; insofar as these may be identified with any model of society that society may be described as 'modern' or possibly 'early modern'. In a third set of cases, gender may be seen as the dominant partner, with family being largely subsumed under wider analyses of gendered processes within a society as a whole. Such societies may be called modern, late modern, high modern or, following Walby, 'public patriarchies' (Walby, 1990). Finally, 'family' and 'gender' may be seen as increasingly problematic and variable theoretical entities with relatively little direct connection between them. This may be roughly identified with the analysis of postmodern society. Most complex modern societies contain elements of all these kinds of relationships and some of these will be explored in the pages to come.

Family Constructs Gender

The notion that it is the family and family relationships that construct gender identities is very widespread and, on the surface, very persuasive. Justifications for differential pay or employment practices were often presented with reference to women's 'family responsibilities' or to the idea of 'the family wage'. Such ideological constructions are often seen as crucial in understanding a woman's relatively disadvantaged position in the labour market.

Beginning with definitions of 'the family' we find that these nearly always revolve around definitions of parenthood and marriage, themselves often broken down into clear gendered identities. Marriage is constructed as a heterosexual relationship which is formally recognized and parenthood is developed from or associated with the idea of marriage. The very constituent elements of everyday understandings of the family cannot be detached from issues of gender.

This is not simply a matter of terminology; issues of gendered identity are very much at the centre of concern here. As Connell (1987: 125) writes: 'The very idea of "the housewife" and "the husband" are fusions of emotional relations, power and the division of labour.' These identities, although arising out of and generated within family contexts, are not confined to the family. They spill over into, have continuity with, wider constructions and understandings of gender identities. The abstractions of gender identities are, as it were, fleshed out or given substance through their anchorage in domestic identities. It does not matter that many households may be headed by a woman and many others are, in various ways, dual-earner households. It is not always the realities of domestic life that shape gendered identities but the constructions of family that are important; the family may only appear to be the crucible within which gendered identities are forged.

Classically, much sociological and sociopsychological analysis was devoted to accounts of the ways in which gendered identities were reproduced through the agencies of socialization located, primarily, within the family and family relationships. Such analyses, it has been argued, are better at explaining how gendered identities are repro-duced over time than they are at accounting for their origins; they tend to give an overdeterministic picture which is weaker when it comes to explaining changes in the gender order; and they are not particularly effective when it comes to assessing the part played by other institutions and processes in the construction of gendered identities (see Henshall and McGuire, 1986).

If we are to retain some sense of the socialization process as contributing to gender identities our focus should be upon the totality of family-based practices and not simply upon those practices which might be overtly identified as 'primary socialization'. Among such practices, a key place must be occupied by the sexual division of labour and understandings of family responsibilities over the life-course. These are patterns which have proved to be remarkably resilient. Vogler argues that 'domestic sexism', especially the sexist attitudes on the part of the male partner, still has a significant impact upon the gendered structure of the labour market (Vogler, 1994). Women are more likely than men to leave or to change their job for 'family reasons' (Scott and Burchell, 1994: 140). Further analysis has focused upon the complex juggling acts, the 'coping strategies' (Evetts, 1988), that women have to perform in order to balance domestic obligations and employment commitments. Men are not conventionally called upon to engage in such strategies. However, this is not simply a question of who *does* what. It is also a question of who *is* what, and much feminist analysis has explored the relation-ships between these various juggling acts that women are expected to perform and the fragmented existence that often follows from this and the very construction, with both positive and negative connotations, of female self and identity.

There are links here with the question of socialization. The patterns of sexual divisions within the home, and the construction of the divisions between home and work, are amongst the most obvious and, one must assume, taken-for-granted features of everyday domestic life, observed and sometimes adopted by children as they grow up. Moreover, the differential expectations of children in terms of their contributions to domestic labour affects their sense of gender identity (Jamieson, 1986).

Thus, gendered identities are bound up with these tasks and the taken-for-granted assumptions that surround and arise out of their performance. Women, as Cornwell points out frequently, see housework and child care as *their* work (Cornwell, 1984). These are activities which they *own*. All the moral qualities which are, or were, associated with the world of employment, with having and keeping a job, are also to be found in analyses of women's household responsibilities.

Questions framed in terms of the sexual division of labour within the household run the risk of obscuring issues of power in the analysis of domestic relationships. To put the matter somewhat starkly, the descriptions of who does what within the home may obscure questions of who decides for whom. Power arises out of the unequal distribution of resources within the home; also, inequalities in terms of power, favouring the man, shape these distributions of resources. Yet, as will be argued later, matters are rarely as straightforward as this and increasingly scholars have been analysing the complex intersections of gender and power in the context of the home (Davis, Leijenaar and Oldersma, 1991).

We cannot, therefore, conclude that family and marital relationships are automatically disempowering for women and empowering for men. It may be suggested that where the experience of power is generally consistent with gendered expectations, then these experiences of power will play an important part in the shaping of wider gender identities. The working man who is emotionally dependent upon his partner and the housebound woman who has clearly marked out areas of control and responsibility have their wider gender identities confirmed. Different and complex mixes of powerfulness and powerlessness, therefore, provide important strands in the construction, and undermining, of gendered identities through family relationships.

An important way in which family and marital relationships can construct gendered identities is around sexuality. The simplest case may illustrate the point. In a context where marriage is defined as the only legitimate site for sexual expression and where, also, legitimate sex is defined in terms of heterosexual 'penetrative' sex, then it could be argued that here marriage constructs gender in a direct way. The central normative sexual act is the one which can lead to the reproduction of the species as well as being the one in which the man conventionally proves to himself and to others that he is a true man. Similarly, a woman has confirmation of her true femininity through motherhood. The nexus linking marriage, sexuality and reproduction is also one which generates and reproduces gendered identities.

Despite greater freedom of sexual expression and sexual representation, this model of sexuality still remains a dominant one and hence the links between marriage, sexuality and the production of gendered identities remain strong. Attitude surveys in Britain would seem to suggest tolerance of premarital sex and cohabitation but strong disapproval of adultery and, to a lesser extent, of homosexuality. Where there have been changes over a period of some decades is in the direction of recognizing sex as a legitimate source of pleasure in its own right and in the enlarged range of sexual expression around the sexual act.

There may be an extent to which greater sexual freedom may have strengthened or at least redefined the ways in which the marital relationship constructs gender identities. With a greater openness about sexual expression in marriage comes an obligation on the part of the spouses to satisfy each other. While some degree of mutuality is implied there may also be the particular obligation on the part of the woman to be 'sexy', responsive and inventive in order to keep her man and to preserve her marriage. There is also an obligation on the part of the man to satisfy his partner; a wife's orgasms might replace the production of children as a confirmation of masculinity.

There is another, darker, side to these links between sexuality, power, family and gender identity and this is to do with sexual abuse and violence within domestic relationships. Many of these violences follow and reinforce lines of gendered power and identity. In particular, although not exclusively, these may seem to focus on specific contrasts between perpetrator and victim and active and passive. In the origins of the acts themselves as well as the wider frameworks of meaning in which these acts are understood and assessed, everyday constructions of masculinity and femininity are part of the context of understanding. Many of the manifestations that accompany domestic violence, the difficulties of escape or of providing a credible account may reinforce these understandings as much as the original act. It may also be noted that violence against husbands by wives might also serve to perpetuate or reinforce conventional understandings of gender insofar as the husband feels reluctance or embarrassment in bringing such events to light.

There do appear to be some very strong ways in which ideas of marriage and the family reinforce or reproduce constructions of gender. Issues of the very definition of marriage, of divisions of labour, of power, sexuality and violence all interact with each other to underline or reinforce themes of gender difference and gender inequality. However, there are further complexities to be explored.

Family Obscures Gender

Family relations may obscure, rather than directly construct, gender identities. For example, dominant models of marriage may construct relatively ungendered narratives about domestic life. In modern times, an understanding of marriage in relational, as opposed to institutional, terms may serve to obscure gender differences. There has been a rise of a dominant discourse about the centrality of interpersonal relationships understood not simply as the formal linking of two or more people but as the deeper psychological and interpersonal interweaving of two biographies. With the rise of this more complex understanding of relationships, there has also been a widespread understanding that marriage represents a central, if not the only, adult relationship which is expected to manifest all these characteristics. People are expected to work at their marriages, the marital relationship is constructed as a desirable end in itself and sexual expression is seen as a key element in the growth and maintenance of marriage.

These narratives about the growing relational character of marriage obscure both some persisting and deep-rooted institutional features and questions of gender differences. Deep understanding of marriage as *the* relationship presupposes some measures of equality, in theory if not in practice, between the partners. *Sexual* differences may be important within marriage given the centrality of heterosexual love and the different psychobiological experiences in childhood, while *gender* differences are assumed to decline in importance. Thus in many middle-class marriages, it may be assumed, women are faced with the complex work of reconciling this ideology of equality with the reality of deep gendered differences in, say, the understanding of a 'career' and what this may mean for domestic identities (Jordan, Redley and James, 1994: 77).

Similar observations about the obscuring of gender inequalities may be made about the growing use of the term 'parenting'. First, it is an active word, emphasizing the work of parents rather than their formal statuses. Second, the term smooths over gender differences and suggests that the work of parents is something that should be shared between mothers and fathers. Earlier understandings saw the active business of parent work as being especially the province of mothers, while issues to do with status, control and linkages to the outside world were the responsibilities of fathers. While the evolving notion of parenting, informed by professional advice and popular manuals, places particular and novel demands and responsibilities on women (Reiger, 1985), it also quite specifically seeks to draw men into the active side of parent work. In many cases, the formal or public presentation of parental activities may be in terms of sharing or of 'give and take', a public presentation that may be at odds with day-to-day realities (Backett, 1982; Cornwell, 1984). In some cases, these differences may reflect the persistence of powerful constraints arising from the organization of the labour market, but this is probably not the whole story.

Sociology and social science in general have played a part in the elaboration and perpetuation of some relatively ungendered images of marriage and parenting. Similar observations may be made about some constructions of child abuse which ignore or obscure questions of gender (Margolin, 1992). Many of the key terms – 'companionate marriage', 'the symmetrical family' etc. – have developed from sociological work, while other terms, not specifically anchored to family studies, may also be deployed in ways to obscure gender differences within the home. Examples, already noted, may include the rise of the concept of the household as a theoretical object within a range of social science disciplines, together with the associated concept of 'negotiation' to describe processes within households.

Family Modifies Gender

Feminist and critical studies of family life have, cumulatively, developed a coherent and complex picture of the various ways in which family relationships and values construct or obscure gender. Somewhat less heralded are the ways in which family relationships may themselves become a source of change within the wider gender order.

In part this is to do with the relative autonomy of domestic life within the wider social system; notions of privacy, however limited and ambiguous, do help to ensure some degree of leeway within family practices. Further, gender is all pervasive and exists at all levels yet we cannot simply move between levels, reading off 'patriarchy' from the particularities of domestic encounters. Wright (1993: 46) refers to '. . . the specific complexity of gender domination – the way it packages together in variable degrees and forms, domination and equality, oppression and reciprocity'. Such an understanding could be readily applied to family practices. Wright (1993: 46–7) goes on to argue for the possibility of '. . . the elimination of gender oppression . . . experienced partially in micro contexts in a society within which gender domination remains'.

Day-to-day encounters within domestic life may always be gendered but they are rarely simply just about gender and it is out of the complex, and sometimes contradictory, unity of gendered family identities that possibilities of change and modification emerge.

It is possible, therefore, to see the family or household as a site for the meeting and working through of a variety of contradictions around gender identities and the gender order. Thus some of the complexities and contradictions of power may meet within the household. A man, feeling that he has little real power in the public world of employment, may become envious of the apparent power and control which he sees in the daily lives of his partner. Women, juggling domestic and employment responsibilities and sharing the experiences of marriage and parenting with other women, may come to develop ironic or critical perspectives on their own domestic situations. If we develop a more fluid understanding of power, one which focuses less upon structures and more upon day-to-day claims and counter-claims and unresolved or unspoken tensions, we may begin to see how family life may be an element in the challenging of the wider gender order.

The family or the household becomes the site for potential changes in the gender order partly through the exchanges between family practices and other sets of practices. Thus changes in the occupational structure have their impact upon the gender order in part directly, through a restructuring of the labour market, but in part indirectly as mediated through domestic relationships. Thus the growing participation of women in the labour market at all levels increasingly produces the possibilities of discrepancies in terms of occupational status between women and men, in some cases with the former higher than the latter (McRae, 1986). Some accommodations to these discrepancies may reinforce prevailing gender patterns but others may allow for some degree of change or modification. In a different area, Wheelock considered the mixed impact of male unemployment on household practices (Wheelock, 1990). She found a general pragmatism on the part of some of the couples inter-viewed, although little sense that men found themselves to be diminished as men through their increasing participation in domestic activity. Some men were developing new, domestically based skills and there was some modest breaking down of stereotypes. This account can be read as indicating the persistence and strength of traditional gender assumptions or the potentialities that exist for change.

However one may read these somewhat fragmentary pieces of evidence, one central point remains. Individuals within family situations are capable of evaluating and responding imaginatively to the forces and processes that confront them. Gender is not wholly 'given'. Insofar as family relationships constitute one major arena where women and men meet and interact, it is not surprising that it is here also that some people may seek to bring about modifications in their day-to-day workings of gendered themes. A minority of men head single-parent households and elsewhere women and men may work together in order to develop non-sexist or less sexist patterns of child rearing. Individuals may explore possibilities of role reversals or more equitable divisions of labour. Men may confront their violences and seek out ways of dealing with them.

Theoretically, the links between changes and processes within domestic relations and changes in the wider orderings of gender may be of several kinds. The simplest level may be numerical where, for example, individual divorces become divorce rates and these reach levels when they become matters of public concern. Or changes and experiments may take place amongst sections of society who have some degree of public visibility, through their professional status and through their access to the media. Or individuals may begin to form support groups or campaigns aimed at translating personal solutions to areas of more public debate and concern. The impact of changes within domestic and interpersonal relations and changes in the wider structuring of gender relationships is not automatic and we need more investigation into how such changes actually come about.

Gender Constructs Family

It may be agreed that the family cannot be seen as the sole site for the generation of gender hierarchies or the sole arena within which such differences are played out. Further, to a very large extent, family relationships are shaped by gender or patriarchal relationships. To put the matter more strongly, it is impossible to write or think about family without also thinking about gender. The reverse is less obviously true.

As we have seen, the key terms that are used in family discourse are gendered. Further, the pairing of many of these terms encourages us to hear them in terms of difference and opposition. Other oppositions and divisions, with a currency wider than the family and which have strong gendered connotations, also impinge upon constructions and understandings of family life. The distinction between public and private is one such opposition. Supposed overlaps between public/private, men/women and work/home are not complete, fixed or unambiguous. Nevertheless, they continue to be influential. Even if it becomes increasingly difficult to pronounce the phrase 'a woman's place is in the home' without irony or modification, it is still the case that the home and domesticity continue to be understood in feminine terms. 'Househusband' still has an unfamiliar ring or a sense of a striving for political correctness; 'houseperson' even more so.

Another relevant gendered opposition is that between rationality and emotion. This has a wide currency, is historically constructed and continues to have complex gendered associations (Seidler, 1994). In as much as family relationships are constructed as sites where a lot of 'emotional labour' (Hochschild, 1983; N. James, 1989) is performed or expected to be performed, then this distinction between the rational and the emotional shapes ways in which family life is understood. The wider gendered distinctions between rationality and emotion partially structure and inform the routine processes and understandings within family practices.

There is an interesting contradiction here. The terms which we possess in order to describe family relationships are key terms in mapping out gender relationships. Who speaks of family also speaks of gender. Yet these terms are, formally, equally weighted and evenly balanced: husband, wife, mother, daughter and so on. Yet, as the discussion around the distinctions public/private and rational/emotional suggest, the family becomes a special sphere for women.

Men often get edited out of the account. Thus insofar as gender constructs family it does so in a complex and double way through the solidifying of gender oppositions and through the feminization of the home and domestic activities.

Within the array of gendered terms associated with the family it is doubtful whether there is a more central term than 'mother'. This is a term which is defined both around the theme of sexual difference and also around constructions of the public and the private and the rational and the emotional. Indeed it could be said that families were 'mothered' rather than 'gendered'. The bond between the mother and the child is being constructed as having at least one foot firmly within the natural order. Mothers who voluntarily relinquish the custody of their children are defined as having *abandoned* these offspring (Rosenblum, 1986: 197). Fathers who leave the mother with their children may be understood as having behaved badly but they are not generally seen as behaving 'unnaturally'.

Gender does not always have a direct or unmediated impact upon the construction of family relationships. It may be mediated through other agencies such as the state or professionals. Law, for example, often has a direct effect in mediating gender constructions into the heart of family relationships through, for example, issues to do with inheritance (Collier, 1995; Finch and Hayes, 1994).

Gender Obscures Family

This is an area which is both controversial and relatively unexplored. Feminist scholarship has been successful in identifying the all-pervasive character of patriarchy and gendered social relations which entered into the most intimate interpersonal relationships and the most apparently innocent representation. Despite some recent criticism from those who stress other differences or who seek to deconstruct the notion of gender further, this critique has remained strong and influential.

This gendered perspective has been especially strong in the context of the analysis of family and domestic relationships so much so, indeed, that it may be possible to speak of an 'over-gendered conception of the family'. This is not to say that it is possible to talk about family processes without bringing in issues of gender but it is to argue that these processes bring in themes other than gender. A chief candidate here is that of age and generation. Recent interests in age – especially childhood and children – should have the effect of allowing for a more systematic exploration of age as a key strand in family analysis.

There are other processes which, while not being gender-neutral, cannot be reduced to gender. One example of these would be the idea of 'family obligations' (Finch, 1989; Finch and Mason, 1993). Constructions of family obligations are complex, subject to flux and negotiation and shaped by a range of considerations. Gender is clearly woven into these patterns but it is not the whole pattern. The notion of obligation itself may be seen in gender-neutral terms, although as soon as it is given content or flesh – through being deployed in concrete plans of action – gender often comes to the fore. Thus there may be very general notions that 'blood is thicker than water' which in principle carry no gender markers. Yet whether these general principles be called upon in conducting a blood feud or in rallying around an unfortunate relative are questions which are clearly shaped by considerations of gender.

Thus it is possible to argue that an over-gendered construction of the family may have the consequence of obscuring those aspects of family life which, while being of considerable importance, do not readily fall within the framework of gender analysis. It might be noted that while feminist theory has been to the fore in putting gender on the map it has not been the only influence. Indeed, it may be possible to argue that modern society itself tends to encourage an over-gendered view of family and possibly other sets of social relationships (Illich, 1983). To argue in these terms is not to say that there are areas of 'family' which should be kept safe from gendered analysis but simply to say that a complete account of family life cannot stop with questions of gender.

Gender Modifies Family

> In all forms of male–female cohabitation . . . the *conflicts of the century* break through. Here they always show their private, personal face. But the family is *only the setting, not the cause* of the events. (Beck, 1992: 105; his emphasis)

The impact of changing relations between women and men at a more general level upon family and household relationships has been well explored. Pride of place is usually given to changes in the labour market both in terms of the overall expansion of opportunities for women, especially married women, and in terms of the particular opening up of areas formerly closed. In terms of their impact upon family relationships the most important would seem to be the steady erosion of the male breadwinner model; the provision for women of alternative sources of income and identity outside the home; the impact upon domestic timetables and the negotiation of time within the household; and the provision of greater opportunities for, if not the actuality of, greater male participation in the home.

A considerable amount of research has been devoted to these and similar issues. Other discussions might note the impact of other factors such as political enfranchisement, legislation dealing with property, inheritance, divorce and custody and so on. There may be discussion of the impact of possible role models such as Baroness Thatcher, Madonna or Laura Ashley.

One more ambiguous area is to do with female sexuality and personal identity. The double-edged impact of the 'sexual revolution' or 'permissiveness' upon women has often been noted. However, a major theme in modern societies has been the linking of hetero-sexual attractiveness with personal identity and a project of the feminine self. Women were encouraged to think of themselves not simply as wives or as mothers but as individual women who could express their femininity through bodily discipline and careful groom-ing. Men have not been immune to these influences either. Of particular importance was the 'democratization' of this process. Gullestad's study of working-class women in Bergen shows how these women sought to make themselves sexually attractive without denying their identities as mothers and as morally responsible adult women (Gullestad, 1984). She points to a tension between sexuality, highlighting a sense of self and personal identity, and sameness, embodied in the restrictions surrounding motherhood.

This discussion of some possible linkages between female sexuality, consumerism and a sense of self highlights some possible ambiguities in the analysis of factors assumed to impact on family relationships. A more liberal interpretation might argue that the cumulative effect of all these changes – political, in the market-place, in terms of freer sexuality and so on – can be liberating in the sense of a gradual enlargement of the field of choice for women. A more sceptical approach might see these changes in the gender order as being of limited significance with an effect that is overall supportive of marriage and the family with all their oppressive and patriarchal features now better concealed but definitely present. Somewhere between these two interpretations would be one which focuses upon the possible contradictions that such changes highlight, contradictions which may give rise to pressures for further change.

Changes in the gender order with their possible impacts upon family relationships are not simply the product of socio-economic changes but also of more direct sexual politics. Certainly, the post-1960s feminist movements, while addressing themselves to the gender order as a whole, paid particular attention to many of the oppressive features of family living. Recent debates about the alleged decline of the family have often cited 'Women's Lib' as a direct or an indirect cause, although this is not necessarily anything new.

The actual impact of recent feminist movements and critiques has yet to be fully explored. One may also include here the impact of action on the part of men, in support of or reacting against women's movements, in support of parental leave or fathers' 'rights' (see, for example, Haas, 1990).

One area where it is possible to see an impact is in relation to violences within the home. It was largely the work of feminist writers that put questions of violences against wives on to the political agenda and that developed institutions or practices to deal with the consequences of such violences. Such a critique called into question much that had been taken for granted, namely the idea of the home as a safe haven, notions of domestic privacy and of the rights and expectations of husbands. It, together with subsequent debates around child abuse, provided some legitimation for external intervention into domestic life and some measure of demystification of the domestic relationship. A more recent illustration would be debates and legislation concerning rape within marriage.

To conclude this section we may cite changes in patterns of divorce, especially since the Second World War, as changes which link issues of family and gender together in complex and diverse ways. Phillips (1991) emphasizes, as explanations for these trends, the increasing opportunities for life outside marriage, rising expectations of the quality of married life and reduced tolerance of abuse within the home (1991: 118). All these factors impinged more upon the experiences of women than of men and this was reflected in the increasing proportions of women as initiators of divorce proceedings (1991: 232). The evaluation of the significance of these trends remains controversial; what remains clear also is that here we have some major changes in family living that have been partly shaped by wider changes in the relationships between and the expectations of women and men.

Problems with Patriarchy

This presentation of the links between family and gender has its limitations. For one thing, it may underplay the degree of *inter-change* between these practices. For another, it only provides the basis for further theoretical analysis.

The word 'patriarchy' is frequently used in the context of feminist analyses of gender although it has not gained universal acceptance. Perhaps one of the best-known definitions has been provided by Hartmann (1983: 194):

> I define patriarchy as a set of social relations which has a material base and in which there are hierarchical relations between men, and solidarity among them, which enable them to control women. Patriarchy is then the system of male oppression of women.

This definition stresses the systemic character of male domination and its materiality. While focusing upon male oppression of women it also includes relationships between men. Walby's definition, by contrast, is stark in its simplicity: 'A system of social structures and practices in which men dominate, oppress and exploit women' (Walby, 1989: 214).

Three particular issues emerge. First, is the definition to be an inclusive or an exclusive one? Does the definition apply to certain kinds of historically located societies or does it apply to nearly all human societies? Second, does the definition deal only with the relations between women and men or does it, as in the literal sense of the word, also include relationships between adult men and children of both genders? Linked to these two questions is one concerning family relationships and their position in the definition and further elaborations of patriarchy. Are family relationships central or marginal to the analysis of patriarchy? Some writers would wish to confine the use of the term to, broadly, pre-capitalist societies (Barrett, 1980; Rubin, 1975). Walby, among others, wishes to refer to a whole range of societies, while recognizing there might be distinctions between kinds of patriarchy. At the same time she wishes to exclude questions of the dominance of adults or fathers over children from her definition and analysis (Walby, 1989, 1990). She focuses explicitly on household rather than family relations (1990: 62).

Walby provides the most sophisticated attempt to date to deal with these basic problems of making the concept of patriarchy work. She seeks to explore six patriarchal structures: the patriarchal mode of production within the home, patriarchal relations within waged labour, the patriarchal state, male violence, patriarchal relations in sexuality and patriarchal culture (Walby, 1989, 1990). This is an analysis which has the potentiality for investigating relationships between and across patriarchal structures and, by implication, the various ways in which these might combine. Such a multi-stranded approach also has the potentiality for investigating contradictions within and between the various structures.

One of the key points about the analysis of patriarchy is that it underlines issues of power within gender relations (Witz, 1992: 3). Walby's discussion deals, implicitly at least, with the multiplicities of sites where patriarchal power is exercised and recognizes the various levels of power and the interconnections between them. Thus issues at the level of the patriarchal state may also interact with inter-personal levels where questions of sexuality and male violence may be at the forefront. However, important questions remain. Are there variations in the degree, as well as in the kinds, of power exercised by men over women? Further, how are power relation-ships between men, or over children, linked to power relationships between men and women? How far do many of the concepts and discussions around patriarchy draw upon routine masculine under-standings of power, derived from quintessentially masculine institu-tions such as war, business, politics or sport?

For example, Kranichfeld (1987) in her discussion of power in families argues that power is generally understood in masculinist terms. She argues that this inhibits the discussion of power in families from the outset since it plays down those areas of power which are associated with women, in their activities as kin-keepers for example. If we understand power as the ability to change the behaviour of others intentionally, then women not only exercise power within families but have an effect over generations. She argues for a much closer attention to micro-power situations. Similarly, O'Connor has argued for a recognition of the complexities of women's experiences of power within the context of marriage (O'Connor, 1991).

Kranichfeld seems to have identified one of the problems with the use of power in the context of discussions of patriarchy and its application to family studies. Walby's argument would seem to treat the family (or the household in her formulation) as simply one site in the shaping of patriarchies and one which has probably become of declining significance in the long-term shift from private to public patriarchy. Nevertheless, she does identify some significant changes around households and their relationships with the wider society and suggests that these changes may have an impact on the degree and form of patriarchy. These include changes in 'reproductive technologies', in the domestic division of labour and in household composition (Walby, 1990: 77–86). Yet there are problems with her limitation of 'family' to household relations and her reluctance to include age in her definition of patriarchy. Gittins (1993: 35), on the other hand, argues that: 'Patriarchy is thus both a gender and an age relationship, based on power, and is essential in understanding families.'

A broader understanding of both family, where age, gender and generation meet, and patriarchy might enable a more complex appreciation of the interrelationships between different levels of power in the context of domestic relationships and hence an understanding of the processes of change and variation as well as of stability and continuity.

However, this is not to dismiss the concept of patriarchy. The analysis continues to draw attention to central concerns about the relationships between the gender order in general and its particular manifestations in domestic and family contexts. Further, the idea of patriarchy possesses, in contrast to many associated concepts, a critical edge, reminding the reader that gender relations are about inequalities and exploitations as well as about divisions and differences.

Sexual Stratification

One of the arguments in favour of retaining the term 'patriarchy' is that there does not seem to be an alternative term which captures the pervasive character of gender inequality while at the sime time maintaining a critical perspective on these practices. However, as we have seen, this sense of all-pervasiveness can also be problematic in that it does not easily allow for variations between and within societies. These variations revolve around some of the complexities of power: the links between power at different levels and the different and contradictory strategies adopted by the relatively powerful in order to maintain or assert their power and by the relatively powerless to resist or to evade the imposition of power.

A possible alternative to the term 'patriarchy' is that of 'sexual stratification', a broad approach deriving from sociology, social anthropology and economics, and one which has developed in the United States with relatively little influence in British debates (Blumberg, 1991b; Blumberg and Coleman, 1989; England and Farkas, 1986; Huber and Spitze, 1983). One possible reason for the development of these approaches in terms of 'sexual stratification', which seem to be a set of converging concerns rather than a fully integrated theory, would seem to be a dissatisfaction with the term 'patriarchy' and a recognition that theories based upon the idea of the 'universal subordination of women' might be limited in their usefulness.

This is not to argue that these approaches deny persisting and widespread inequalities between men and women and that these inequalities are often of an exploitative character. The term 'sexual stratification' carries with it strong reminders of other systems of stratification which are also characterized by marked inequalities and where the subordinates find the relationships oppressive. Yet there is also an interest in change and variation.

Thus, for example, we might wish to focus on the unevenness of change in the 'roles' of men and women between the 1950s and the 1980s (England and Farkas, 1986: 17). Here we see both change and stability or resistance to change. It also raises questions of who benefits; if women have been doing most of the changing, do they lose or gain as a result? These are important questions and it is by no means certain that the general concept of patriarchy helps us a great deal at this level of analysis.

There are similar questions when it comes to developing a comparative analysis. Social anthropologists such as Sanday (1981) have pointed out the multi-dimensional and multi-causal nature of gender differentiation and inequalities in all societies and have sought to develop models and understandings that are more sensitive to such variations. Some of this work has been influential in the development of analyses of sexual stratification.

Much of this analysis may seem overformal or difficult to use, with lengthy lists of propositions and assumptions confronting the reader. However, some of the key ideas may be outlined fairly briefly. First, sexual status is treated as a variable rather than as a fixed 'given'. Variations may be between societies, between individuals within a single society or within an individual's life course or parts of a social network. In the terms of one writer: '. . . sexual status is the consequence of the interplay of productive relations, social relations and ideology' (Schlegel, 1977: 34). Huber and Spitze provide a more elaborated but similar account of the key elements of an adequate theory of gender stratification (Huber and Spitze, 1983: 6–7). While such an interplay may be seen as coherent and converging, producing a relatively fixed and oppressive gender regime, this is not necessarily the case. The influences may be seen as contradictory and uneven in their effects, generating not only differences but also potentialities for future change.

What runs through these varied accounts of sexual stratification is a more multi-faceted understanding of power which seeks to explore the interplays between macro- and micro-levels. Chafetz (1991) distinguishes between power based upon the resources that one may possess or have access to and 'definitional power', the power to determine the basic rules of a particular encounter or social situation. Blumberg stresses the variations between relative male/female economic power and the relationships between these at the macro- and the micro-levels (Blumberg, 1991a). A particular example of these complex workings of gendered power is provided by England and Farkas. In their discussion of marital power they explore the different relational investments made by men and women in marriage, seeing these investments and the strategies associated with them in the context of a wider system of structural constraints and cultural expectations (England and Farkas, 1986).

These theories of sexual stratification point to sources of variation in the structure of relationships between women and men and, with this, to potential sources of strain, contradiction and possible change within the system. They point to some of the mechanisms and processes that link the deployment of power at a micro level with the wider structure of institutional and cultural constraints. In many respects the sexual stratification approach is more capable of generating interesting research questions and strategies, together with middle-range theorizing, than more globalized notions of patriarchy. Yet the two broad approaches are not necessarily incompatible. Theories of and approaches in terms of patriarchy direct attention to a critical understanding of the connections between different clusters of practices (sites or structures) within a society, whereas the analysis in terms of sexual stratification focuses more readily on the micro-level and on the links between that level and macro-structures. 'Patriarchy' is probably better at explaining elements of stability and continuity in the ordering of gendered inequalities. Sexual stratification may perhaps more readily explore variations and some sources or potentialities for change.

Conclusion: Towards Complexity

If there is one thing that theories of patriarchy and theories of sexual stratification have in common it is a tendency to adopt a relatively unproblematic approach to the key variables, gender and family. Yet, as we have seen, these are complex and contested terms: indeed, the very language of variables seems unable to capture these complexities even where pointing to variation.

New and complex questions are beginning to emerge out of the substantial and cumulative body of theory and research identified with feminist scholarship. In some cases, these have focused upon the complexities that arise when gender is woven into other themes to do with class, race or ethnicity. Elsewhere, there has been a focus on the complexities associated with the concept of power, sometimes deriving inspiration from the work of Lukes, Foucault or Giddens. Thus, Kathy Davis argues that there has been a tendency within the 'feminist common sense on power' to treat women as 'cultural dopes' (Davis, 1991: 79) and seeks to adapt Giddens's work on the interplays between agency and structure. In the same collection of articles, Meyer argues for the inclusion of discussions of both power and love in our discussions of gender (Meyer, 1991).

Such considerations throw up further complex questions. Is it possible to understand gender and gender relationships apart from approaches informed by ideas of patriarchy or sexual stratification? At a first glance, the answer would seem to be a clear 'no' unless our discussion refer to some future 'post-patriarchal society', the equivalent of a classless society. Yet, if we see gender as a question of difference as well as of inequality then, theoretically at least, it is possible to conceive of gender relationships around this theme of difference which are not themselves characterized by dominance, oppression or exploitation. The ideal of the heterosexual relationship, however much the reality may depart from it, may be an example of this. Further, if we see patriarchy as referring to properties of a system as a whole rather than to the individual actors who make up that system, it may be possible to find at the more individual or interpersonal level, examples of non-patriarchal yet gendered practices. Such practices may be defined as gendered insofar as the categories of women and men are held to be relevant, if not all-embracing, considerations for understanding that relationship. They may be defined as non-patriarchal in that they are non-oppressive or have non-oppressive elements.

It may be recognized that such relationships are theoretically possible but that they are marginal in that, while they may exist, they are numerically insignificant and even to draw attention to them runs the risk of obscuring the dominance of patriarchal structures. Alternatively, such practices may be seen as Utopian in that, even where they do exist, they are tainted or nullified by the wider patriarchal structures. Yet it may be possible to see patriarchal and non-patriarchal gender relationships as two threads, not necessarily of equal thickness, which, together with other threads, may be wound around each other. There are contradictions within most relationships and it should be no surprise if such contradictions are at their sharpest where matters of gender are concerned.

Further, it may be argued that human relationships are not simply shaped by past or present constraints or structures. They are also shaped by potentialities or images of the future. Such open-ended understandings are part of what it means to exist in a modern or postmodern society. Potentialities of non-exploitative or less exploitative gender relationships, within and outside marriage and families, can be important influences in shaping present understandings of family and gender.

Another complex question suggested by these explorations is whether it is possible to talk about family relationships apart from gender. Let me illustrate this by taking something which many people would regard as one of the most highly gendered aspects of married life, that of violence against women in the home. These incidents do raise questions of gendered differences such as contrasts between strength and weakness, aggression and vulnerability and so on but they are much more to do with gendered inequalities and exploitations, with constructions of men's rights and female duties and with power and intimidation. Yet is this simply about gender or patriarchy? What makes violences in the home different from other violences between men and women? While theories of domestic violence based upon systems theorizing or psychoanalysis can and have been misused and may often have the effect of obscuring the gendered oppression that constitutes the main theme of marital violence, it is by no means clear that they are wholly irrelevant to the analysis of such practices. Treated with care, such approaches may provide part of the framework for understanding such violences and hence for controlling them.

To argue more generally, it may be suggested that there are several family themes which do not directly relate to issues raised by gender theorizing. These might include kinship and patterns of family obligations or issues to do with age and generation. However, the point is not one of substituting a 'family' analysis for a 'gender' one. Rather, it is to see gender as one theme, often the most important theme, that runs through and helps shape family and household relationships.

What this points to is a more fluid understanding of the key terms 'family' and 'gender'. It has already been recognized that 'family' is a contested term and that the response to the difficulties that this poses is not to ban the use of the word or to define the problem out of existence but to see definitions and understandings of the term 'family' as topics for inquiry in their own right and part of the process of analysis.

Similar issues arise with the term 'gender'. In practice, talk of gender often tends to reproduce all the characteristics associated with 'biological sex'. Thus it is often understood in dichotomous terms or it is assumed to be a key 'face-sheet' variable, with a degree of fixity greater than some other variables such as class or age. However, more phenomenologically informed discussions of gender seek to introduce a more fluid set of understandings, a tendency also encouraged by postmodern theorizing. The attempt here would be to suggest that gender is a dependent rather than an independent variable or that it is possible or feasible to see gender this way. Gender is not a fixed set of characteristics which people routinely carry into each and every situation. The salience and character of gender is something which emerges out of and in contexts of particular social encounters. It is a property of interactions rather than of individuals or social structures. It is a set of potentialities rather than of fixed actualities. The fact that gender themes so often come to the fore in social encounters does not detract from this general orientation.

Another way of thinking about this is, as noted earlier, to understand people as 'doing gender' or doing 'gender work'. 'Doing gender' may not necessarily be confined to heterosexual groups or encounters (Fenstermaker, West and Zimmerman, 1991: 296). In a study of 'gender play' amongst schoolchildren, Barrie Thorne develops the idea of 'border work', the construction of gender distinctions seen as 'short fences that are quickly built and as quickly dismantled' (Thorne, 1993: 84). She goes on to argue that we need to develop a parallel idea around the notion of 'neutralization', processes whereby gendered differences are muted or neutralized in particular contexts. We may do gender consciously or unconsciously,

naively or ironically. Gender may be embraced, reinforced, modified or rejected in the course of doing gender work.

The importance of family and domestic relationships is not simply
that it is within such contexts that much gender work gets done. It is
also that domestic life provides the site for the interweaving of the
public and the private, the structural and the interpersonal. There
was a popular song called 'Good for Nothing' which contrasted the
public image of the man in evening dress in the opera box with how
that man appears to his wife as she washes his socks. Family life may
become a back stage where the participants are aware of both the
public and the private faces of gender. Yet family life may also be
another stage where gender performances take place. We are only
beginning to explore such complexities.

4

Care

Introduction

Issues of caring have been very much part of the discussions around the interrelationships between family and gender but they are important enough to deserve a separate chapter. Very schematically we can identify a series of steps through which caring entered into feminist and sociological agendas. First, there was an analytical understanding that was based upon a separation, but functional interdependence, between home and work. Insofar as issues to do with care were considered, they tended to be considered outside the ambit of mainstream sociological research within the separate disciplines of social administration or social policy. In the second stage, when feminist and Marxist perspectives were beginning to make their impacts on the study of family relationships, the separation of home and work was maintained in theory but there was a more critical and searching focus on relationships within the home and particularly upon women both as houseworkers and as employees in the formal economy. This consideration merged into a third stage where the boundaries between home and work became much more blurred and the focus was upon the home as a site for work. This was when we began to get a focus upon the household and upon divisions of labour within and between households. At the same time, feminist research was engaging with caring practices and responsibilities especially as they affected women. The final, or rather most recent, stage could be seen as a coming together of themes to do with work, the household, gender and caring. It is this current stage of development that will be the main focus of this chapter.

In this chapter I explore the interactions between three main shifts in focus or perspective. The first, and most central theme, will be a shift from a focus on the carer to a more generalized focus upon caring. This more generalized focus includes a consideration of the caring relationship as a whole, rather than separate considerations of the carer and the cared-for, a more processual understanding of caring and an exploration of the deployment of rhetorics of caring. Thus one way of considering the caring relationship is as a site where rhetorics to do with care, family and gender interact.

The second shift is one that has been considered in the previous chapter, that is a shift from gender to a focus upon the process of gendering. In other words this entails a shift in emphasis from seeing gender as a relatively straightforward face-sheet variable to a process whereby gender becomes more or less significant in particular contexts and in relation to other dimensions of social difference and social inequality.

The third shift is one of the main themes of the book as a whole, namely a shift from an exclusive focus on 'the family' to a consideration of constructed understandings of family seen in a wider context. In the case of a study of caring this entails a shift in terms of empirical focus, looking, for example, at patterns of formal and informal caring outside the home and in the context of formal organizations not centrally concerned with caring practices. This shift is also one in terms of theory whereby we begin to consider caring practices, inside and outside the home, in wider contexts to do with emotional labour, the rationality of caring and so on. As an example of this cumulative growth of analysis, I could cite Carol Thomas who identifies seven dimensions in the concept of care (Thomas, 1993).

Discussions of care have increasingly focused upon care of the elderly and the shifting and contested boundaries of public and private responsibilities for this care. The main features of this debate are well known and do not require greater elaboration here. They include demographic projections of the increasing proportions of the elderly within modern societies (Grundy, 1995), a growing critique and a widening awareness of the defects of institutional care, and an increasing desire on the part of successive governments to reduce levels of taxation and public expenditure. In the case of Britain and

North America, at least, these combined with a reassertion of the centrality of family life within the nation as a whole.

In the context of these cross-currents, the idea of 'care in the community' developed in relation to the care of the elderly, the sick, the disabled and the mentally ill. Ideally the focus of care would rest with the immediate family relations of the person requiring care, supported by local social services and professionals where appropriate and possibly by wider links within the neighbourhood. In practice, as feminists were quick to point out, the reality meant a focus on the caring work of women, often with relatively little support from other family or kin or from social services. The notion of 'community', which like the 'family' had strong rhetorical and emotional connotations, was shown to be an inadequate representation of the daily reality of many women's lives. For example, Oakley and Rajan (1991) were critical of the assumption that working-class women at times of pregnancy could call upon the resources of a close-knit community. It is not that such supportive networks are necessarily absent (see Wenger, 1984); rather their extent and significance may be less than might be claimed.

For a variety of reasons, therefore, the theme of 'care' and its links with ideas and constructions of the family became a major theme in the 1980s, in Britain certainly but also in many other societies, especially Nordic countries. The growing complexity of the analysis of care and the way in which it is woven round themes of family and gender will be the main theme of this chapter.

Distinctions

In this analysis a variety of distinctions came to be developed. First, there were distinctions made between the kinds of person who were the recipients of care. Thus Waerness distinguished between (a) caring for dependents, (b) caring for superiors and (c) caring in symmetrical relationships (Waerness, 1987: 211). In conventional family terms these relationships might be illustrated by the care of a child by its mother, the care of an elderly relative by a daughter and the care of a spouse by the other partner. It is clear that while there might be some similarities in the caring responsibilities in all three cases, there are also important relational differences between them.

A second major distinction is one between 'caring for' and 'caring about'. This distinction was devised to differentiate between the actual tasks associated with caring and the emotional meaning of the relationship between the carer and the cared-for. Caring is therefore a complex relationship involving both activities and feelings (Graham, 1983; Waerness, 1987: 210). Parker is sometimes identified as having originated the distinction, although he does not quite use this precise form of words (Parker, 1981). His particular concern was with the activities involved in 'caring for'; here he prefers to use the word 'tending' rather than the more ambiguous 'caring'. This distinction, and its use by feminist writers such as Graham, has become a commonplace within the caring literature. For example, Traustadottir (1991) uses the distinction between 'caring for' (work) and 'caring about' (love) in an ethnographical analysis of the meaning of care. She also adds a third term, emerging from her analysis, to do with the 'extended caring role'. This refers to those situations where a specific caring role (for example a mother caring for her own disabled child) is generalized (for example care for disabled children in general).

This distinction between 'caring for' and 'caring about' has been very influential. However, as with all such distinctions, the separation is often easier in theory than in practice. Many marital and family disputes arise, in fact, from the shifting boundaries between caring for and caring about. If you really cared for me, you would cook my meals, clear up after you, have sex with me and so on. The boundaries are up for dispute and negotiation. However, it was important to stress at the outset that there was no necessary connection between the two forms of caring.

Further, the phrase 'caring about' does seem, in English at least, to carry largely positive connotations. While pointing to the important emotional dimension of caring work, such a phrase tends to smooth over the complex and contradictory mix of positive and negative emotions that are involved in any long-term caring relationship. Nevertheless, despite these problems, the distinction remains a necessary point of departure for the analysis of caring.

Another set of distinctions concerns those between informal and formal care. In a sense this was the point of departure for the current debate; an ideological support for and sometimes celebration of the former as opposed to the latter. The former is often unpaid and carried out by persons who are usually linked to the cared-for by ties of marriage or parenthood or on some other personal basis. The latter is paid and normally supplied by persons who have no such ties. These include various professionals, the social services and paid carers in the private sector.

We are dealing with a complex mesh of cross-cutting distinctions: formal/informal, paid/unpaid, public/private. Leira, for example, considers a range of institutions that provide child care (family and household, social networks, informal labour markets, state services and formal labour markets) and notes whether these might be paid or unpaid. A reformulation of these distinctions leads to a fourfold classification according to whether the child care arrangement is contractual or non-contractual and whether it is paid or unpaid. Marriage may be seen in this framework as involving child care which is unpaid yet contractual (Leira, 1992). There may be any combination of these caring practices over time the actual mix depending upon resources, the kind of care required, the duration of care and so on.

Thus the distinction between formal and informal systems of care is itself a compound and complex set of distinctions. Further, we can see interconnections between them. Thus within the caring professions, nursing and social work for example, there may be some carry over of expectations derived from women's work within family relationships. This association of professional caring work with the traditionally feminine may contribute to the 'semi-professional' nature of these occupations (Abbott and Wallace, 1990b). Conversely, some informal caring work within the household, especially perhaps in relation to children, may take on quasi-professional characteristics. Such caring work may be increasingly informed by expertise and monitored by paid professionals even where these professionals do not take on a regular involvement in the business of caring.

Care and Family Relationships

The terms 'care' and 'family' are frequently and effortlessly bracketed together in social science analysis as well as in ideological or policy statements. These links may be analysed at a variety of levels. In the first place, we may be concerned with what actually takes place; who provides the bulk of the care, for whom and of what kind? In all the studies dealing with patterns of care, other family members, often a single family member, are heavily involved (Clarke, 1995; Parker and Lawton, 1994). However, we may also be concerned with values and norms concerning the centrality of the family in society on the one hand and the supposed correctness or naturalness of meeting caring responsibilities within immediate family ties on the other. We may here be dealing with the ideological construction of the nuclear family and its supposed crucial role in carrying out caring responsibilities (Dalley, 1988) or the more immediate and more complex set of understandings around family obligations (Finch, 1989; Finch and Mason, 1993). Or, indeed, we may be concerned with the complex relationships between the two, the processes by which ideological constructions of the family and family obligations become part of the common-sense and taken-for-granted expectations of household members. For example, Arber and Ginn argue that not only is the spouse, in practice, a key caring resource but that this is expected as a right (Arber and Ginn, 1992: 96). Conversely, legislators and those responsible for the public construction of the family may draw upon popular, experiential, taken-for-granted assumptions about family responsibilities. It is probably best to see the relationship between the two, the ideological and the everyday set of assumptions around caring responsibilities, as being less one of the former determining the latter but rather the latter drawing upon and deploying, selectively, ideological resources in the day-to-day business of constructing and making sense of family obligations.

Concern about the ideological use, or misuse, of the term 'family' with its powerful emotional input, has led several critics to recommend caution when using the word especially in connection with the organization of care in a modern society. Gullestad's analysis of the *passepike* or 'baby-walker' not only serves as a reminder that children may care for other children but also that care may be organized within social networks which do not always consist of persons related by ties of kinship. What matters in this Norwegian practice, where an older girl looks after a younger child for a few hours in the afternoon, is a context of trust (Gullestad, 1992). More generally, Balbo suggests the use of the term 'survival units' in preference to 'family' (1987). This term has not attracted widespread use but nevertheless may serve as a reminder that, in considering issues to do with the deployment of care in modern society, we need to be particularly cautious about the terminology we use.

Care and Gender

The involvement of women in all aspects of the provision of care has been a major theme in numerous texts and articles. Finch and

Groves provided an early statement (1980) while, more recently, Arber and Ginn point out that men are less likely to be disabled than women, that they have greater access to caring resources and, when occupying the position of the 'cared-for', are more likely than women to preserve some sense of self-identity rather than perceiving themselves as a burden (Arber and Ginn, 1992). Dalley pointed out that women are involved in both 'caring for' and 'caring about'. In the case of the former it is noted that women are routinely found performing all the tasks and responsibilities associated with caring. This applies as much in the distribution of caring activities in the formal sectors, public and private, as it does in informal care. Formally or informally, women are supposed to be 'natural' carers. The link here is with constructions of motherhood, an unbroken circle linking a set of highly specific tasks with 'natural' maternal sentiments (Dalley, 1988).

This discussion links with the more general discussion of gender in the previous chapter. The links, mutually reinforcing, between caring for and caring about, are parallel to the links between gender as a set of activities and responsibilities structured by the sexual division of labour and gender as a core sense of identity. Gender, to repeat, is not simply a matter of who does what but who is what, although the relationships between the two are rarely straightforward (Graham, 1983). To be expected to undertake to do certain kinds of activities is to develop a particular gendered identity. To develop a particular gendered identity is to expect to undertake certain kinds of tasks and to undertake these willingly and as a matter of course. Caring tasks and emotional labour are not just any set of tasks, they constitute a central set of tasks in constructing gender identity and sexual difference.

Some modifications need to be made to this picture. In the first place men are not absent from caring work and, indeed, their involvement in such activities may have been underestimated by some previous commentators (Applegate and Kaye, 1993; Arber and Gilbert, 1989; Clarke, 1995; Parker and Lawton, 1994). The involvement of men in child care has been a much debated and controversial development since the early 1980s; again this discussion applies as much to the involvement of men in the formal paid sector as it does to men in the home, as fathers. While women tend to live longer than men this is clearly not universally the case and men may be found caring for an aged or infirm partner. It is not that men are incapable of caring activities nor that they are not to be found engaging in such activities; it is that the meaning attached to the involvement of men in these tasks and the kinds and amount of support that they receive from others in order to fulfil these obligations are shaped by considerations of gender.

Similarly it is clear that not all women are involved in caring activities or that their involvement in such activities is identical. For one thing, class remains an important line of division for women, and men, engaged in informal care (Clarke, 1995). Further, women do not necessarily passively and unquestioningly accept the 'caring role'. Indeed one of the main reasons for abandoning the language of role theory is because it seems to provide too structurally determined a model of male and female practices. In a modern society, gendered identities are increasingly faced with a number of competing and contradictory currents. Traustadottir, for example, considers a variety of ways in which women may experience caring, at least from the perspective of the carer (1991). To engage in caring may be seen as empowering, it may be seen as disrupting, it may be compartmentalized as one part of life or it may be combined with a career in a variety of ways.

As was argued in the previous chapter, the understanding of gender has becoming increasingly complex and this is as true in the discussion of caring as it is in other aspects of the sexual division of labour and gender work. Nevertheless, caring in all its aspects continues to be closely linked to discussions of gender, in a reciprocal way.

Extending the Scope

The scope of the analysis of caring is being extended in a variety of ways. In the first place, considerations other than gender are being introduced. Graham noted that feminist accounts of gender had generally focused upon 'white, heterosexual women in established family networks' (Graham, 1993b: 127). The analysis of caring needs to be extended to include considerations of age, race and class as well as gender. Again this may be seen as an application of developments in the study of gender more generally.

Chief among these considerations are those of race or ethnicity and class. The broad category of 'women as carers' is being subjected to greater scrutiny and refinement. However, while this move may serve as a useful corrective to an over-gendered view of care it does bring its own problems. Gunaratnum (1993), for example, has noted that popular stereotypes exist about Asian families and their apparent greater 'propensity for care'. The category 'Asian' is certainly too broad, while the linking of Asian families with the notion of extended care also needs greater analysis. If the metaphor of the kaleidoscope is to continue to be an influential one in feminist or postmodern discourse it should be remembered that this model implies new sets of overlaps as well as a multiplicity of differences. In other words in the interplays of class, gender and race, Asian women (or men) may come to have some experiences in common with their white counterparts while also having other different experiences and sets of meanings.

A second way in which the analysis of care is being extended is through a focus on social actors other than the 'carer'. As Graham has pointed out, the feminist analysis tended to focus upon the activities and expectations surrounding the 'carer' rather than the 'cared-for' (Graham, 1993b). Similarly, Arber and Ginn point to a one-sided view of the caring relationship in many studies (Arber and Ginn, 1992). Indeed, there is perhaps relatively little sense of a 'relationship' in some of the studies of carers; it is rather like listening to one end of a telephone conversation with the voice at the other end seeming muffled, distant and indistinct.

The call to extend the study of the caring relationship from the carer to the cared-for, a move associated with the development of critical or radical perspectives on disability, is to be welcomed on a variety of counts. First, gender also enters the analysis of the cared-for as well as the carer. Second, it goes beyond looking at the cared-for as being simply objects of care to seeing the ways in which they seek to maintain a sense of self-identity in the face of the loss of certain socially valued skills and an increasing sense of dependence. And finally, it represents an ever widening movement whereby voices, hitherto excluded or marginalized in dominant discourses, are being given a hearing. The extension of the analysis of caring to the cared-for represents, in potentiality at least, an extension of the notion of citizenship.

Clearly such an extension represents further complications in the analysis but it should be seen as an extension of existing and developing analysis of caring rather than a simple substitution. At the same time it cannot itself be a final stage. While it is clear that a focus on carers should be augmented by a focus on the cared-for, it is also the case that the analysis cannot stop there. The culmination must be the focus upon and the exploration of a range of caring relationships. The kinds of distinctions made by Waerness and cited above may be one point of departure, distinctions based upon the perceived and actual power relationships between giver and receiver.

Finally, the analysis of caring may be extended by looking beyond immediate family or household situations. Again, Graham has noted that the early feminist discussions focused upon the unpaid labour performed by persons related to the cared-for through either marriage or birth (Graham, 1993b). There is relatively little, she argues, about paid work within the home, that is domestic service, although this has been the subject of a fair amount of historical analysis. In the analysis of paid domestic labour, issues of gender frequently interact with issues of class and race.

Beyond the home, it has already been noted how there have been analyses of caring in professional or semi-professional relationships both in the public and the private sphere. There is also scope for more analysis of informal caring work or emotional labour within the context of formal organizations not overtly dedicated to caring work; the work of secretaries or female colleagues, for example, in largely male-dominated organizations. Caring work in a hospital may take place in its administrative wings as well as on the wards or in the surgeries.

Thus we have seen a considerable extension of the research agenda concerning caring. It has been taken beyond gender, beyond the carer and beyond the family. But this extension could develop into a series of fillings-in rather than a systematic analysis of caring and caring relationships. There needs also to be some development in terms of theory and conceptualization, going hand in hand with this broadening of the research agenda. This has indeed been the case.

Developing Theory

A variety of concepts have developed around the theme of caring. Their significance is that, in each case, they serve to extend the analysis beyond the unpaid work of, largely, women in the home to wider theoretical or philosophical considerations. These conceptual developments, therefore, complement and to some extent derive from those developments in the scope of the empirical analysis discussed in the previous section.

The first concept to be considered is the idea of emotional labour. This may be seen as an integral part of a desire to include the analysis of emotions within the sociological agenda, traditionally much more concerned with various modes of rationality (Craib, 1995; Duncombe and Marsden, 1993; Jackson, 1993). The idea of emotional labour shows, implicitly at least, that emotions are not simply personal 'feelings' generally inaccessible to sociological analysis but that they may be seen as having observable characteristics.

Existing usages of the term tend to focus upon certain forms of paid employment, such as airline stewards or nurses, where the management of emotions, other people's emotions, represents a key feature of the employment being described (Hochschild, 1983; N. James, 1989). It can be seen that such work is itself highly gendered and can with little difficulty be applied to work within the family. In one sense it can be seen as a variation on the theme of the extension of the concept of 'work' analysed in chapter 1. Paid emotional labour is gendered in that women tend to be found doing it more frequently than men and that, more profoundly, it is equated with common-sensical notions of femininity.

There should be no difficulty, therefore, in applying the ideas derived from the analysis of paid emotional labour in formal organizations to the analysis of unpaid emotional labour in the home. Indeed, the classic functionalist discussion of the division of labour within the household assumes just this. The expressive role involves a multiplicity of skills designed to control or to handle the emotions of others, to smooth tensions and strains between other family members as well as providing a refuge from or a counter-balance to the tensions of the public sphere. In the context of caring the interplay between caring for and caring about could readily be redescribed as emotional labour. What the woman gives in this work is emotion as much as any kind of physical labour, while she is also supposed to be able to handle the emotions and tensions on the part of the cared for both individually and in relation to other members of the family. Thus, to give a simple example, caring for a sick child involves all of the following: physical care and monitoring, handling the fears and frustrations experienced by the sick child, handling the adjustments required on behalf of other members of the family who may be resentful of the attention being accorded to the sick child, and drawing upon one's own emotional resources and exercising emotional control while doing all of this. Even this very simple example can highlight some of the complexities of emotional labour when it is applied to work in the home.

What this example suggests is that emotional labour is not something which is confined to caring within the home but that it has continuities with all kinds of other routine domestic activities not conventionally associated with caring. It may be noted that a similar kind of extension may be made within the formal spheres of paid employment. It is relatively straightforward to see emotional labour in nursing or social work. It is perhaps less obvious in other occupations although a moment's consideration of a policeman or woman dealing with the parents of a missing child, a manager initiating procedures for dismissal or denying promotion or a railway employee confronted with a host of stranded passengers will make it clear that emotional labour is very widespread indeed.

The concept of emotional labour has, therefore, a variety of points in its favour. As with the earlier analyses of housework, it stresses that many of the everyday routines within the household and elsewhere are 'work' in the sense of the expenditure of effort and personal resources if not in the sense of receiving payment. Further, the idea of work can be extended to the receiver of care as well as to the carer. Just as clients or patients have to work at being clients or patients, so too do the cared-for. The cared-for are expected to deploy their own emotional labour; they as much as the carer are required to 'cope'. Thus the sick child, in the example earlier, is expected not to make unreasonable demands, to co-operate in the process of a likely restoration to health, to accept the temporary incapacities, to recognize the strain the sickness may present to other family members and to engage in a certain amount of self monitoring or surveillance.

What this analysis is pointing to is a way of going beyond an over-gendered concept of caring and, more important, to an analysis which focuses upon the caring relationship rather than the feelings and activities of the carer and the cared-for in relative isolation. In households, just as in more formal organizations, men are supposed to engage in emotional labour as well as women. This is not to say that they are required to do so as much as women or that, necessarily, they do emotional work in the same way. Yet, if men are cared for as well as caring then they too are expected, from time to time, to engage in emotional labour.

There are some problems with the use of the term 'emotional labour' in the context of caring. It may allow us to lose sight of some of the specific features of the caring relationship within a wider generality. From the point of view of a study of the emotions it may still marginalize these through a focus upon the more overt, perhaps more rational aspects of emotional work. It certainly tends to leave the notion of emotions themselves somewhat undertheorized. But it certainly enables an analysis of caring in relational terms and highlights the complexities of the interplays between caring for and caring about. It also underlines the senses of continuity between the formal and the informal in the analysis of caring.

The themes of emotional labour are elaborated in two further sets of ideas. In the first place, Waerness argues for an understanding of a 'rationality of caring' (1987). All rational systems, she argues, require the existence and use of emotions and feelings; such elements are not simply deviations from an otherwise rational order. Conversely, all apparently emotional or informal situations have their elements of rationality. In the case of the rationality of caring, for example, there is the role of practical experience and personal knowledge and the flexibility that is required and comes from the use of such knowledge.

What such an approach, like the discussions of emotional labour, provides is a way of thinking through the distinctiveness of care as it is to be found in family relationships while also arguing for continuities between family life and other areas of life. A somewhat similar argument is developed in Kathleen Lynch's discussion of 'solidary labour' (1989). Her general argument, in common with some of those already advanced, is that: 'Labour and love cannot be completely analysed separately without doing injustice to both' (1989: 2).

In traditional (for example Marxist) discussions of labour or work, the term 'labour' implies a relationship between subject and object. Solidary labour, on the other hand, is to do with relationships between subject and subject. Solidary labour is not something which is confined to family relationships; it can be found in all kinds of other systems and organizations and, indeed, is required by them. Again, it can be argued that there is nothing especially new about this argument and that, for example, the analysis of the functioning of small groups argued as much. But to be reminded of existing theoretical insights through the use of novel language is part of the process of theorizing.

It might be felt that some of this discussion of emotional labour, the rationality of caring and solidary labour is not sufficiently gendered. Thus it might be felt that while there is an implicit presupposition that such forms of activity are especially identified with women, the processes by which this identification is achieved are not clearly developed. Further, it might be argued that the continued use of words like rationality, labour and so on attempts to understand the practices of caring within a framework and a terminology developed within mainstream and 'malestream' social science. The use of such words, it may be argued, reflects masculine activities and preoccupations. In other words, the specifically gendered character of caring is played down.

A more overtly gendered approach is provided in the philosophical discussion of caring by Noddings (1984). Part of her analysis revolves around a distinction between ethical caring and natural caring. The latter sounds as if it is calling upon some notion of innate human goodness, although she is eager to dispel this impression. Rather, the argument is that all human beings have some memories of caring and tenderness and these become part of the stock of autobiographical resources which shape and give meaning to subsequent experiences. This is a theme within those versions of psychoanalysis most frequently considered in sociological discussions (Rustin, 1991). Clearly, such memories or echoes of caring are often complex, contradictory and sometimes painful but it seems likely that they are sufficiently universal to enable such experiences to be shared across other differences in terms of cultures or more specific experiences. To give a parallel illustration, although there are many different languages it seems reasonable to suppose that all human beings have some idea of what it is to understand another human being and to be able to indicate when they do not understand. The idea of natural caring would seem to be an important one since it serves to highlight how issues to do with caring and family often become so emotionally charged.

Ethical caring, on the other hand, is more to do with a sense of obligation. It is more codified, formally and informally, and appears to derive more from sources outside the individual although it may readily become part of that individual's sense of self and identity as an ethical person. Ethical caring does not, it would seem in Noddings's argument, derive simply or directly from natural caring although there are clearly connections. However, ethical caring is more open to specifically cultural or ideological pressures although these pressures may call upon images or memories derived from the idea of natural caring.

It is not difficult to see that the ethic of caring is frequently linked to the experiences of women. Again, the argument has to be unpacked with some care. It is not, as far as I can see, being argued that women are natural carers or that men are excluded from the experiences of natural caring. Rather, the sexual division of labour in most societies, especially around mothering and caring for young children, tends to identify women more closely with caring and this is carried over in most people's recollections of caring and tenderness. Such an identification is readily reinforced within patriarchal societies. Indeed, it is interesting to note that one of the rationales for encouraging men to play a more active part in parenting and fathering is in order to develop 'the feminine side of their character'. Thus conventional understandings of sexual divisions are reproduced even where attempts are being made to subvert them.

One particularly important feature in Noddings's discussion is the emphasis on caring as a relationship. She points to a necessary interdependence or reciprocity in the relationship between the one caring and the cared-for. Indeed, this would also seem to be implied in some of the other discussions, namely in the concept of solidary labour. If caring is caring about/for somebody rather than something, then some degree of reciprocity and interdependence is necessarily implied. There may, indeed, be pressures within both formal and informal settings to shift from an interpersonal reciprocity to a more impersonal definition of the situation, although it is doubtful whether such interdependencies can ever really be totally submerged.

Noddings's discussion opens up the possibilities of a more complex discussion of care and the caring relationship. We move beyond the particularities of the care for the elderly, or the infirm or for children in a particular society to more general concerns focusing upon ethics, responsibilities and the nature and origins of altruism. It is relatively straightforward, using sociological and historical analysis, to understand how a system which has been referred to as 'compulsory altruism' (Dalley, 1988: 17; Land and Rose, 1985) comes into place and becomes especially focused upon the activities and expectations of women. Similarly, it is relatively easy in principle (although considerably more complex in practice) to understand the development and evolution of a 'moral politics of caring' (Rodger, 1991). What perhaps is less easy to understand is the apparent effectiveness of these processes. This must be something to do with the relative ease with which connections are made between the routine practices of tending for a sick or aged person and something which is understood or constructed as the natural order of things. The experiences associated with birth, sickness, aging and death are, however various the meanings and interpretations, part of the human condition. So too are the reciprocities and interdependencies that arise in the production of social beings. As Durkheim argued, ethical issues and social life, in the deepest sense, become intertwined since both, ultimately, refer to the same thing. But these deep social reciprocities and interdependencies need to be given concrete historical and social forms. These are organized around particular structures of the gender order and of the familial order.

Thus the gendering of care is a heavily overdetermined phenomenon. As Finch and Mason (1993) argue, individual women in family contexts build up a series of commitments over time in the course of their gendered biographies. They do not assume such caring responsibilities through an abstract notion of obligation or equally remote ideological pressures. Yet notions of obligations and ideological bracketings of women and care arise out from and give meaning to the everyday commitments with which women are confronted. Such commitments seem natural and this sense of naturalness in part derives from wider, more pervasive, notions of care, reciprocity and human nature.

Issues to do with caring, therefore, point to the ways in which deeper social and ethical issues are mobilized and shaped in particular historical contexts and given meaning in particular institutions and sets of gendered relationships. One of the more specific features of a modern society which is woven into these themes is the notion of citizenship and the relationship of the individual to the state. First, as has often been noted, the idea of citizenship while being formally gender-neutral is, in practice, highly gendered (Walby, 1994). Historically, the notion of citizenship and the bundle of rights and duties associated with it, was bound up with the public sphere, with the worlds and activities of men and notions of masculinity. In the second place, as Hernes has argued with particular reference to Nordic societies, women become more dependent upon and determined by the state than men (Hernes, 1988). She considers the various strands linking women to the state, as citizens, as clients and as employees. As citizens, despite the extension of the franchise to women and despite increasing rates of participation in the formal political process, women tend to remain at a more secondary or indirect level. In the shift from private to public reproduction, their involvements as mothers, spouses and carers become more the focus of public and professional attention. This means, among other things, the greater and specific involvements of women as clients of the state. Finally, the institutions of the state themselves come to employ increasing numbers of women, although this employment tends to be more focused upon caring or quasi-caring activities. With the growth of systems of state welfare, therefore, there are increasing links and interchanges between the formal and the informal, the paid and the unpaid, in the organization of caring.

Increasingly the debates around caring have led to a broadening of theoretical scope as well as of the number of empirical issues involved. Such theoretical discussions could be extended into topics considered in subsequent chapters, such as the sociology of the body or the sociologies of time and space. In considering the actual nature of care, we are taken beyond the immediate concerns of particular, largely family based relationships, to consider wider issues to do with altruism, ethics, obligations and citizenship. It cannot be pretended that these theoretical extensions constitute a single coherent story and much remains to be explored and investigated before these themes are brought together.

Conclusion

The stage at which, I believe, we have reached may be characterized in these terms. Imagine initially a series of clearly bounded boxes, labelled gender, family and caring. These boxes are linked to each other by a series of two-headed arrows. The general picture is one of mutual influence although it may be possible to establish particular causal chains linking these boxes. However, the overall impression of such a modelling is one of relatively discrete variables.

If, however, we abandon the imagery of boxes, variables and causal relationships we move towards an understanding that explores a caring nexus both constituted by and constituting the ideas of family and gender. Thus, women may be found to be engaging in caring practices within the home and elsewhere but it is also the case that the identities of women and gender are constructed and shaped within the caring process. Similarly, a focus upon caring not only entails a focus upon the family and its central role in community care but also and more importantly on the processes whereby the ideas of family are constructed and modified through a gendered focus upon caring practices. We are returning to the metaphor of the kaleidoscope whereby shapes and colours are merging into each other, each deriving a meaning through its fluid interaction with the others.

A focus upon caring practices in many ways points to what is defined as or understood to be specific about family relationships and obligations. Understandings, popular and professional, about the family focus not simply or solely on specific and relatively fixed sets of relationships but more fluidly upon ideas of obligations or upon the more qualitatively defined aspects of these relationships. In this context, notions of caring and caring obligations help to define what is family, the boundaries of family obligations, however fuzzy or lacking in permanence these may be. Claims are made about the special nature of family obligations and this sense of specialness has much to do with ideas relating to caring, both for and about.

At the same time the focus upon caring practices takes us beyond the specificities of family relationships and the constructed boundaries of the family. Through looking at the interfaces between formal and informal caring and through looking at the processes whereby gender, family and caring are constructed as a particular nexus, we go beyond the particularities of family. We gain insight into family processes through ideas derived from an analysis of emotional labour or the rationality of care or a more philosophically based exploration of the nature of caring relationships. And finally, the exploration of some of the specific patterns of caring practices within family and household relationships can enrich our wider understanding of these theoretical notions.

5

The Body

Introduction

The sociology of the body represented a major new development in
the 1980s (O'Neill, 1985; Scott and Morgan, 1993; Shilling, 1993;
Turner, 1984, 1992). These accounts began with a discussion of the
lack of attention to the body in previous theory and research, a
major theme being sociology's overcommitment to models of rationality. Yet it might also be argued that an embodied sociology
represented a continuing, if sometimes submerged, theme in social
analysis (Shilling, 1993). Durkheim, Weber, Elias and Goffman may
be cited as key authors in this respect.

However, despite these new explorations and developments
around the sociology of the body it may be argued that there has still
been relatively little systematic treatment of family and family issues
under the heading of the sociology of the body. Certainly, the
possibility is present – in Turner's discussion of anorexia nervosa, for
example (Turner, 1984) – but the systematic linking of family
sociology and the sociology of the body remains to be achieved.
Perhaps it is O'Neill who provides the strongest and most explicit
linkage between family, body and social knowledge (O'Neill, 1985:
19). Yet such suggestions have not been followed.

To some extent this absence is curious. Family practices are, to a
very large extent, bodily practices. Family themes and family
concerns revolve around issues of birth, death and sexuality and the
connections and relationships that are made and unmade through

these. As Shilling argues, although without mentioning the family: 'Our daily experiences of living . . . are intrinsically bound up with experiencing and managing our own and other people's bodies' (Shilling, 1993: 22). The body is very much present in family sociology even if its presence is not always welcomed or recognized.

Control and Regulation of the Body

It is perhaps not surprising that many of the emphases in the sociology of the body dealt with issues of control and regulation. In part this reflects a core interest within sociology generally to do with order and in part it reflects the concerns of some of the key influences on the developing sociology of the body, namely some feminist writings, the works of Foucault and, linked to these, some concerns in the sociology of health and illness.

Following Elias and others we may see bodily control as having two related aspects: control over others and control of the self. In the case of the former it may be argued that issues of bodily control have been very much to the fore in at least one area of family sociology, namely the study of socialization. In the classic studies of the Newsons, for example, issues of bodily control are very much to the fore even if the somewhat abstracted language of the sociology of the body is absent from these empirically based accounts. There is the control of children's bodily activities, such as toilet training, masturbation, the touching and display of genitals and more general issues of gendered bodily comportment.

There is also the use of the body as a means of control. The Newsons and others provided detailed analysis of the use of physical punishment and possible class differences in these parental practices. But the body is also implicated in many other systems of control and rewards and punishments including the deprivation of favoured foods or the use of such foods as inducements, the restrictions on liberty or physical movement and, less directly, various forms of emotional control. It could be argued that the implied or actual threat of the withdrawal of love is just as much a bodily form of control as smacking, since the emotions that such sanctions arouse are felt in bodily terms and the effectiveness of such sanctions often rests upon the physical memories of love and closeness and its withdrawal or absence.

'Socialization' does not end with the attainment of school age or even adolescence. Julia Brannen and her colleagues have provided a rich account of the relationships between family practices, young people and health (Brannen et al., 1994). A young person's illness is something which is given social recognition, negotiated and managed within a family context. Further, the behaviour which puts youthful bodies at risk (to do with food and diet, sex, drink and drugs) are matters of parental concern and interventions.

Our discussion should not be confined to the relationship between parents and children. Use of bodily control is also a feature of relationships between spouses. The role of violence or the threat of violence in the relationships between men and women is well known and documented (R.E. Dobash and R. Dobash, 1979). But bodily control within marriage is not simply to do with violence or with the control of women by men. It is also to do with the use and denial of sexuality, the threat of the withdrawal of love or control over the use and preparation of food. Turner's suggestive discussion of 'the hand' may be helpful here (Turner, 1992). Hands are giving, open and caressing, expressing concern, love and connectedness. But hands are also raised and strike blows and withhold. Hands represent the two faces of intimacy.

Another bodily part which is also crucial to understanding family processes is the eye or, more particularly, the gaze associated with the eye. Parents routinely exercise surveillance over their children, an activity which is not simply an expression of concern but also, implicitly at least, a statement of the right of parents to gaze upon their children's activities at all times and in all places. The family setting is a panoptical setting. Conversely, children's 'rights' to gaze may be severely restricted, as witnessed in the sanctions on 'staring'. Similar, although more contested, issues of surveillance arise between spouses or lovers. Consider the frequency with which conflicts over reading another's mail or diary feature in fictional treatments of family life. Married or cohabiting partners have, among many other things, to negotiate issues to do with the use of space and these in part are to do with space which is relatively free from the surveillance of others.

As the illustration of toilet training indicates, the control of others is linked intimately to the control of self. The overt aim of toilet training (although probably hardly the only aim) is to instil in the child some sense of control over her or his own bodily functions. In theoretical terms also, control by others and control of oneself are often closely linked. However, self-control is never purely self-control. Not only do we learn self-control through interaction with others but it is often, if not always, for others or a performance in the face of others. Dieting is a case in point. It is clearly an example of self body management but this self is managed in relation to others, actual or generalized. Moreover, especially in domestic contexts, it is carried out before an audience of others and with possible consequences for *their* food and domestic practices.

Professional discussions of the routine practices of family life are full of references to the intimate connections between self-control and control by and for others. Parents are advised to provide firm boundaries for their children not as discipline for the sake of discipline, but in order to enable the child to control her emotions or desires and so to become a competent social performer in an ever widening range of situations. Much middle-class socialization consists of, in theory at least, a finely nuanced balance between liberal notions of autonomy and self-discovery and a recognition of the requirements of that section of society within which the children are being brought up (Brannen et al., 1994).

Again, the themes of self control are not confined to parent–child interactions. The increasing perception of marriage as a relationship rather being simply an institution (Lewis, Clark and Morgan, 1992) would seem to entail similarly delicate balances between self-expression and self-control. A contrast is often made between a patriarchal past where the husband simply imposed his will on his compliant wife and a more egalitarian present where the needs of both partners are recognized and this mutual recognition becomes part of the elaboration of the marital relationship. A good illustration of this may be in terms of sexual relationships, where the shift is seen as being one from the fulfilment of male needs (together with the wider needs of family and society to produce heirs and new generations) to a situation of mutual pleasure giving. The reality is much more complex and ambiguous than these accounts recognize; the important point here, however, is that these definitions of the situation are widely promulgated and frequently expressed.

It has been argued that family relationships constitute a particularly appropriate, although not exclusive, site for the exercise of these bodily controls, over others and over the self. However, as has already been indicated, such control is never purely a family matter. Obviously, in talking about socialization or social reproduction, processes which involve themes of bodily control, we are talking not simply about the needs of immediate and intimate domestic groups but of the expectations that prevail in a wider social order. Clearly there is some element of functionality here, although one which is combined with a degree of relative autonomy on the part of the socializing or reproducing agents. Further, there may be elements of dysfunctionality or lack of fit between the controls exercised within family relationships and those manifested or required elsewhere. For example, modesty in terms of nudity and bodily display may have to be unlearned or at least modified in the context of school changing rooms or showers.

Further, the exercise of control, especially parental control, within a family context is not necessarily an exclusive concern of parents or other family members. A major theme in the historical analysis of modern families has been the extent to which and the ways in which controls within the family have been shared with or exercised on behalf of other agencies. These would include agencies concerned with the nation's health, with education and with policing in both the specific and the more general sense. Again it would be misleading to assume too high a degree of functional fit here. There have been numerous examples, both historical and current, of contestations around the exercise of control over the bodies of family members. These would include, for example, programmes of family planning, programmes of sex education, laws relating to school attendance and issues to do with domestic violence and child abuse. In all these cases what has been at issue has been the boundaries of the family and the competences of family members to exercise controls over the bodies of others.

A neat illustration of the ways in which family relationships exist as a site for the exercise of bodily controls is provided by Alan Prout's discussion of children being 'off school sick' (Prout, 1988). Children are expected to attend school on a regular basis and parents are expected to ensure that they do so. Absences from school need to be supported by some kind of legitimate excuse provided by the parent. Hence when a child is sick, or manifests apparent symptoms of sickness, the parent, usually the mother, has to exercise some fine judgements. Prout notes that the parent who successfully gets the child out of bed and off to school, despite apparent manifestations of sickness, may be seen as encouraging or exercising 'stoicism training'. The example is a good illustration both of the intersections of the embodied control over others and the training for self-control and of family relationships and other agencies.

The Public and the Private

Issues of control overlap with concerns to do with the fluid distinctions between the public and the private in modern society. The routine bracketing of the home and privacy is a key social and historical accomplishment. It is also clear, although perhaps less heralded, that much of this discussion deals with bodily issues. The public arena is where the body is either concealed or idealized and where bodily movements or expressions are kept under control. The stays and corsets of the Victorian era may serve to symbolize the contrast between the public and the private expressed in bodily terms. The corseted body presents an idealized female shape in the public arena (an arena which may on occasion include the wearer's own home) and is also a demonstration of the wearer's social and bodily competence. The stays are unlaced and the wearer relaxes in private.

We see, therefore, that issues of control are very much linked to the nexus around the public and the private focused simultaneously on the home and on the body. In the first place, there is the concern with keeping certain activities out of public view. The public performer is expected to avoid those activities which detract from or threaten to undermine that public performance or which draw attention to the work that goes into that public performance. The unwitting display of braces or bra straps at a formal dinner may serve as a somewhat trivial example. In particular, the taboos, prohibitions or sources of embarrassment often revolve around the unwitting or unwelcome reminders of the embodiment of the performer such as yawns, farts, belches and erections.

In the context of the home there is often not just one front and back stage but a series of overlapping front and back stages. The home may represent a back stage to the performances in the public sphere but it is also the case that public performances may take place within the formally private sphere of the home where there may be other back stages: bedrooms, kitchens and so on. This is particularly the case in middle-and upper-class entertaining but it also has its working-class manifestation in the often observed front drawing-room which is kept neat and spotless and out of bounds except for special occasions (Chapman, 1955). Further, even between persons understood to be members of the same family and household, there may be a series of front stages and back stages, zones which are held to be private and which require special rituals (for example knocking) to permit entry. Again, all these nests of front and back stages very often are to do with the body and with bodily concealment. Thus children may not be allowed in their parents' bedroom except under certain conditions and bathroom and toilet doors are kept locked.

In a sense, much of the work of 'the civilizing process' is devolved upon women within the home; the bodily controls exercised within the home are in part in anticipation of competent social performances in public. However, the home is also constructed as a site where relaxation from the demands of civilization may be expected or permitted. Hence the home does not simply 'prepare', in some functional sense, its younger members for public performance. It is also very much involved in the business of constructing or reproducing the selfsame boundaries between the public and the private. The child in this context may also learn the rule of 'don't do as I do, do as I say'.

The maintenance of boundaries around the public and the private, however contested and fluid these boundaries might be, is linked to issues to do with the construction and control of the self mentioned earlier. Yet bodily control within the home is not to be simply identified with the generation of guilt or shame. Matters are more complex. The competent self is one who can maintain a range of performances, who understands what is the appropriate performance in a range of situations and who, in other words, deploys an increasing repertoire of bodily controls and displays. To be in control of one's body in the multiple transitions between the public and the private (or, rather, between publics and privates) is to be in control of one's self. To be able to make such multiple performances coherent, as part of a consistent evolving autobiography, is to engage in the successful construction of a self.

One obvious illustration of these processes is to do with sexual modesty. The work of the Newsons deals in some detail with control over a child's bodily display, over issues to do with nudity and the touching of genitals, sometimes revealingly described as 'privates'. Such controls are shaped by considerations of class and gender and may be seen to relate, to some extent, to issues of sexual danger and the way in which women in particular are expected to present themselves in the presence of men.

The issue of masturbation is a particularly significant one in the exploration of bodily controls and the borders between the public and the private. On the one hand, it represents one of the most private acts; even defecation is publicly acknowledged in the form of, again significantly, public conveniences. Yet it has also been the case that this most private of acts has been the object of a variety of controls ranging from the most obviously physical to more indirect deployments of guilt or fear. Such sanctions almost certainly have not ceased, although they now coexist with a range of more positive constructions running from the neutral, arguing that it is a harmless practice which most individuals grow out of, to a more positive recognition of masturbation as a legitimate form of self bodily knowledge and, in an AIDS era, of sexual self-expression. However, in British culture at least, 'wanker' is still a popular term of abuse.

But perhaps the most revealing example of the interaction between the body and the public and the private is to do with defecation. In most Western societies, this continues to be the subject of control and taboo, a fact reflected in its relatively infrequent treatment in sociological writings (Murcott, 1993). This is not to say that other societies are necessarily significantly more libertarian in this respect (Loudon, 1977: 168).

A whole host of issues converge around excretion. These include constructions of dirt and cleanliness, some of the most tangible evidences of embodiment and, in more complex and concealed senses, issues of sexuality. In discussions of care, whether of small children or of the elderly, the cleaning of another's excretia represents the most powerful symbol of caring practices. A rich store of language and expressions revolve around the toilet; familial identity and individuality is often manifested in 'private' usages of words to denote going to the toilet and the activities involved in this practice.

A particularly revealing illustration of the shifting boundaries in relation to the public and the private around the embodied family is recent debates concerning violence and abuse. The body is centrally implicated in these questions both as the object or victim of violence and as the perpetrator. What is at stake is not simply the degree of physical injury or pain, mental or physical, that is caused but the very status of the body and its links to senses of self and personhood. A unilateral violation of another's body, especially within family contexts where there are clear inequalities in terms of power and frequently few opportunities for escape or immediate redress, is felt by the victim as an assault on the self and an uncoupling of the integrated links between body and self. The body becomes an object, an extension of another's desires or projects, while the sense of self if it remains, becomes detached from that body. What is at issue here also are notions of ownership, a questioning of the taken-for-granted understanding of 'my body', 'my self'. The perpetrator, on the other hand, sees the other's body as an extension of his or her own bodily field.

However, the very notions of self and personhood, rights and citizenship, that are being deployed or implied here have their own historical and cultural antecedents. Cross-cultural analysis, considering for example such issues as circumcision or initiation rituals (Korbin, 1981), open up possibilities for considerable variation in what is regarded as legitimate or illegitimate in relation to the infliction of injury or pain on another's body or the use of that body for a project which, formally at least, might appear to be outside the volition or desires of the recipient. A variety of overlapping considerations are relevant. There is the extent to which the violences perpetrated by family members on another family member are visible to those outside the immediate family circle. There is the extent to which these violences are perceived by the witnesses as legitimate, within reasonable bounds, or illegitimate or excessive. Further, questions of legitimacy may be linked to questions of the rightness or otherwise of the ends for which these violences are perpetrated; generally speaking, individual gratifications might be disapproved whereas publicly acknowledged legitimations, ritualistic or just punishment, for example, may be reinforced.

Questions of legitimacy are also linked to questions of control or lack of control. Generally speaking legitimate violence may be seen as controlled violence, that is, violence perpetrated by an agent who is seen to be in full control not only of the other but also of himself and herself, whose violence seems to be carried out according to clearly defined and publicly available rules. The violence committed by an agent apparently out of control will not be so publicly acknowledged. However, in modern times at least, violences committed by agents apparently out of control at the time may be seen as understandable if not fully legitimate, and may themselves be the subject of lesser sanctions as a result. Legal notions of provocation revolve around such issues.

The fact that issues of violence and abuse within family relationships have entered the public agenda is itself a reminder of the shifting boundaries between legitimate and illegitimate, and between public and private. The problematization of violences within the family has occurred in the following sequence: physical violences against children, physical violences against wives, sexual abuse of children, sexual abuse of wives. Each of these has its own history, set of key concerns and contested features. Thus even though physical violence against children has probably had the longest history of public concern, there remain areas of contest and debate, for example the extent to which a parent has a right to inflict any physical punishment on a child, the extent to which a child has public redress against a parent who inflicts such punishment or the extent to which outside agencies have a right to involve themselves in family matters.

The processes whereby gender becomes woven into these shifting concerns are equally complex. In some cases (for example violence against wives, rape in marriage), activities of feminists have been central in placing the issues on the agenda. Sometimes, men have been identified as the key, if not the sole, perpetrators, and the violence or abuse has been understood as being strongly linked to issues of masculinity and patriarchy. In yet other cases, men have been implicated not so much as the perpetrators but as the agents responsible for the legitimatization or public definition of the issues under consideration. Yet, just as issues of violence and abuse raise issues of the contested boundaries between the public and the private so too do they often raise contested discussions as to the gendered nature of such practices and of the nature of gender itself. Thus, women have also been identified as the perpetrators of physical violence or sexual abuse of children. Or, where men have been identified, questions remain as to whether this is an issue of masculinity in general or a question of particular and identifiably problematic areas of masculinities.

Such discussions of bodily violence, abuse and control might give a somewhat pessimistic picture. It is worth stressing, therefore, that the body can also be identified with sources of pleasure, especially pleasures connected with the erotic. Thus many of the pleasures that people routinely enjoy are to do with the body and have particular associations with family and domestic relations. A whole range of bodily pleasures and sensations may be associated, ideologically, actually or through the work of memory, with family life: memories of warmth, bodily freedom and the comforts of food and countless minor tendernesses. It is true, of course, that the reverse is often true or that such comforts may not always be unalloyed. It is also true that bodily freedoms and pleasures may often be associated with an absence of or a distance from family relations. Nevertheless there is a particular linking of bodily pleasures and family life which is not simply a question of ideological mystification.

One of the central sets of pleasures associated with domestic life focuses upon marriage as a site of legitimate and positively sanctioned sexuality. It need hardly be said that this is not exclusively the case and it is increasingly likely that one's first sexual experiences will take place outside marriage. Further, however much people may formally disapprove of adultery, extramarital sex, heterosexual and homosexual, plays an important if complex part in the lives of many people and couples (Lawson, 1988). Yet with all these qualifications, marriage represents the key site for the legitimatized expression of sexuality. Further, it is not simply permitted within marriage, it is increasingly positively encouraged. Sexual expression is seen as an integral cornerstone in the elaboration of a marital relationship (Lewis, Clark and Morgan, 1992; Clark, 1993). Yet, outside the prescriptions of marital or sexual therapists, marital sex may come to be seen as routine, as simply part of the man's pleasures and generally lacking in excitement. In the popular imagination, exciting sex takes place outside marriage. Further, it seems likely that there remain considerable differences in the sexual experiences and expectations of women and men both inside and outside marriage.

Yet in talking about the body and its pleasures in association with family life, we should not confine our discussion to expressions of adult (hetero)sexuality. As Bologh (1990: 218) writes:

> Because we are embodied beings, all sociable relations have an erotic dimension (the body and senses are affected); all sociable relations are erotic relations. We all find the actual presence or some trace . . . of another more or less pleasurable, more or less affective.

Bologh is talking about the erotics of all social relationships; not just those that exist within family or marriage. Again we see many continuities between family living and other spheres of social life. However, to put the case negatively, family relationships are not excluded from such a general statement. Further, it is possible that legitimized or positively sanctioned bodily pleasures continue to be most closely associated with family living and one does not necessarily have to elaborate a wholly Freudian analysis to suggest that there are important continuities, autobiographically, between experiences within the home and the capacity to enjoy and share in the erotics of everyday life. Most touching, positively connotated as well as negatively, takes place between intimates in domestic or familial relationships.

The pleasures and erotics of family living cannot, however, be detached from issues of risk and danger. Thus it is true that family relations provide the most unambiguously positive sanctioned site for physical contacts between adults and children: comforting, physical horseplay, routine caresses and embraces. Yet, as we have seen, such contacts, which are often pleasurable to both parties, carry with them their own risks. These include risks of being misunderstood, of shifting from routine expressions of concern combined with mutual gratification to contexts where the gratification becomes more dominant and less mutual. Parents, especially fathers, may express confusion as to what is now expected of them in the context of widespread concerns about the sexual abuse of children.

A more embodied approach to the study of family relationships highlights aspects of bodily control but also legitimized pleasures and expressions. We are dealing with an area of considerable tension, contradiction and ambiguity. One person's farting or belching within the confines of the home may be perceived or remembered by another as disgusting, as thoughtless or as just another example of masculine ways of being in the world. Many of these ambiguities and tensions arise out of the contested barriers between the public and the private around the site of the home and family relationships.

Social Divisions

While the facts of birth, death and ageing, together with questions of health and illness, affect all human beings, there is scarcely a statement that we would wish to make about these processes which we would not also wish to modify or qualify in some way according to divisions of gender, age, class or ethnicity. The interplays between embodiment and these divisions, in the context of family life, need some consideration.

Gender

Sexual differences are conventionally understood in biological or bodily terms. The complex process whereby biological and cultural differences are converted into or mask social inequalities has been discussed in chapter 3. A key element in the linking of gendered inequalities and the body is the family, using the term to refer to an ideologically constructed entity, as a site for the legitimate procreation and rearing of children, combining this with the social constructions around motherhood. 'After all it is women who have the babies' remains a key argument in debates and battles around questions of sexual equality. Yet motherhood and its socially sanctioned site in the nuclear family reflect less the direct impact of biological considerations than the interplay between biology and culture and social structure.

The expanded understandings of reproduction developed by Marxists and feminists remind us that not only is biology shaped by cultural and social structural factors but also that practices within families and households around parents and children are linked to the wider society. At various times and in different places there have been concerns with lineage and the provision of legitimate heirs, the disposition of property, the provision of a socialized and disciplined labour force or the divisions of labour around questions of informal care. These linkages seem to suggest some kind of functional analysis. Yet it may also be the case that the linkages between social and cultural reproduction and gender differences and inequalities within the home are weakening.

The proximate reasons for this are relatively familiar ones to do with female participation in the labour force, weakenings of the necessary relationships between biological reproduction and the conventional nuclear family and, in some cases, declining birth rates. More distant or more theoretical causes revolve around shifts in the gender order, although the extent to which there has been a clear march forward in the direction of sexual equality is less obvious. Yet one of the implications of these shifts would seem to be that the relationships between bodily differences and gendered inequalities become less and less straightforward.

This may be illustrated with reference to two themes that have already been considered. First, sexual modesty is to do with the control of the body, by self and by others, and with ways of relating the self to the body. However, it is not merely something to do with the body, its control and concealment, but is also something that is expressed in bodily terms, with lowered eyes or blushes. It is a gendered set of practices since the requirements of sexual modesty fall more heavily upon women than men.

This particular model of sexual modesty does, however, appear to be more relevant to those cultures where modesty within the home is clearly linked to modesty or control within the public sphere and where some of the central concerns linking these are to do with themes of honour and shame. While practices to do with sexual modesty undoubtedly still occur within the home and elsewhere, they would seem to be more individualistically based and more open to disagreement. It would appear that the strong links between bodily behaviour, themes of modesty and gender within the home are weakening. High modernity, with its concerns with the self, introduces a tension between traditional expectations of gender deportment and individual self-realization. Given that self-realization is increasingly associated with bodily perfection and that constructions of the ideal body are also linked to sexuality, we can see another strand in the tension between identity and stability within marriage (Askham, 1984). The cultivation of the sexually attractive body is not simply something that is imposed upon women by a patriarchal society, nor is it something which is only required of young or unmarried women as part of the process of attracting a mate. Women, in an increasing range of contexts, do not see any contradiction between developing or maintaining a sexually attractive appearance and a continuing concern with motherhood and domesticity. Gender inequality remains an issue here around the fact that the pressures to construct or to maintain a sexually attractive body bear less heavily upon men than women.

Another illustration is to do with the various claims that individuals may make in relation to the bodies of others. These rights of access, assumed or agreed, exist in all interpersonal contexts but take on a particular significance in the context of family life. We may also include here rights in terms of gazing upon the bodies of others or of commenting upon another's body. Chief among the rights of access will be those acts which are sexual or defined as being largely sexual in content.

Generally speaking, these rights or assumptions are unevenly distributed between men and women with women being more likely to be the recipients of and men more likely to be the initiators of such access. Within the home these accesses are more likely to be claimed as rights rather than simply assumed as part of normal everyday gender conduct. Again, the key example may be to do with sexual relations. However, as we have seen, the apparently unambiguous nature of marital rights has been challenged through a variety of rulings in relation to rape within marriage and it is likely that this challenge will be part of an overall critique of taken-for-granted masculine assumptions within intimate relations. Concretely, the mere fact of being married does not give a man an automatic right to pat his partner's bottom or fondle her breasts at all times, nor does it provide an open-ended licence to comment on her physical appearance, especially in the presence of others.

Age

Similar considerations arise in relation to age. Once again, for example, we are dealing with differential rights of access with older individuals, especially parents, claiming more rights of access to the bodies of juniors while simultaneously denying these rights to their children. This is not simply in terms of direct physical access such as smacking, kissing or touching, but also in terms of surveillance and comment. Transitions in terms of age may be accompanied by a redrawing of the boundaries in relation to physical access. Children may, where circumstances permit, be allowed separate bedrooms after reaching a certain age or may be allowed some measure of privacy with parents, for example, being expected to knock on the door of their daughter's or son's bedroom before gaining admittance. And again, as in the case of gender, we see some wider challenging of these practices and assumptions in the contexts of debates about child abuse and domestic violence as well as wider notions about personal autonomy.

Similarly, the ambiguities and tensions to do with care of the elderly within the home frequently focus upon the body. Ideas of 'second childhood' are frequently highly embodied and elaborated within the context of family relationships. Supposed bodily correlates of ageing to do with increased deafness, failing sight or absent-mindedness may be subjects of comment in domestic contexts. Yet again, physical signs of the ageing process such as the development of a paunch, baldness or the menopause may be recognized, commented upon and made concrete in the face of an audience of familiars, spouse or children.

Whether we are talking about relationships between parents and children or about the care of the elderly or yet other aspects of ageing we are talking about a process whereby biological signs are given meanings within domestic contexts. It is not that these meanings are not also developed in other contexts. However, since age and age differences are built into family processes and since family members claim greater licence to comment upon such matters, it is likely that the work of constructing age divisions continues to be especially associated with the home.

Class

Many images of class are bodily and masculine images, from the muscles and upraised fists of the proletariat to the rounded bellies of the members of the bourgeoisie. In the context of the home, class divisions have two aspects. First, there will be class divisions within the home and the way in which these are expressed or maintained in bodily terms. Living-in servants were segregated from their employers and their employer's families and the formalities of the relationships between master and servant were coded in bodily terms. This codification was especially important where servants had physical access to the bodies of others. Thus servants attended to the bathing of their masters or the physical grooming of their mistresses.

But more important in a modern society is the way in which class and status differences between households might be expressed or symbolized in bodily terms. Thus, in the time-honoured distinctions between the rough and the respectable, rough children are defined as being noisy, their bodily movements violent, clumsy or undeniably physical, their general appearance as unkempt or scruffy. Respectable children are defined as being quieter, more apparently in control of their bodies in public places and more obviously bearing the signs of prior grooming. Often such physical signs pointed to many fine distinctions and gradations. When I was a child, it was the normal practice in my home to smooth down my hair with brilliantine or Brylcream. Such practices were scorned as being 'sissy' by boys from more working-class families while also being scorned as unnecessarily pretentious by more securely middle-class families. Bodily appearance stands for the social status and standing of the individual while that embodied individual also stands for or reflects the social status of the family from which he or she comes.

Many of the concerns treated earlier in this chapter derive much of their meaning and significance from their location within wider social divisions. The interplays between external controls and self control within the home not only vary between social classes but also serve to maintain and to reproduce class and status boundaries. Further, notions of the public and the private, as they are expressed in bodily terms, are also located in and given meaning by the wider stratification system.

Ethnicity

Beyond the more obvious differences (skin colour, for example), ethnic differences are often constructed around forms of bodily appearance such as dress and deportment. Sexual and reproductive practices also often appear to the fore in the construction of ethnic stereotypes. Clearly these practices are in some cases linked to families but it may also be the case that perceptions of 'threats' of 'invasion' are linked to the practices of families rather than individuals. Thus the idea that 'they' are taking over the neighbourhood is based upon the bodily presence of family units, occupying space, as well as upon the perceived dense links (whether these perceptions are accurate or not) between separate household units. The common perception that Asians have a much stronger or supportive family life is linked to perceptions not so much of a collectivity of individual strangers but a series of familial or kinship linkings, in other words not single bodies but a series of linked bodies.

In contrast, other family practices attributed to different ethnic groups may focus upon themes of disorganization. In this case the 'other' family units are too noisy, too irregular in their habits, too obviously embodied in their mode of being in the world. Whatever the ethnic group being described and whatever set of practices are attributed to that ethnic group, the point is that such practices are both embodied and located in family practices.

Thus conventional social divisions – gender, age, class and ethnicity – may be seen as having bodily dimensions and these may be seen to be reinforced through family practices. However, changes that have affected family relationships and wider relationships between women and men also serve to confuse the relationships between embodiment and social divisions. Issues of gender and age, while still important social divisions in all kinds of ways, appear to lose their essential characteristics based upon embodiment and seem to be more free-floating and open to challenge and negotiation. Even so, we are referring to differences that exist, of necessity, within family relationships; of necessity because any definition of family relationships must include some reference to age and gender.

Differences between households, those in terms of class and ethnicity, are perhaps of a different order, although their importance is somewhat variable. However, it is likely that at a time when there is a common perception that the family is under threat, then social differences between households, differences expressed in perceived or actual modes of embodiment, may become important.

Wider Issues

Mind and Body

It is important not only to see discussions about the relationships between the mind and the body as not simply belonging to the realm of ideas but to recognize that these ideas themselves have a social and materially based history. That material is not simply or solely economic in the more narrow sense but in part relates to some of the key social institutions within society, among which we would consider family and domestic relationships.

Within modern society, distinctions between mind and body are partially related to distinctions between the bourgeoisie and the proletariat and divisions between mental and manual labour. Distinctions between mind and body may be mapped on to distinctions between those who work with their brains and those who work with their hands or with things. These differences themselves take on embodied forms, in popular imagery and everyday practices. Those who work largely with their brains are rationally organized in bureaucratic hierarchies and wear clothes which seek to deny the body. The intellectual is the egghead.

Weaving into these distinctions are other, highly gendered, distinctions between the public and the private and between the home and the workplace. Running through and across the class and status distinctions defined in the previous paragraph there are also distinctions between men and women. The hierarchically divided and ordered public sphere is largely the sphere of men, dominated by men. The hegemonic masculinity is less one of the deployment of physical force and more one of the deployment of rational argument and rational controls. The private sphere is organized by women, partly on behalf of men, and is more embodied, more associated with emotional labour or the rationality of care. Thus the history of the distinction between mind and body has a materiality in terms of gender relations and family practices as well as class relations. The history of rationality is the history of masculinity and femininity (Seidler, 1994).

However, as Hernes and others have argued, this particular model is probably more appropriate to the early stages in the development of a liberal state (Hernes, 1988). In the context of a liberal state, minimally interventionist and seeking to preserve or enhance the liberties of its (male) subjects, the mind/body distinction has its most developed expression. The social changes that developed subsequently tended to undermine these sharp oppositions. These developments include the increasing presence of women, especially married women, in the public sphere and the increasing interventions of the 'mature welfare state' (1988: 122) into the home and domestic relationships. Family and domestic relationships become shaped by wider rationalities, while issues of caring and emotions enter the market place. If today there is less of a tendency to think in terms of sharp mind/body distinctions and oppositions (one thinks of the rise of holistic medicine here), this in part reflects the increasing fluidity of the boundaries between the public and the private and the partial reshaping of the gender order around the home and family relations.

Rationality and the Emotions

In the conventional divisions between home and work, the home becomes the site for the emotions. It is a site for their legitimate expression or for the discharge of emotions kept under restraint in the public sphere. Emotional labour, as we have seen, was constructed as chiefly the work of women within the home, work involving managing the interpersonal emotional economy of domestic relationships. We see that this labour is very much tied up with the body and its control and maintenance. The body is the site for emotions just as family relationships are the context specializing in the management of emotions.

It is important to consider some possible modifications to this account:

1 There is good reason to suppose the modern household to be a site for rationality as well as for emotions. Models of the puritan or the bourgeois family clearly include notions of order, rationality and moral and financial bookkeeping. The nuclear family was never simply an emotional counterbalance to the rationality of the public sphere. For one thing, to see the family as a little commonwealth implies some kind of rational hierarchical organization. More prosaically, the timetables of the public world come to take precedence over the less predictable rhythms of domestic life; individuals have to organize their lives in keeping with the demands of work time, transport schedules and school timetables.

2 The language and theories of social science have contributed to perceptions of the family and household as being other than a site

for emotional labour. Functionalist or Marxist theories emphasized the links between household and the rationalities of the
public sphere while more recent discussions of family life in terms
of strategies or rational choice reinforce this perception of the
rationality of domestic life.

3   There has also been the increasing encroachment of other
agencies, linked to the state and relevant professions, into the
routines of family life. This is part of what Reiger calls 'the
disenchantment of the home' (Reiger, 1985).

4   Finally, there has been a growing recognition of the importance
of emotionality within sites formally designated as belonging to
the public sphere. This includes the discussions of emotional
labour in areas of paid employment, the interplays between
formal and informal and between paid and unpaid in the area of
caring and more recent discussions of sexuality at work.

Thus family relations become a particularly contradictory site. On
the one hand, professional analyses and interventions emphasize the
emotional interdependencies that are said to characterize marital
and family relationships. On the other hand, other understandings,
as well as the logic of developments within the public sphere, suggest
that family life is not apart from other rationalities. Thus the
conventional distinctions between the rational and the emotional
become blurred, just as the distinctions between the public and the
private become more confused.

The Body and Familial Boundaries

The boundaries of family relationships can be extremely flexible and
various, shaped by the demands and concerns of the moment. One
way of thinking about this variation is in terms of a kind of bodily
density. This does not simply refer to the close spatial proximity of a
particular set of persons over longish or repeated periods of time.
This is certainly an important aspect of the bodily density referred to
here, involving knowledge, control and care of the others' bodies in
numerous repeated and often unacknowledged ways. But this kind
of bodily density extends across and between households linked
through ties of marriage or descent including reconstituted households. Even where the notion of bodily density does not necessarily
entail the daily monitoring of one's own and others' bodily behaviour, it also extends to the possibility of such monitoring and to the

knowledge that people have of others' bodies even where they no longer live under the same roof. Thus, individuals may anticipate caring for a sick or aged relative even though, for the present at least, they are living in a separate household.

We may see family relationships as being particular clusters characterized by bodily density. This is not the only way of viewing family relationships but, it is hoped, an additional and a potentially fruitful perspective. Within these clusterings we have claims made about certain bodily rights and certain knowledge, perhaps guilty knowledge, about other family members. The statement that no man is a hero to his valet may be extended to cover a wide range of family and domestic relations. One example of this is the continuing debate as to whether family members, grown-up children or ex-partners, should provide public accounts of other family members while they are still alive.

It can be argued that while family relationships have some special or particular significances in terms of understandings and uses of the body, this is by no means exclusive to family relationships. Prostitutes, physicians, psychoanalysts, secretaries and lovers may well have guilty bodily knowledge of others and bodily density is clearly a feature of many work and leisure situations. Nevertheless, the particular clustering linking family obligations and reciprocities with notions of the body, control, caring and density, is worth exploring.

Conclusion

While this chapter may have demonstrated ways in which the developing sociology of the body can contribute to our understanding of family processes, can it also be argued that family studies has something to contribute to the sociology of the body? Further, is there anything special about the body/family linkage? Superficially it might be argued that I do not cease to have a body when I leave my front door and, indeed, it might be argued that some of the strongest bodily images relate to non-familial settings. These would include sports fields and gymnasia, war and the military, pornography and many areas of culture and the arts, especially dance and theatre.

Certainly, much of the writing on the body highlights the fact that family practices do not exist in isolation and have continuities with values, sites and practices outside the family. Everingham's study of motherhood, for example, stresses that motherhood is never purely a family affair and extends to playgroups, social networks and neighbourhoods (Everingham, 1994: 84). More generally, notions of 'body rights' (Shaver, 1993/4) or citizenship (Turner, 1992) have informed and shaped concerns about the body and such concerns are by no means confined to family situations. Here, as elsewhere, the family setting has a part to play but it is by no means an exclusive one.

Yet, while we cannot see family practices as being exclusively concerned with bodily matters, is it possible to speak about 'a family body' or familial body practices? O'Neill's proposed three-level model of body politics suggests that this might be possible. These levels are the 'bio-body', focused upon the family and dealing with matters to do with well-being, health and sickness; the 'productive body', focused upon work and dealing with self-control and exploitation; and 'the libidinal body', located around the personality and dealing with such matters as happiness and fulfilment (O'Neill, 1985: 80). Such a model would need to be developed in ways which move beyond an implied (and possibly essentialist) base-superstructure model with the bio-body located in the family constituting the base. Rather, it would be more helpful to see a series of exchanges between the various levels which need not, diagramatically, be located on top of each other. Thus it is not the case that family practices are embodied while practices elsewhere are disembodied; it is that family practices are embodied in different sorts of ways.

What is distinctive about family bodily practices?

1   There is a widespread understanding that family and body are closely linked. When family matters are on the agenda, bodies are rarely far behind. Family processes and relationships are shaped by and given their dynamism by their linkage to processes of birth, sexuality, death and ageing. These are all clearly embodied, although never exclusively biological or determining.
2   Much family work is conducted with the physical co-presence of others, and where issues of physicality are (in contrast to, say, work situations) very much to the fore. Here the affinities between the words 'family' and 'familiar' may be helpful. To be familiar with another person is to have some bodily knowledge of that other, through the hand or the eye.
3   In various ways and to varying, and sometimes contested, degrees, family members have bodily licence. This licence may be in terms of the bodies of others or in terms of one's own body under the gaze of others.

4 Family bodily practices operate at the interface between the
   public and the private. Thus it is not true to say that these
   practices are exclusively concerned with the private sphere.
   Rather, they are conducted in the context of an awareness of the
   boundaries between the public and the private or between back
   stage and front stage. Thus, family members are best placed to
   judge whether a politician who pronounces on family values
   matches his words with his deeds.

Again, exceptions to each of these points may be produced to
show that family practices are not exclusively involved in the bodily
themes described. However, taking these four points in combination
does suggest a particular, significant and distinctive linkage between
family practices and bodily concerns. Further, our understanding of
family processes may be greatly enhanced by the development of a
more embodied sociology. But, at the same time, discussions of the
sociology of the body need a greater awareness of developing
discussions of family practices and processes.

6

Time and Space

Social contacts are extended in space and quickened in time, and
in the same degree the mental unity they imply becomes wider
and more alert.

C.H. Cooley, *Social Organization*

Introduction

The explicit analysis of issues to do with time and space has become
more prominent in recent sociological theorizing. This interest may
be reflected in middle-range theorizing, as exampled by Goffman's
discussion of front and back stage, or it may be reflected in more
general theorizing as, for example, in some of the work of Giddens
(see Adam, 1994). While these discussions are relatively recent in
terms of sociology, the more comparative discipline of social anthropology has always given more attention to these issues. Starting with
Durkheim's key observation about how some of the most fundamen-
tal categories through which we order our social being and understanding of the world have themselves societal origins, social
anthropologists have often been more sensitive to the ways in which
societies may live with concepts of time and space very different
from our own. Social historians have also, necessarily, been sensitive
to issues of time; E.P. Thompson's discussion of the relationship
between clock-time and the disciplines of industrial capitalism is an
influential example.

Discussions of time and space have not been absent from family research and theorizing, either. Discussions of the home are clearly dealing with issues of social and domestic space. Similarly, discussions around the ideas of lifecycle and lifecourse inevitably deal with time. It may be argued, however, that such discussions, obviously deploying ideas of time and space, are not usually central to family analysis which is more readily focused upon structures and relationships. Yet time and space are key axes around which the analysis of family processes should be developed. Family relationships are relationships that are established, and broken, over time. Definitions and distinctions between family and household revolve in part around issues to do with time and space: the latter is defined largely in terms of place (although time is implied), while the former is defined in terms of time, of past relationships shaping and influencing present relationships and obligations. There are also questions to do with the impact of geographical mobility on family relationships. Again, the more specific discussion of 'bodily density' developed in the previous chapter is to do with the co-presence of social bodies in time/space locations.

Even in this brief discussion so far it becomes apparent that the themes of time and space cannot be separated, although there are times when it is convenient to do so. Giddens's analysis centrally recognizes the interdependence of ideas of time and space and this will be reflected here. Even where one or the other term is being emphasized it should always be remembered that the other is waiting in the wings.

Definitions and Distinctions

Time

A host of definitions and distinctions exist here and these may be located in two broad groups.

1   There are those distinctions which attempt to capture different ways in which time might be conceptualized or understood, at both the personal and the cultural level. These include:
    (a)   distinctions between linear and cyclical time (for example Hernes, 1988). Notions of career or conventional understandings of autobiography might be examples of the former; notions of the seasons, or the academic year might be examples of the latter;

(b) distinctions between linear and spatial time (for example Cottle, 1976). Whereas linear time deals with pasts, presents and futures which may or may not be unitarily spatially located, spatial time deals with the allocations of times in relation to specific spaces or locales, such as the working day or a period set aside for housework.

2   The next set of distinctions deal less with social actors' definitions of time and more with theoretical or methodological concerns facing social analysts. The aim of these distinctions is to clarify different times that might be thought to coexist within a given theoretical framework or research problem. These include:

(a) distinctions between historical time, personal time and situational time (Wallman, 1984: 4–6). Similar distinctions include Evans-Pritchard's distinctions between microcosmic/ ecological time and macrocosmic/structural time (Gell, 1992: 16) and Wadsworth's distinction between individual human development and different social/historical times (Wadsworth, 1986: 118);

(b) distinctions between Cohort, Age and Period effects. These are especially important in the analysis of social mobility, essentially an account of individuals moving through social space over time (Goldthorpe, Llewellyn and Payne, 1980: 68);

(c) distinctions between calendar time, social time and personal time (Blaxter, 1992).

These and other concepts have attempted to recognize that in any one social situation a variety of different times may coexist. Roughly, these distinctions may be seen to deal with contrasts between the historical and the personal levels of analysis. Linked contrasts are those between external and internal and between time as a constraint and time as a resource. In all these contrasts, there are senses in which the family and the household may be seen as occupying some mid-point, facing both ways, between the various alternatives (Morgan, 1985).

Space

Concepts and distinctions to do with space are possibly less elaborated, at least within the sociological literature. The central distinction is that between physical space and social space, although this is probably of limited usefulness. Is it possible to provide any description of space which is not in some way touched by human, that is to say social, concerns? The drawing-room, as far as the eye can see, the North of England and twelve acres are all terms describing space and although they represent physical distances, areas and locations the terms used to describe these locations are necessarily drawn from our cultural repertoire and have meaning in terms of human projects. This distinction can only serve as a point of departure.

Perhaps more useful is an approach which begins with a recognition that space is about boundaries and which goes on to ask questions about how these boundaries are drawn (Morgan, 1985). We can distinguish between administrative boundaries, those boundaries such as postal districts or parishes which are set up for certain ordering purposes by the state or some other agency; personal or affectual boundaries, which have some meaning to social actors themselves; and theoretical boundaries, which are constructions of the social analyst seeking to make some kind of generalization about the social world. Research may be seen as a movement between and across these different boundaries. In terms of 'family', the same term may represent all three usages, the family of the census, the family of my day-to-day understandings and the family drawn up in the process of sociological analysis.

Alternatively, or in addition, we may draw up distinctions similar to those used in the analysis of time. Thus it might be possible to distinguish between space as a set of constraints and space as a resource. Or we may distinguish between historical space, family space and individual space. The first term is used to present the whole range of constraints and possibilities that exist in a given time period. This points to the interdependence of time and space.

Multiple Times and Spaces

One purpose of making these distinctions is to argue that there is not, even within a given culture, one time and one space but a multiplicity of times and spaces all weaving into and interacting with each other (Hernes, 1988: 104). Multiple times and spaces would seem to be a key defining feature of modern society but such multiplicity does not make for harmony: '. . . time and space should be seen as produced and producing, as contested and determined and as symbolically represented and structurally organised . . . there are a variety of times and spaces . . .' (Urry, 1990: 160).

These contested concepts of time (and space) are well reflected in Hernes's use of the term 'chronopolitics' (Hernes, 1988). She is writing specifically about the relationships between employment and social policy over the life course. Current discussions of 'flexibility' in terms of work and organizational practices are being seen as not merely matters for workers as employees but also in terms of their impacts on women and domestic relationships and the extent to which and the ways in which domestic patterns may be taken into account in the ordering of working time (Hewitt, 1993).

Issues to do with the multiplicities of times and spaces, therefore, are not simply matters of theoretical concern but have daily practical and political significances. In terms of family relationships, the recognition of these multiplicities is important in the following ways.

(1) Such an understanding underlines the variability and flexibility in the notion of 'family' itself. For example, Chandler includes in her discussion of families without fathers families where the father is away for longish periods of time (Chandler, 1991). These include the wives and children of men in the Navy, deep-sea fishing or some similar occupations which necessitate fairly long, if regular, absences from the domestic base. This analysis recognizes that the notion of the nuclear family is not fixed but variable once the dimension of time is taken into account. We may similarly explore multiplicities of times and spaces within 'reconstituted families'. The extent to which and the ways in which family relationships are constituted and reconstituted can only be appreciated over time and through considering the complex linkages between several different social, domestic spaces.

(2) Thus questions of the variable understandings and definitions of family and household can be re-posed in terms of differences of time and space. We may, therefore, describe a given family situation as any particular combination of relationships, times and spaces. However, even within a given family situation there exist a multiplicity of individual times and spaces. These may be variously described as projects, careers, auto/biographies or any terms which imply some linkages between pasts, presents and futures. Thus we may speak of a 'pregnancy career' involving not simply the biological changes associated with pregnancy but the individuals' understandings of stages and growth, projections into the future and the incorporation of past pregnancies of the individual concerned or of others connected to or known to that individual. Further, the pregnancy career

involves not only the mother-to-be but also often involves the father and other persons, partially defined by the central pregnancy as being family members with differing interests in the outcome.

Up to now these multiplicities of times and spaces have focused upon the different careers, as threads of linear time running through a given family situation. However, it is also to be remembered that the multiplicities of times include times, and spaces, not simply defined in linear terms. The fact that different members of a family may also have different concepts or usages of time and space is as important as the fact that they have different projects or individual biographies. Put another way, individuals within family contexts not only have different time/space experiences and practices but they also may understand time and space in different ways.

(3) The recognition of the multiplicities of times and spaces within given family situations also leads to a consideration of the temporal and spatial politics of family life. Much family interaction is around such issues. Claims to a particular chair or for exclusive use of a particular room, times spent in the bathroom, attempts to co-ordinate multiple timetables around mealtimes and the planning of family holidays; these and many other everyday illustrations constitute the micro-politics of family life and are to do with contested times and spaces. Again, such contestations and negotiations do not simply arise out of family relationships; they also and simultaneously constitute or reconstitute those relationships. Thus discussions around the timing of meals at weekends are not only necessitated by the facts of family living – shared household and acknowledged family relationships and obligations – but they also constitute a family set, a range of people whose projects and timetables need to be taken into consideration. Further, in the process, individuals may draw attention to past arrangements or conventions or, in the case of reconstituted families say, arrangements in different domestic contexts.

Discussion of the multiplicities of times and spaces might suggest links with themes of postmodernity. Certainly issues of flux, multiplicity and many-sidedness are key themes in postmodern theorizing. However, it may be said that while postmodern theorizing might have sensitized analysts to a greater awareness of these multiplicities in family living it cannot be said that these characteristics are a unique feature of a society that might be defined as postmodern. Given the coexistence and co-presence of social actors with different backgrounds, expectations, experiences, ages and genders within everyday family situations, there can scarcely be any great novelty in the fact that different uses and understandings of time and space are necessitated by and constitute those family contexts. Whether and in what ways these timetables and usages of space have become more complex is a matter for further discussion and empirical analysis.

Time, History and the Life Course

Discussions of the life course in family sociology are now fairly extensive (Allatt et al., 1987; Bryman et al., 1987; Morgan, 1985: 176–80). First, there has been a growing awareness of the differences between life cycle (the older term) and the life course, with the latter now being preferred. The reasons for this preference are that the constructions of the life cycle deployed an inadequate metaphor for family processes which tended not to be simply cyclical; that models of the life cycle tended to suggest a relatively fixed series of stages through which individuals moved; that there often seemed to be an implication that these stages and processes were normatively central, with other stages and movements seen as deviations or branches of the main cycle; and that the focus tended to be on the individual without any reference to other collectivities or processes. The idea of the life course was chosen because it more adequately suggested linkages between changes in households and changes in individuals; it suggested that these changes were linked to wider movements of historical change; and it did not seem to imply any normatively dominant model of *the* life course.

Part of the debate was around the metaphors used to describe differing conceptions of time. Misleading cyclical models were replaced by a complex and interweaving set of linear models. However, it is possible that social actors still might tend to think in cyclical terms (with, for example, ageing as a return to a childlike dependence) and these understandings might still be influential. Further, there is still some danger that a relatively unitary model of the life cycle might be replaced by an equally unitary model of the life course. Harris (1987: 27–8) stresses: '. . . a life course is not a progress through a structure but the negotiation of passage through an unpredictably changing social environment'.

One of the advantages claimed for life-course analysis is that it provides opportunities for the linking of questions of age and time.

Ageing is a complex interlinking of biological and sociocultural processes, essentially to do with time and its passage and often focusing upon the time of one particular individual (Elder, 1978). The process of ageing is intermingled with various elements structuring social time, including a variety of social timetables, notions of turning points, generalized age-grades or categories (1978: 25–6). Cheal's suggestive metaphor of the 'social convoy' conveys a linking of ageing and time in a way not anchored to single individuals: 'A social convoy is a set of individuals who collectively experience the passing of time' (Cheal, 1988b: 101). My sense of both ageing and the passing of time is realized, reinforced or sometimes mediated in the presence of significant others who engage in routine memory work such as commenting on obituaries, recalling past family events or poring over photograph albums.

It is difficult not to think about age and ageing without also thinking of a variety of social markers: school-leaving age, age of majority, appropriate age to get married or be a parent, retirement age and so on. Age is linked with wider conceptions of time and constructions of normal life spans. Hence the movements of individuals through household and family relationships are located in changing historical time. To give a very simple example, as I write there are continuing discussions about the respective ages of retirement of men and women within the European Union.

Another claimed advantage for life-course analysis is the shift in focus from stages to transitions or turning points (Hareven, 1978: 2). Stages refer to relatively fixed notions of periods of time through which individuals are supposed to pass and which often have clear points of demarcation. In the case of transitions we refer to social turning points which are given significance in family contexts, which may or may not take place and which may vary in terms of their timing, the numbers of significant others involved, their overall significance in terms of, say, ritual recognition and many other variables. We need, therefore, to consider not merely those transitions which demographers, historians or sociologists might take as being of significance but those transitions which social actors themselves find important. The significance arises, in varying degrees, for the fact that these transitions entail some realignment, additions and subtractions within the set of relationships described in family terms. Outside the familiar trinity of births, marriages and deaths there may also be other significant transitions in terms of divorce and re-marriage, change in job or educational transitions.

The idea of the life course still carries with it strong connotations of linearity and a forward or future orientation. Even within this framework there are a variety of complexities. Individuals do not simply move from stage to stage or through a series of transitions. They also carry with them memories, selective and distorted, of earlier transitions and times, relating to their own life courses and those of others. Thus, rather than a simple set of moves from past to present to future, we have a series of continually modified inter-actions between present, selected pasts and projected futures.

Perhaps of particular interest here are the various uses that are made of pasts in the development of a life course. As has been increasingly recognized, the practice of autobiography and the use of autobiographical memory are by no means straightforward tellings of tales in an orderly sequence (Conway, 1990; Stanley, 1992). We select from the past, edit out, add to or embroider our pasts according to present or imagined future audiences, or to the occasions giving rise to these memories. Part of what family living means is the sharing, not necessarily harmoniously or consensually, of memories of past events and transitions. Again, it is not simply the fact that 'families' do this memory work; they also constitute or reconstitute themselves in the process. Family members, it might be argued, are those who claim certain rights to the access of memories of others. These uses of memory and the past are nicely illustrated in John Urry's discussion of the importance of 'imaginary co-presence' in family life. Thus the others with whom people interact in family contexts are not simply people who are physically co-present in time and space but are also people who are physically distant or even dead (Urry, 1990: 170).

Such everyday, informal monitoring of family pasts and memories sometimes takes on a more formal character. The growing interest in personal family history in many modern countries is a reflection of two broad sets of factors: first, individuals have the leisure, education and resources to conduct such searches; and second, the multiple discontinuities brought about by migration, war and divorce and separation perhaps provide much of the motivation to achieve some sense of temporal stability.

Yet it is also possible that such projects, and the less formal memory work conducted within and about family relationships, have a wider significance. The Australian historian Ann Curthoys notes the growth of the 'massive industry' of genealogy (Curthoys, 1993: 167) and the high public profile that historians have in Australia, arguing that there are links to be made between individual and national senses of and searches for identity. But Britain too has its own concerns about identity reflected in the development of the 'nostalgia industry' (Samuel, 1994). The heritage industry in part gains its effectiveness through its links with individuals' sense of and searches for their own pasts, part of the normal work of family living, while family relationships and pasts may derive new or sharpened meanings through the explorations of a national heritage, real or imagined.

These explorations of time, either in terms of an analysis of life courses or the more intimate exploration of family memory work, are not simply about time. In these analyses, issues to do with space are also present. The family members and significant others are also located in spaces as they move through time. Leaving home, for example, is a turning point which is also to do with the re ordering of space and distance. Memories are of places and sets of relationships, social spaces, in time.

Finally, in considering issues such as time and the life course we should emphasize, once again, that our attention cannot be focused upon the family narrowly conceived. The careers and trajectories that individuals follow through families and households are not confined within the boundaries of these domestically based units. They move through employment, through education and through a variety of other spheres, public and personal. The concept of the life course may indeed provide a more sensitive appreciation of the ways in which family times are woven into other times and timetables.

Physical and Social Space

However limited the distinction between physical and social space, it does have some meaning in the context of family studies. The notion of 'overcrowding', for example, is never simply a question of the number of bodies in relation to a given area or number of rooms. Whether or not a situation is defined as being overcrowded is shaped by who is doing the defining and by social conventions and current levels of expectations, relative to a particular social grouping or strata.

Social or symbolic space refers to the sets of meanings which are assigned to particular physical locations; much of this will be discussed further in chapter 8. More specifically we are dealing with those spaces which are given meanings in family contexts and these may include not merely the dwelling identified as 'home' but the place where we regularly go on holiday, the house where we used to live, the houses of grandparents or aunts which were especially welcoming when we were children. Even where these other spaces might not, in some formal sense, 'belong' to family members they may be invested with meaning through the fact that they become part of the shared nexuses of meaning developed over time in family contexts: a local church, a particular pub, a favourite picnic spot or certain shops.

One particular aspect, already discussed, of symbolic space is to do with the distinction between front and back stage. This refers to the particular usages and meanings which are attached to sub-areas within a domestic location. Family relations not only determine what and for whom particular spaces are defined as front or back stage, public or private; the prior or ongoing designation of such areas also helps to shape the relevant circle of family or other intimates. As noted in the previous chapter, there is often considerable fluidity in these distinctions and they may not always be subject to consensus or agreement.

One way of distinguishing between families or households, indeed, is in terms of the degree of spatial openness or closedness. It may be assumed that families differ according to the fixity and clarity of the distinctions between front and back stage. This may be one aspect of Bernstein's distinctions between 'positional' and 'person-orientated' families (Bernstein, 1971: 152–3). In positional families we may imagine relative degrees of fixity in these designations, with clear lines of demarcation both in terms of the location of these symbolic spaces and in terms of those who are allocated to them. In person-orientated families, the allocation may be less predictable and may be the subject of negotiation or contest. Bernstein is also concerned with other aspects of the symbolic ordering of space within the home, with the degree of formality and demarcation that may obtain. Thus some households may have lavatories which are decorated with posters or pictures or which may have reading matter to hand for those who use them. Others, located in more positional families, may be more austerely functional, not welcoming the blurring of boundaries that books in the toilet might suggest. Such distinctions, between positional and person-orientated families or in terms of the use of front or back stages, do not simply reflect social status distinctions; in a real sense they *are* these distinctions.

As well as organizing differences within the household, family members also maintain various distinctions between inside and outside, ways of organizing social space around family themes of relatedness and reciprocities. Such boundary drawing may relate to 'my' house or the House of Windsor. Such processes of boundary drawing have a long-established history within sociological thought, ranging from distinctions between in-group and out-group, reference groups and membership groups, through to more recent discussions of the processes of drawing ethnic boundaries. From these examples it is clear that such boundary drawing work is not confined to families. Family relationships may, however, provide the basis for such boundary drawing; distinctions between them and us may begin in the nursery. They certainly provide a readily available source of images and rhetorics of 'kith and kin' with which to describe, explain and justify the drawing of ethnic and other boundaries.

Family relationships and obligations may provide models for the drawing up of wider social maps, symbolic and cognitive orderings of social space and one's place in it. The development of the notion of 'truancy' from the nineteenth century onwards may serve as one illustration of this process (Paterson, 1988). Clearly, the concept of truancy cannot exist outside the development of compulsory schooling and the development of such schooling also entails 'schooling the family', instilling into family members responsibilities in terms of the attendance and appearance of school-age children. Truancy is a matter of being in the wrong place at the wrong time. In this case, external agencies require family members to develop these social mapping skills; in other cases, adults in the family may provide a more direct and more independent role in the social mapping process, as when designating certain places as off-limits, as rough or dangerous or in some way inappropriate locations for subordinate family members. Family work entails a great deal of continuous social mapping, tracing out not merely the key and ongoing familial and kinship relationships but also the wider symbolic ordering of social space.

Once again these examples and themes bring us back to the essential interdependence of time and space. In the Languedoc village where I am writing this chapter, there is a traditional 'hour of silence' formally extended to two hours from noon to two. Adults, especially visiting adults, are expected to keep their children quiet and off the square during this 'hour'. We are also familiar with the idea of 'night' as a frontier (Melbin, 1987) and the controls that parents seek to exercise over the after-dark activities of their children. Families may not be the only institutions where individuals learn that there is a time and a place for everything but they would seem to continue to play a major role in this respect and, what is perhaps more important, are expected to do so by more formal agencies.

Gender and Time/Space

In dealing with divisions within the family I concentrate on the idea of time and space as resources and as constraints. Here the constraints are not abstract, externally derived forces but, in many cases at least, the other side of the coin to resources; one person's resources are another person's constraints. Time and space may be seen as aspects of power differentials within family relationships, although this is not the whole story.

To follow through these complexities let us consider the well-explored theme of housework. Despite some evidence of increasing participation on the part of men, housework is still identified as women's work. Common understandings of housework see it as a series of externally derived constraints on a woman's labour and, most importantly, on her time in relation to a fixed spatial location.

Accounts of housework tend to see such work as directly servicing the man to whom the woman is married or otherwise attached (together with other household members) and indirectly as functioning to maintain patriarchal structures or possibly capitalist relations of production. However, such accounts are probably not so much inaccurate as incomplete. As Bernice Martin's discussion of housework argues, it also introduces an element of control over time and space (Martin, 1984). Housework, as a regularly repeated activity, imposes a form of control over the temporal order of the household and control over and privileged access to certain spaces, most typically the kitchen. It may well be argued that, with the deskilling of domestic labour, these factors of power and control have become less important; however, it is likely that they are still a feature of housework. It is also the case that much housework continues to be regarded as drudgery and the rights and controls that a housewife might derive in the process are often in the absence of rights and controls elsewhere. However, the point is that the temporal and spatial controls are not all one way and that they may also be seen as resources as well as and at the same time as constraints.

Another example which perhaps more clearly shows the relationships between time, space and inequality within the household is to do with leisure, again a highly gendered concept (Deem, 1986). For men the concept of leisure is often relatively straightforward. It is defined in opposition to or complementary to paid employment and is conventionally understood as time which is under the control of the individual. It may be enjoyed at home, sometimes in a particular space such as the garden, or outside the home. For women, matters are not so straightforward even if they, like the men, are in full-time employment. Their concepts of leisure time are less clear cut; indeed, in some cases, work in paid employment outside the home may take on some of the features associated with leisure as a form, if a limited form, of freedom.

Thus a consideration of leisure in the context of the home highlights some important interconnections between gender, time, power and control. It has a bearing both on gendered *inequalities* within the home and on gendered *differences*, that is, in concepts of leisure and conceptions of time. However, it is likely that, once again, matters may be a little more complicated than this. Insofar as marriage is defined in relational terms, shared leisure may be seen as an important activity for both partners. Issues of leisure and the time associated with it may become matters of contention and contestation within the home. This may not simply be a question of the time spent away from home by the man in his sports activities or hobbies, but also the impact that this leisure time has upon other household timetables. Leisure may therefore be seen as a particular thread within domestic life which, if followed, may highlight some of the complex dynamics of power, gender, time and space.

The two aspects of gender, gender as inequality and gender as difference, are linked together in all kinds of complex ways around issues of time and space. It is not simply a question of the unilateral imposition of power, although this may be seen, theoretically and practically, as the bottom line. There are also questions of gendered conceptions of time that may meet and sometimes collide in domestic life. Men may have a more linear, forward planning model of time, one linked to a greater market or rational public orientation (Cottle, 1976). Women may have a more fluid concept of time or times, one which is partly cyclical and one which is spatial, involving the allocation and juggling of a multiplicity of times. These different conceptions of time derive from structured gendered inequalities but they still tend to take on a life and a meaning of their own in the context of everyday household situations. Households then are both organized around and reproduce gendered conceptions of time and space.

To argue that different concepts of time and space coexist in household settings and that these concepts are partially at least mapped on to gender differences is not to say that this coexistence is easy or harmonious. Hernes's (1988) notion of 'chronopolitics' can be applied at the more micro-level of everyday domestic life. Time and space here can be seen as a series of claims which actors may make; this is my time, this is my place. These claims may also be on the time of others or around the right to encroach on the space of others. For example, Davies argues that night-time might be seen as private time by many husbands and fathers; women, with open-ended caring responsibilities, may not be able to maintain such clear-cut temporal boundaries (Davies, 1990: 42). Clearly, these claims and counterclaims need not necessarily mesh. Indeed, some systems theorists argue that time and space are among a set of key resources around which different patterns of family functioning may be mapped (Kantor and Lehr, 1973).

Issues of time and space are frequently and centrally woven around issues of gender within the home and family situations. This is not simply the question of the day-to-day working out of a patriarchal order within the home, although this may well be a central theme. Gender is not simply a variable which influences behaviour and outcomes within family processes. It is in these processes themselves, organized around issues of time and space, that gender is constantly being created, shaped and modified.

Age and Time/Space

Issues to do with age and generation are centrally to do with time. Further, they are key aspects of family life; part of any definition of family would include some reference to generational differences as being one of the main axes around which that life revolves. Yet the concept of age is far from straightforward, dealing as it does with social constructions rather than clearly marked out biological processes and differences (Finch, 1986).

Social definition enters into the process in a variety of ways including the definition of stages and transition points, of the characteristics that are thought to be associated with particular ages or stages, and the allocation or limiting of various rights and duties at different stages. All this makes for considerable complexity and means that, for example, a simple concept of 'ageism' cannot be developed as an exact parallel to sexism or racism (Bytheway and Johnson, 1990; Ginn, 1993).

Again, as with gender, questions of age do not arise specifically in relation to the family. Indeed, many of the social categories to do with age in a modern society arise out of external definitions to do with education or employment relations. Where family relations enter is, firstly, in questions to do with 'generation'. A person's location in terms of generation is often, although not exclusively, in relation to that person's position within a temporally ordered set of relationships, as a parent, say, in relation to that person's children. Up to a point such rankings may be individual and highly variable, although this variance is reduced through the introduction of another sense of generation, that is to do with historical time and cohorts passing through time. Thus the notion of 'my parent's generation' combines a family position with a historical location. Such constructions of generations may constitute important social variables (Mannheim, 1952) and are certainly central channels through which history and autobiography are linked.

Family relationships are also important in that they provide contexts through which many locations to do with age are given substance and meaning. For example, birthdays and anniversaries are typically focused upon, although not exclusive to, family relationships. While there are wider social constructions of age (voting age, age of majority, for example), family relationships provide a context within which these administrative definitions are elaborated. Discussions as to whether a child is too old or too young for particular activities frequently take place in the family with the family members making use of material and expert advice provided outside the confines of the home. Such arguments, say about the wearing of make-up or high heels or taking alcohol or tobacco, simultaneously seek to define age-appropriate modes of behaviour while also reworking definitions of age, and gender, and family relationships themselves. Thus a mother who claims that her daughter is 'too young' to wear make-up is not merely defining age-related forms of appropriate behaviour but also making certain claims as a parent or as a representative of an older generation.

Thus parent work is also age and generation work. But definitions and constructions of age need not necessarily be confined to relations between parents and children. Some of the complexities of 'caring' outlined in chapter 4 revolve around complex decisions to do with age-related notions of dependence and independence.

Further, family relationships provide an arena where stereotypical notions of age and ageing are deployed, including the sending of ageist birthday cards, references to middle-aged spread or to having one foot in the grave. Parents, like children, may be constructed as engaging in age-inappropriate behaviour or of 'not acting their age'. While doubtless such age work and age negotiations take place outside the home, in workplaces or centres of leisure, it is likely that they take on a particular set of meanings in the context of family relationships.

While age is commonsensically understood to do directly with time, it is also to do with space. Children are kept out of or confined to certain spaces, for example, and older generations may lay claims to particular spaces. Once again we see that issues of time and space as resources come to the fore. These claims in terms of time and space as age-related resources are well illustrated in the following quotation from Blake Morrison's autobiographical recollections of his father:

> We talk about my father's sense of family – his failure to let go of his children, his assumption that he had the perfect right to invade whatever space they had, even as adults: how he would walk in on Gill and Wynn without knocking, take over projects of theirs, organise them without bothering overmuch if this is what they wanted. (Morrison, 1993: 121–2)

Inside and outside the family, age has a spatial as well as a temporal dimension. Children are excluded from public houses or certain places of entertainment or are encouraged or expected to attend other places. The elderly may 'feel out of place' in modern society, a society which seems to be radically different from what an individual experienced in his or her younger days but which also seems indifferent to his or her needs. Notions of age are constructed and challenged within family contexts and between family members, although the material that is often used in these constructions comes from outside the nexus of family relationships. Retirement, for example, is not simply something which is imposed upon individuals or which, through these individuals, also happens to families; it is also within families that retirement is defined and given meaning. Patterns of intergenerational conflict are doubtless shaped by overlaps and interconnections between domestic relationships and wider patterns of inequality and political mobilization (Johnson, Coward and Thomson, 1989).

Age, therefore, is not simply and directly to do with time but it is also linked to the use of and meanings assigned to time. We may consider, for example, the use of the term 'quality time' to describe desired relationships between parents and children or between spouses. Some of the complex interconnections between different aspects of time and age may be explored by considering the term 'waiting' (Adam, 1990: 121–5). Conventionally, it is assumed that lower status individuals are kept waiting by higher status individuals. Within the home, many of the routine day-to-day conflicts between parents and children may be around issues of waiting and imposed deferred gratification: 'Daddy will read to you later' or 'You can have some ice-cream after you have finished your main course.' Yet children may also keep parents waiting, through last-minute visits to the toilet or searching for missing items of clothing. Such conflicts around waiting may also take on a gendered dimension.

Conclusion

Developments that have focused on general issues of time and space may also enhance our particular understandings of family life. They give a materiality to family life, but one which is not narrowly economic. A focus upon themes of time and space enhances an awareness of the complexities of family life and serves as a safeguard against reification. To say that family relationships are woven around themes of time and space is to introduce a flexibility into our understanding of family processes. Time and space are notoriously slippery concepts to grasp and to use and this very slipperiness reminds us of the fluidity and many-sided quality of family living. The treatment of family issues in terms of time and space should not be seen as an optional extra, something to be tackled once family relationships and structures have been analysed, but as being at the heart of family life and its analysis.

But family studies may also contribute something to our understanding of general issues of time and space.

1   At the simplest level, family life constitutes a readily available and widely understood source of illustrations for more general themes to do with time and space. Take the following quotation from Adam, for example.

> The second law therefore expresses explicitly what is known tacitly in everyday life: that all systems tend toward disorder; that things, just like people, are impermanent; and that every time

something occurs, some amount of energy will be unavailable for
future work (Adam, 1990: 62)'.

The 'everyday life' referred to here could, of course, refer to any
areas of activity. But it is likely that this relatively abstract
statement fits in most readily with routine experiences of family
life, experiences which are certainly gendered.

2   At a more theoretical level, specific concepts developed in the
analysis of family processes might also have a wider applicability.
The concept of the life course, originally developed on the
frontiers of sociology, demography and social history to explore
the linkages between individual time, historical time and family
or household time, could well be applied to institutions 'outside'
or other than family relationships. Thus formal organizations,
which also have movements in and out of them and individual
careers within them, themselves undergo processes of structural
change and growth and exist in and interact with historical time.

3   Family relationships may be seen as constituting key elements in
the understanding of wider social processes. This is the case, for
example, in the analysis of social reproduction, a theme centrally
connected to issues of time. While this is not simply a matter of
biological reproduction and nor is it a process that is confined to
the family, it is also the case that families and households
continue to be key sites for the reproduction over time of
structural relations: relations of class, gender and ethnicity, for
example. Similarly, the analysis of social and historical memory,
again not confined to but still an important feature of familial
relationships, may be enriched through more finely based
analyses of family life.

All this points to the Janus-faced quality of family life that I
discussed in a previous book (Morgan, 1985). This refers to a
theoretical location of family relationships between the individual
and history and between the macro and the micro. Temporally and
spatially, the family may be constructed as looking both ways and as
combining and comingling elements from the immediate, the individual and the everyday with the historical and the structural.

There are a number of reasons why family relationships may be
particularly appropriate for these investigations in time and space.
None of these taken singly would be overwhelming but taken
together they provide a strong argument for taking the family
seriously in these wider theoretical inquiries.

1   The mixing of different ages and generations is a central and not accidental feature of family relationships. Places of work will certainly have people of different ages and will probably have people of different generations but this is not a theoretical requirement of such places. Further, workplaces will encompass a limited range of ages, excluding, for example, the very young and the retired. This required mixing of ages and generations necessarily gives rise to work to do with time and the meeting of the historical and the autobiographical.

2   A second reason is the particular nature of family relationships, obligations and reciprocities. This is not necessarily to argue that family relationships are 'really' special; it is just enough at this stage to argue that they are constructed and understood as such by family members and by agencies outside particular families or households. Thus, individuals may feel both constrained and empowered by family relationships and by the particular usages of time and space as resources within family contexts. The multiple meanings of 'home' which are explored in chapter 8 are to do with locations in time and space and with gendered understandings of these locations as prisons, areas of freedom or something in between.

3   Associated with this is the idea of the family as being constructed as the legitimate agency or site for a variety of activities. We have seen how this works in the case of the body but it is also the case in terms of the usages of time and space. Family and marriage may be seen as sites in which we are expected to give time and space to our relationships, to our partners and to our children.

4   Family relationships are understood to have greater density and intensity than many other relationships. Battles over timekeeping or personal privacy within the home have a particular intensity because of their multi-stranded character. They carry with them memories of previous similar conflicts, both on the part of those currently engaged in the struggle and in the memories of those recalling other struggles in other family contexts in the past. Much of the negotiation that takes place in reconstituted families, for example, involves these complex and intense, emotionally charged deployments of time and space as resources and constraints.

5   This links with chapter 5, dealing with the sociology of the body. Here it was argued that there were special, if not exclusive, links between family life and the body. It may also be argued that bodily/family life is likewise bound up with questions of time and

space in several complex ways. Social memory is embodied (Connerton, 1989) and embodied social memories are frequently shaped or mediated through family practices and rituals. In going through the photograph album, for example, we are recalling bodies located in family time and space, past practices and rituals which, while they have special and private meanings in terms of the individual relationships involved, also point out to wider more generalized memories and pasts.

Considering all these factors together and in interaction with each other provides a strong case for taking family relationships seriously in the empirical and theoretical investigation of wider issues to do with time and space. Family time and space is both special and shared. It is special in that it is bound up with highly specific memories and practices but these memories and practices are also located in wider space/time locations. It is the fact that family time and space continues to be seen as something special, and the fact that family practices overlap with and are shaped by other non-family practices, that together underline the case that developments in family studies may have a lot to contribute to the analysis of time and space in society.

7

Food

Introduction

Food represents another of those areas which is central to human life but which never quite seems to get the detailed and systematic treatment within sociology that it deserves. Insofar as there have been developments in the sociological study of food, these have tended to focus on a variety of issues:

1 studies of food itself, upon the amounts and types of foods available, their modes of preparation and their symbolic significances;
2 studies of the political economy of food production in the context of a global division of labour;
3 analyses of divisions of labour in the processes of food preparation;
4 studies dealing with divisions in food consumption.

These various discussions have been concerned with food within family and household relationships and/or food within the wider society.

Food and Definitions of the Family

Some definitions of the household make explicit reference to the preparation of food; the sharing of at least one meal per day may be seen as a key defining characteristic of household membership. A group of students or a commune could, in this definition, constitute a household. Households could consist of single persons, couples of the same sex, or any combination of adults and children. If the breaking of bread together constitutes some sense of belonging, then this unity could be based upon a very wide range of social arrangements.

Family relationships, as opposed to household relationships, may also be defined, although somewhat more loosely, in terms of food. These may not simply be family members located within a particular household but also family members who belong to different households. Sharing meals on family, religious or national festivals may play an important part in the ritual life of families. These meals may serve to define who belongs or does not belong to particular families or map out areas of social and interactional significance. Again, there is nothing inevitable here and shared meals may equally take place between people who are not defined as family related. The sharing may be based upon reasons of convenience or economy rather than on any strong sense of family unity (Dobson et al., 1994).

Food also marks out differences within families and within individual and household life courses. Part of the processes of mutual accommodation within marriage will almost inevitably be around questions of food, the 'right' way to brew tea or the definition of what constitutes a proper meal at weekends. Food comparisons will be part of the dynamics of living in reconstituted households where children compare, favourably and unfavourably, the food being served in their current household with that served in the previous household (Hughes, 1991). Food and food preparation, therefore, do not simply create or reinforce unities within family groups; they may also provide the resources around which differences and divisions can be expressed.

Food, Power and Divisions: Gender

Perhaps the major axis around which the micro-politics of food revolves is to do with gender. The most obvious aspect of this is to do with the preparation of food, an important aspect of the sexual divisions of labour within households (Mennell, Murcott and Van Otterloo, 1992: 95–111). Generally speaking, women largely assume responsibility for the preparation of food, including deciding the menus, buying the food and preparing it for the table. They may also bear a large measure of responsibility for clearing up after the completion of a meal. Husbands and other men may help in these activities, with washing up being a favoured task, although here as elsewhere the participation of men is largely seen as helping rather than assuming routine responsibility. The alleged incompetence of men in the kitchen is frequently the subject of considerable humour and wry comment.

However, the picture is not so straightforward as might at first appear. This is not simply the fact that some men do develop expertise in cooking and food preparation and in the organization of meals. It is also the case that while men are less likely to be involved in the preparation of food, they also have food preferences and notions as to what constitutes a proper meal (Murcott, 1983). Marital relations are expressed in these contradictory relationships to the preparation of food. Countless numbers of British sociology students have recorded how Yorkshire miners threw fish and chips, bought from outside the home rather than prepared within the home, at the back of the fire, declaring them not to be a proper meal (Dennis, Henriques and Slaughter, 1956). That this may not simply be a quaint echo of past times may be reflected in the fact that disagreements over food may constitute an important precipitating factor in episodes of violence against women in the home. The division of labour around the preparation of food need not be a harmonious one.

Food preparation also represents divisions in terms of knowledge. This knowledge may be about particular cooking techniques, about dietary needs, about the combinations of various textures and flavours. Sources of this knowledge may be informal, passed down from mother to daughter, or they may be more formal through classes in home economics or domestic science, through regular articles in women's magazines and newspapers and, increasingly, in programmes on television or radio (Mennell, Murcott and Van Otterloo, 1992, 88–94). Cookery books are now an important part of publishing, as are specialized weekly or monthly magazines devoted to food and food preparation. However, whether the knowledge be passed down through kinship relations or acquired through formal or semi-formal instruction, the processes of the acquisition of food knowledge frequently reinforce gender differences. In the former, it is the informal relationships between different generations of women that are important; in the latter, it is the development of skills in a craft which is defined as being especially, although not exclusively, the sphere of women.

There have been some subtle transformations around the work of food preparation and their connections with gender. Earlier cookery books, where they used photographs, tended to emphasize bulk and nourishment. More recently, incorporating lavish photographs of the dishes taken from above, cookery books take care to present the food as a work of art as well as a source of sustenance. While in both cases the presentation of food is supposed to demonstrate that time and skill have gone into its preparation, earlier generations demonstrated the 'tender loving care' that housewives deployed in keeping family members well fed. More recent generations continue to demonstrate this, of course, but also show the development of more cosmopolitan skills less immediately anchored to particular family relations. Whether these shifts represent professionalization or deskilling is a matter for some fine judgement. Some of the mystery departs, however, when it is learned that today's dish appeared on last night's *Food Programme* on television.

Knowledge represents a form of power and control. In other circumstances, such a power base in terms of an access to specialized knowledge, one that was important in terms of the well-being and livelihood of others, would seem to be unequivocal. This would seem to be the case in top-class restaurants where the customer is normally expected to defer to the expertise of the chef. In the case of the sexual division of labour within the home, there would appear to be certain limiting factors on this potential power to be yielded by the housewife. A husband could always take his custom elsewhere and make use of take-aways, restaurants, the services of other women or, indeed, his own more limited skills. More important, perhaps, is the fact that to a large extent the wife/mother feels obligated to provide nourishing and attractive meals for other family members. She may be encouraged to do so by folk wisdom about the ways to a man's heart, or by the advice columns in newspapers and popular magazines or by a suspicion that if she doesn't do it no one else will. In many cases, the provision of proper food, in all the complex and negotiated sense of the term, may be closely bound up with a sense of self and feminine identity.

One way of considering the provision of food within the home and the reasons why the possession of food knowledge does not straightforwardly bestow power on the possessor is to see it as an important aspect of caring work. This is clearly the case when we are considering food for infants, sick members of the family, the elderly or those with special dietary needs. This expression of care, associated with the linked theme of sacrifice, may also be discovered in the many cases in poorer families where the mother ensures that her husband and the children have the best items of food that are available. But more generally, the provision of food has some aspects of caring and emotional labour perhaps because food itself is not an emotionally neutral subject. Few subjects evoke such an extensive range of emotions as food: from the heights of pleasure and satisfaction to the extremes of revulsion and disgust (Fisher, 1991). In providing food, the provider is not merely undertaking a series of tasks or chores, although they may seem like that, but also handling past, present and potential future expressions of emotion.

Yet there remains some element of power on the part of the food provider. In part this relates to the divisions between front stage and back stage, focused upon the kitchen, the power being the greater, the clearer the lines of demarcation. In fact as well as fiction, the possibilities for administering doses of poison in a husband's food become greater, the more clearly the kitchen is marked off from the view of other family members. Less dramatically, the cook may jealously guard this part of domestic territory and gain satisfaction in the secret knowledge of how the dishes were really constructed. One television commercial showed the housewife serving instant coffee to her guests, having first made realistic coffee percolating noises in the backstage area of the kitchen.

Up to now we have considered the production of food in the home and its association with gender. It is also important to consider aspects of consumption (Charles and Kerr, 1988). First, there are all kinds of ways in which the housewife or provider of food will sacrifice herself in order to provide the best items of food to her husband or to the growing children. This, of course, is especially important, the closer we are to the poverty margin; lone parents, for example, may use the apparent freedom they have to choose the weekly diet in order to serve others (Graham, 1987: 69). Again, the provision of food may be seen as not simply just another task like sweeping or washing but a key aspect of caring work.

Second, food is not always gender neutral when it comes to its symbolic connotations. For example, alcoholic drinks have clear gendered connotations with the distinction between beer and wine roughly, at least in Britain, corresponding to differences between men and women (Mennell, Murcott and Van Otterloo, 1992: 55–7). Salad may be regarded as women's food while rare steaks may be seen as more appropriate for men. In the case of bull's testicles, the gendered connotations are fairly unambiguous. Vegetarians tend to be more frequently women rather than men (Beardsworth and Keil,

1992). Food is part of the symbolic order as well as part of the economic order, and themes of gender differences are interwoven with themes of nature and culture, the raw and the cooked and the animal and the vegetable. These patterns are by no means straightforward – in the case of food, men may seem to be closer to nature rather than to culture for example – but cannot be explored in greater depth here. Nevertheless it remains true that differences in food preferences and food practices in part reflect and reinforce gender differences. And, again, while the connections are not complete, the nexus linking food and gender is especially strong in the context of the household and family relationships.

Food, Power and Divisions: Age and Generation

If the civilizing process in general is to do with the control of the appetites, then family relationships between parents and children constitute one of its main mechanisms. From birth, if not before, issues of feeding dominate the relationships between mother and child: questions of the timing of feeding, foodstuffs that are thought to be appropriate to particular ages and more general issues to do with the morality of food. A whole host of expressions link food and morality in the exchanges between a parent and a child. 'Waste not, want not', 'Wilful waste makes woeful want', 'Think of the starving millions'; these and many other phrases indicate that the business of eating is not simply a question of satisfying immediate needs but is enmeshed in issues of morality and social being. Parents differ in their approaches to feeding children just as the advice books oscillate between regularity and individuality. Nevertheless, in most cases, feeding the child is never a single-stranded operation but involves wider issues to do with deferred gratification, order and control, generational differences and parental rights and obligations.

One simple example of the linkages between food, family relationships and morality may be provided by sweets (A. James, 1990). Sweets may be rewards or their denial a punishment. The control of a child's sweet-eating represents the convergence of a variety of themes: growing concerns about dental health, commercial interests clearly targeted at children, sweets as small gifts from other relatives, and the pleasure the child experiences in exploring different tastes, colours and textures. 'Never take sweets from a stranger' is doubtless sound advice but its frequent use highlights both the desirability of sweets and their links with friendly or intimate relationships. There are concerns about the nature of 'real food'; parents may be concerned about a child's 'spoiling' its appetite, blunting its appreciation of real food prepared by its mother.

The associations between the provision and preparation of food and issues of power and control are perhaps clearer in the case of generational relationships than they are in the case of adult gender relationships. The specialized knowledge and expertise around diet and age-appropriate foods work with rather than against the caring obligations of the mother. Similarly, other dimensions of power, economic and physical, also overlap with the power deriving from food knowledge. This is not to say, however, that the mother or parent has it all her or his own way. Mothers frequently complain about the eccentric food tastes of their children and their inability, apparently, to provide an appropriately balanced diet (Murcott, 1983). Such limitations on the part of a parent to feed a child appropriately may well be a source of anxiety and emotional distress. Again, the obligation to care may sometimes undermine the power derived from the possession of specialized knowledge and expertise.

There are other ways in which generational differences may be expressed around food. Generations may be family-based or based on cohorts moving through a period of historical change. One feature of modern societies is the availability of an increasingly wide range of foods from different parts of the world, suitably adapted to the tastes of the host country. The Chinese take-away supplemented or sometimes replaced the traditional fish-and-chip shop, and these in their turn have been augmented by Indian restaurants and take-aways, pizza parlours, kebab houses, baked-potato chains, as well as the international hamburger chains. The expansion of these different food outlets becomes identified with questions of taste, individuality and the self. Generational differences are reflected in differences between those for whom such a range of food outlets is part of normal everyday experience and those whose memories are firmly with the era of fish and chips and meat pies. It is likely that these wider generational differences are expressed in the more specific generational differences within the family, with the younger generation socializing the older generations.

Age and generational boundaries may be marked out around food. Certain foods are defined as children's food, while children are excluded from foods that are thought to be more properly the food for adults. The grounds and legitimations for these differences vary considerably but there is little doubt that they are constructed in many family situations. Some, as is the case with alcohol, have wider legitimations and controls but usually the parent has to rely on phrases such as 'You won't like it, dear' or 'It's not good for young stomachs'.

These age and generation differences do not simply revolve around appropriate or inappropriate foods; timings of meals, for example, may also mark out such differences. One mark of age transition may be to participate in the evening meal with other family members or even guests, although such practices differ between countries and groups within society. Further, rights to control or monitor the eating practices of others clearly follow along generational lines. In a variety of ways, therefore, age and generation, as well as gender, are constructed in sites where family and food practices meet.

Food and Differences Between Households

Differences between households are often expressed in terms of food. Perhaps the sharpest differences may be around questions of ethnicity, where food habits and practices serve as symbolic boundaries marking off one group from another. Since feeding is especially associated with households, it can be seen that the household and its practices concerning food (real or imagined) play a key role in the maintenance of symbolic ethnic boundaries. Similarly, themes of multiculturalism, at their more popular levels, may be expressed in terms of attempts to share in different foods and food practices.

Ethnic boundaries represent perhaps the clearest example of the relationships between food practices and differences between households but they are not the only ones. Food may enter in to measures of standard of living or poverty. While definitions of poverty remain controversial, it can be seen that a sense of poverty is mediated very sharply through the whole business of food buying, preparation and consumption. For the poor, food shopping has few of the pleasurable connotations found at other levels of society and coping and managing remain overriding themes in the lives of women in such households. They become aware of household differences in comparing the food trolleys in the local supermarket (Dobson et al., 1994).

More generally, class remains an important variable in the analysis of differences in food practices (Warde and Hetherington, 1994). The interaction between class and food is a central illustration of Bourdieu's approach to 'distinction' and although not all of these practices centre on family or household relationships, a lot of them do (Bourdieu, 1984). In the English language the two linked usages of the word 'taste' are illuminating as are the overlapping usages of the word 'discriminating'.

Numerous illustrations come to mind. Differences between the rough and the respectable may be maintained or expressed around themes of real or imagined differences in food practices; the mother who feeds her children on chips is one popular stereotype. Status differences may be expressed in invitations to dinner parties or cocktail parties, or whether entertaining is done at home or in a restaurant. While occupationally based measures of class may be important independent variables in the analysis of different food practices, the actual practice and experience of class and status differences revolve around much finer distinctions and more care-fully nuanced series of practices.

The point is probably worth stressing that household practices in relation to food do not simply express or reflect differences of class or status. It is through such practices that we come to understand the very notion of difference itself. If food is bound up with personal identity, a personal identity which is nevertheless located within particular households, then this personal identity is built up through a growing sense of difference in food tastes and food practices. Whether or not different households routinely entertain individuals or other households at home; the kinds of food that may be served on those occasions; the extent to which guests are expected to bring some small gift for their hosts; whether or not there are prayers before the meal: in numerous ways the sense of difference is built up through an understanding of different food practices and preferences.

Food, Time and Nostalgia

Muriel Spark begins the first volume of her autobiography with recollections of food: bread, butter and tea (Spark, 1992). Such recollections are, indeed, a common feature in recalling the past; another example would be the loving recreations of food in Richard

Hoggart's account of working-class life in the Leeds of his childhood. (Hoggart, 1958). Food represents a particularly strong form of anchorage in the past, its strength deriving in part from the familial relationships in which the serving and preparing of food are located. The apparent changes in the tastes of everyday foods, the disappearance of some foods and the arrival of new ones often serve as important ways of locating oneself in historical time. Historical events, such as the association of the Second World War with rationing, may be recalled through food.

Food, then, serves as one of the links between historical time, individual time and household time. But time is relevant in other ways as well: '. . . having meals together leads at once to temporal regularity . . .' (Simmel, quoted in Mennell, Murcott and Van Otterloo, 1992: 3).

More cyclical notions of time, daily and weekly, are involved in the timing of meals. Annual festivals are also marked by special food and meals. Households clearly vary in terms of the timing and ritualization of meals – another aspect of the differences between positional and person-orientated households perhaps – and it is also likely that these issues of time are sources of tension and conflict as well as of consensus and unity. The myth of the family meal table may ignore the conflicts around the timing of such a meal and the particular emotional labour and mental juggling that a mother might have to undertake in order to establish such temporal regularities. The complaint that young people use the house like a hotel is in part a complaint about the lack of recognition of regular meal times. One feature of the social fluidity of 'high modernity' may be the increasing frequency of 'grazing' food practices and a greater individualization of meals and eating located, often, in the increasing numbers of single-person households.

Food and the Body

Much of the body work that takes place within households and family relationships revolves around issues to do with food. It is clear, for example, that the issues of bodily control associated with eating disorders have a marked family dimension. Whatever the causes, anorexia is a family matter in that it is within family relationships that its effects are most clearly felt, observed and monitored. That such disorders revolve around issues to do with the control of the body is hardly beyond question: the control over the body by others and by oneself.

Eating disorders probably constitute some of the most dramatic illustrations of the connections between body work and food within domestic relationships. But issues of control run through the use and preparation of food within the household. Particular diets and food controls are conventionally administered or monitored through family relationships: the managing of diabetes, for example. Individuals who go on diets, for medical, political or cosmetic reasons, have to consider the question as to how these diets are to be woven into other eating practices within the household.

One particular example may be found in the use of alcohol within the home (Holmilla, Mustonen and Rannik, 1990). As with the case of anorexia, alcoholism affects not merely the individual but also significant others, often located in families or households. But, outside the specific case of alcoholism, there are all kinds of ways in which couples may monitor and regulate each other's drinking. There may be straightforward attempts on the part of one partner to limit the drinking of the other; or each may encourage the drinking, or abstinence, of the other. Legitimations and accusations and counter-accusations may revolve around gendered conflicts. The question of drinking in the home may be one of these key linking issues, drawing together questions of food, the body, gender and domestic relationships.

Conclusion: Wider Sociological Issues

The exploration of food in the context of family relationships has largely concentrated on themes that have also appeared in other chapters: class, gender, age and generation, the body, time and so on. However, there are some other issues where we can see the developing sociological interest in food interacting with ongoing discussions around family relationships. Here, we go beyond family relationships to look at food in a wider sociological context.

(1) The first is to return to the theme of food, family and stratification. In chapter 2 it was argued that there was a growing recognition of the importance of family and household relationships in the analysis of stratification. Here we have shown some of the ways in which household differences revolve around issues of food and food

preparation. It remains to bring these two levels of analysis together. At the crudest functional or Marxist level, the provision of food within the household ensures the healthy reproduction of the labour force and the class and patriarchal relationships of capitalist society. Notions of a living wage or the family wage revolve around what is necessary to keep a worker and 'his' family fed and sustained in order to ensure the reproduction of capitalist relations of production. A somewhat more subtle level of analysis would examine the way in which meal times are important sites for the socialization of rising generations, places where values to do with timekeeping, deferred gratification and social order are rehearsed and demonstrated.

In terms of class struggle, food may provide a major rallying point for the development of working-class identity and goals. In more individualistic terms, food may provide a powerful source of motivation for social mobility: the desire not to see one's family go hungry or to experience hunger oneself. Memories of actual hunger – the hunger marches, for example – may be woven into these aspirations. In more Weberian status terms, the well-stocked larder, access to restaurants and wine cellars may provide key elements in status aspirations. Conversely, the traditional puritan values of moderation and sobriety may focus particularly upon the dinner table. Status relationships are said to focus upon issues of consumption (not, of course, confined to food), and the household, however composed, tends to be a major site for consumption. Hence there are links in terms of Weberian as well as Marxist approaches to stratification.

It might be felt that all this has a somewhat old-fashioned ring to it and that it does not come to grips with the complexities of stratification in a modern, or postmodern, society. One modification may be that food may not simply be seen as reflecting class differences or status differences but that it may be a source of stratification in its own right. In other words, just as some think that it might be possible to talk of 'housing classes', so too might it be possible to talk of 'food classes'. Such classes would be compounded of dimensions to do with the sheer amount of food or the proportion of income spent on food, the overall salience or centrality of food as a life interest, the location of eating practices and so on. Even if the idea of 'food classes' may, ultimately, seem a little fanciful, it is possible that certain measures to do with food consumption might enter into compound indices of class or status position.

This digression serves as a reminder of the relationships between ideas of food and the self. Whether or not one is a vegetarian, whether or not one feels oneself to be over- or underweight, whether one sees food as something to be enjoyed in interaction with others or as a simple piece of refuelling are all forms of distinction and are all bound up with a sense of self and personal identity. One might consider, for example, the elaborate hierarchies around the purchase and consumption of wine. These careers of the self are major themes in a modern society and are subject to constant evaluation and monitoring. Food, then, is not simply a reflection of class practices (although class factors will still present important limitations to the potentialities for self development here) but becomes a source of evaluation and distinction in its own right. That these food practices are not solely linked to family concerns is clear; but households and families still continue to play an important part in the distribution of life chances and the practices of styles of life.

(2) As well as differences between households there are also differences between nations and food practices located in the household. Nations are often identified or stereotyped according to their eating habits and food practices. There are complex links here between the ways in which nations present themselves or are presented to or by others, the invention of traditions and the development of tourism. Food tourism is at least as significant a development as sex tourism. At the simplest, least theoretical level, one of the facts that a traveller is first made aware of is to do with food practices: the appropriate times of meals and the sequences of courses, as well as, of course, the actual content and taste of dishes themselves.

Discussions of national differences in terms of food practices do not simply map on to family and household practices. Indeed, most of the reasons suggested by Mennell for the differences between French and British cuisine would appear to have relatively little to do with family relationships: the relationships with the court and courtly society or the different relationships between town and country, for example (Mennell, 1985). Families and family practices may be a theme in such differences, in the construction of peasant food, for example, but it is only one among several. However, there are also suggestions in Mennell's work that there were important historical differences in, for example, the development and distribution of cookery books. He argues that the classic emphasis in English cookery books was on the housewife and the domestic scale and that this may have contributed, more generally, to differences between the two countries (1985: 87).

Insofar as family relationships constitute one major arena through which senses of regional or national identity are constructed, there remain important links between food, family and senses of national identity. Every time a French person buys a *baguette* or visits a *charcuterie* and every time an English person stops for fish and chips or prepares a Sunday lunch, they are also reproducing a sense of national distinction and national identity. Households continue to provide key points of reference in these processes.

(3) Finally, we return to the theme of the civilizing of the appetites, already discussed in chapter 5 as well as alluded to earlier in the present chapter. Mennell draws out the connections between this theme and food practices (Mennell, 1985) and hints at possible links with issues to do with family and gender. In other words, the work of the civilizing of the appetites is not uniformly spread through society but is subject to some of the familiar divisions of labour by gender and by generation. The civilizing of the appetites refers not simply to exercising control and discipline over the amount of food that is consumed but also to the preparation of the food, the elaboration in the processes of cooking, and the manners and etiquette associated with its consumption. One may hypothesize that the civilizing of the appetites is in some way related to the size of the consuming group and the growing emphasis upon the conventional nuclear family was therefore an important intervening variable. The co-presence round the table of women and men, adults and children, might also have been another factor. The controls that are exercised over the consumption of food and the wider social and cultural meanings that the exercise of these controls might have all bring us back to practices within the household and family relationships across households.

Food, then, may enter into our family story in two very general ways. It can be a kind of 'trail' or set of linking practices, drawing lines between family and household, class and gender, time and space, the body and numerous other themes. However, it could be argued that the choice of food is not entirely arbitrary. Clothing could be another fruitful point of departure, although here it has to be recognized that there are not the same set of close symbolic linkages with family practices. And here, then, is the second way that food enters the family story. It is not simply the case that developments in the sociology of food may illuminate understandings of family practices. It is also the case that family studies may enhance understandings of food practice by showing the multiple strands of meaning that are woven around food and eating. If it be the case that, under conditions of high modernity, links between food, family and household are weakening or even disappearing then this too is a matter of some significance.

8

Home

Introduction

Clusters of words and phrases litter my pages after early attempts to put something on paper about this topic: living space, overcrowding, social distance, homely, home-making, home-breaking and happy home, identity and stability, gender and generation, no fixed abode, burglar alarms, rough and respectable, housing classes and housing careers, moving home, nostalgia, institution and relationship, surveillance and the body, public and private, an Englishman's home, a place in the country, upstairs and downstairs and inside and outside, the civilizing process, coals in the bath and feet under the table. Even this abbreviated list merely hints at the range of themes that threaten to break loose. This chapter is an attempt to bring some of these together through exploring the links between domestic space, personal space and theoretical space.

'Home' may be seen as part of the trilogy consisting of 'family', 'household' and 'home', although it is probably the least explored item of the three. However, there are clear signs that this early neglect is now being rectified. There have, however, been some important earlier studies. Dennis Chapman's Liverpool-based study, *The Home and Social Status* (1955), poised before the rapid expansion of television and central heating, may in part be seen as an anticipation of later discussions of housing classes or 'distinction'. At roughly the same time, but light years away in terms of approach and content, was the Canadian study of the suburb, *Crestwood Heights*

(Seeley, Sim and Loosley, 1956). They provide a text for all studies of the home: 'The house is . . . much more than a repository of artefacts; it is in its own right and *par excellence* an artefact to which deeply buried meanings are attached' (1956: 43). Of particular importance is their exploration of the overlapping meanings of the house as property, as stage, as home and as nursery, weaving into this discussion reflections on privacy, access, gender and generation.

More recently, Lyn Richard's study of a Melbourne suburb, 'Green Views', explores the multiple meanings and contradictions around the book's title, *Nobody's Home* (Richards, 1990). Australia is reputed to have one of the highest rates of home-ownership in industrialized countries and this study shows how property has a national, even international, economic and social face as well as being a source of personal and private meanings.

In the first section I shall consider the theme of 'address', or issues to do with location in space. In the second section, I shall focus more specifically on the home and the use of space and meanings within it. These are two ways of looking, externally and internally, at the same phenomenon and in the penultimate section I shall look at some ways in which these two broad themes might be drawn together.

Address

In using the term 'address' I am using a shorthand term to refer to questions of location in space. In a modern society, people are frequently called upon to supply an address, often together with full name and date of birth. There is an acceptable format for such an address: '73 Acacia Avenue' rather than 'the house on the corner by the postbox'. A postal code provides additional pinpointing.

Yet there are considerable variations in the mode of addressing. These can range from the most impersonal to the most personal, whimsical or idiosyncratic. Names may be assigned by present owners denoting locations of honeymoons, combinations of the owners' names or domestic ideologies as in the case of the notorious 'Dunroamin'. There is a lot of work to be done in teasing out the way in which these individual distinctions work and how they are linked to other social distinctions in British society.

The ubiquity and quasi-naturalness of having to provide and having an address reflect developments in the state and in notions of citizenship. Without an address we cannot be taxed, we cannot vote and we may be excluded from official population statistics. Claimants need an address to which their welfare benefits may be sent and it would be difficult to imagine the working of the school system or the national health service without knowledge of addresses. Outside the public sector, the obtaining of credit requires the ability to provide an address and, in some cases, a 'right' address. There are close links between housing, address and citizenship (McCrone, 1994: 95).

In Foucauldian terms we may see this as yet further manifestation of surveillance and the panoptic gaze. The cost of not being able to provide an address is to be denied all kinds of services and benefits. However, the cost of providing an address is, in addition to tangible costs associated with taxation, to open oneself up to the possibilities of all kinds of surveillance. As well as state agencies there is an increasing range of commercial interests (with computerized address lists) but this does not exhaust the range of gazes to which a resident may be subject. Others include neighbours and kin, prospective buyers, burglars, tourists and visitors.

Patterns of surveillance and gaze encourage patterns of resistance. With neighbours it is possible to draw the curtains or to call upon legal sanctions. Agencies of the state may, as was the case with the introduction of the so-called 'poll tax' in Britain, be met with straightforward non-registration. Potential burglars may be met with alarms or with neighbourhood watch schemes, although this latter option may increase the possibility of legitimizing the neighbourhood gaze.

Much sociological analysis has focused upon the residence in terms of property and property relationships, seeing these as relationships between people rather than relationships between things (Saunders, 1990: 95). Different property relationships are, in part, the basis of Chapman's analysis, while the authors of *Crestwood Heights* place their analysis in the context of struggles around the use of land (Seeley, Sim and Loosley, 1956; see also Perin, 1977; Richards, 1990 and Zukin, 1988). Distinctions between ownership and tenancy and between public and private run through analyses of housing, and such explorations see property not merely in terms of sets of economic relationships but also in terms of relationships of power with wider political and ideological significance linked with themes of democracy, individualism, citizenship and choice.

Combining the themes of property with the themes of locating individuals in space leads to links between housing and various forms of social division, most notably class, ethnicity and gender. Saunders, for example, has argued that life chances are a product of both access to home-ownership and access to secure employment (Saunders, 1990: 323). Halle's American blue-collar workers would probably agree with this analysis; for them, 'home ownership is a major goal, a rarely questioned ambition' (Halle, 1984: 11). There would seem to be a need for a more explicit linking of housing and stratification studies, even if the specific notion of housing classes may be thought to be too one-dimensional. At present, housing only appears as part of some composite indices of social stratification.

Perhaps one of the difficulties in developing the notion of housing classes lies in the combination of class relationships around property with status relationships which deal with the relative evaluations of different kinds of property according to size, amenities, location and so on. A private tenant may have a good address while an owner-occupier may live in a low- or declining-status neighbourhood. Suburban development might be the object of status snobbery while also, for the residents, be the basis for a preferred family living (Oliver, Davis and Bentley, 1981). However, there can be little doubt that class processes and subjective class identifications are at least strongly influenced by questions of housing. The abstractions of class based upon income or occupation are in some measure given concrete realization in property relations. Strategies of social closure may be most apparent in struggles over neighbourhood and housing.

Of course, within apparently class-homogeneous neighbourhoods finer status struggles may continue. The important point here is that the interplays between class and residence are complex and dynamic and that the focus should be upon the work carried out by members in maintaining boundaries and in elaborating strategies of social closure. Much of this work, it should be noted, is carried out by women. Collins argues that much of the activity of housewives is in the area of status production, transforming the larger categories of class into the more immediate groupings of status group membership (Collins, 1991: 60).

Much of the attention within this section has been upon those who 'have' an address. Yet, increasingly, attention is being paid to those who are 'homeless', whether they be people sleeping rough on the streets of most Western cities, refugees resulting from civil wars or famines or people seeking a living on the margins of growing Third World cities. As several commentators have noted (for example Watson, 1984), there are ambiguities around the notion of 'home-lessness' and there are no clear-cut distinctions between 'the homed' and 'the homeless'. Single-parent families living in 'bed-and-breakfast' accommodation may have an address but often refuse to give it the label of 'home'. Discussions of 'homelessness' and the concept of 'no fixed abode' inevitably raise questions about the concept of 'home' itself and the multiple and complex meanings attached to this term.

Home

As Chapman (1955) pointed out, the number of proverbial and popular expressions around the idea of 'home' are numerous. While the focus today tends to be upon the familial and domestic connotations associated with home, the term often has much wider associations. Schutz's analysis of 'the homecomer' (beginning with the return of Ulysses and ending with the reabsorption of American veterans) can be seen as a return to a native land as well as to a particular set of domestic relations (Schutz, 1945). However, it is likely that the narrower, more specialized use of the term 'home' was well established by the nineteenth century in Britain (Munthesius, 1982). Munthesius's account of the development of the English terraced house argues that the idea of the 'ideal' family dwelling is of relatively recent origin and gained in momentum with the growth of speculative building in the south-east of England from the 1900s (1982: 145) .

It becomes very difficult, certainly, to disentangle family and domestic relations from property relationships in the increasing use of terms to do with 'home-making'. Discussions of 'broken homes' indicate the range of usages attached to this expression and underline the positive work and connotations of 'home-making'. Leaving and moving home are experiences which deserve greater sociological attention. The latter is frequently identified as one of the major sources of stress in modern society, partly because it provides an occasion when a whole host of assumptions about locality, property and family and domestic relationships are reassessed.

It is all too easy to tell an apparently straightforward tale of the growth of domesticity as reflecting the ideological dominance of bourgeois values (Richards, 1990); in such an account the home and domestic life become a means both of the oppression of women and of masking other forms of oppression within society. Such an account, apart from elaborating a highly passive model of the modern home-maker, also fails to explore the complexities and contradictions within this process. I should prefer to see a variety of ideological themes being woven and deployed in the context of the home, themes which may sometimes come together but which on other occasions may contradict each other.

Janet Askham's distinction between 'identity' and 'stability' within marriage may provide one possible framework for exploring these themes (Askham, 1984). While Askham has little to say about the physical location of marital relationships it is possible that this analysis could be extended to the wider, although overlapping, area of the home. Indeed, something of a similar distinction is made by Rakoff (1977) between permanence and identity. Permanence is identified with such popular expressions as 'sinking roots', 'nesting' or 'settling down'. Interviews suggest a possible tension between the values of geographical mobility and permanence, and that stability is not always positively evaluated.

Home, therefore, may be a source of identity and stability, of one of these or of neither of these. Residences which provide neither identity nor stability are probably at the fringes of everyday understandings of 'home' and would include much transitional accommodation. Dwellings offering stability but without much in the way of identity are the familiar butts of popular social criticism from Pete Seegar's 'Little Boxes' to condemnation of high-rise dwellings. More sensitive analysis may recognize that the actor's frame of reference may differ from these stereotypes and acknowledge the abilities of residents to create small distinctions between adjacent properties. Largely imposed uniformity was welcomed by the inhabitants of the Melbourne estate, 'Green Views' (Richards, 1990), where the residents perceived a link to the idea of 'security' (1990: 120–1). But insofar as this security depended upon the ability to maintain mortgage payments, there was always an element of insecurity waiting in the wings.

Cases where identity is stressed at the expense of stability are probably best illustrated by, although certainly not confined to, artistic and intellectual careers in modern society. A good example is to be found in the autobiography of Noel Coward (Coward, 1986), which begins with accounts of his mother's frequent changes of address and continues to list a bewildering variety of other people's homes, hotels, clubs and flats. Such apparent lack of stability is not seen as any kind of deprivation and it can be argued that his very personal identity is bound up with this highly mobile existence.

It is likely, however, that the most common mix is where elements of stability and identity are combined. This would certainly seem to be a prized goal, especially at the more affluent end of the scale (Seeley, Sim and Loosely, 1956). Such a delicate balance may, however, be easily upset, as estates change as the result of other developments, changing patterns of transportation or demographic changes. Changes in personal circumstances, such as unemployment or divorce, may also threaten this balance between identity and stability in the home.

Another opposition that has frequently been developed in the analysis of marriage is that between institution and relationship. The idea of a long-term transition from the former to the latter is more complex and less certain than is sometimes claimed (Lewis, Clark and Morgan, 1992) but it is undoubtedly true that 'relationship' in the strong sense of the word has become one major theme around which actors understand their own and other marriages. Here again, this distinction might tell us something about the home and its gendered character. In Chapman's study, couples taking over a dwelling for the first time concentrated upon those features which underlined the location of a marital relationship in a home of one's own: the bedroom and the living room (Chapman, 1955: 42). In setting up, in creating, a home they tended not to think about forthcoming children; the needs of the husband and wife were seen as paramount (1955). A slightly ironic comment on the significance of home in the context of marital relations is provided by Lawson's study of adultery, where she discovered that nearly one third of the women in her sample had taken their lovers home (Lawson, 1988).

Thus the work of home-making and setting up home seems to provide strong reinforcement of the theme of relationship, especially insofar as this is focused on the conjugal bond or its equivalent. But we may also see such a strong linkage between home and relationship as potentially masking continuing institutional underpinnings of marriage. These features become apparent at times of divorce when the division or ownership of the property becomes an issue or, later, in the case of inheritance. Marriage may be less obviously about property than it was in the past for at least some sections of society but these themes have not been completely eclipsed in the marital relationship.

Discussions of marriage as a relationship often run the risk of obscuring gender divisions. We have already noted how women play a major part in the status work around the home in its wider locality. Women often have a particular responsibility in mediating between the public and the private across the threshold of the home. To some observers, the curved bow windows and softer exteriors of suburban semi-detached homes spoke directly of femininity and maternal warmth (Oliver, 1981). Whether such close identification of the home with the feminine has been oppressive for women is a matter of some controversy (Saunders, 1990: 308–9). It would seem reasonable to suppose that there are complex, and shifting, balances between a sense of sharing in a joint endeavour, a more or less shared sense of being trapped in a domestic setting and a highly gendered differentiation of experience and understanding.

However, the gendering of the home does not end with the degree to which it, as a whole, is identified with women and the feminine. There are also differentiations within the home around gendered space. The Crestwood Heights study (Seeley, Sim and Loosley, 1956) is only one which documents the ways in which different genders, and generations, establish and maintain boundaries within the home (see also Roberts, 1991). Especially relevant is Richards's (1990) subtle exploration of the different meanings of 'mine' for men and women, a discussion which takes us to the heart of the multiple significances of property in modern society. Men tended to see the home as the property of the male individual, as the outcome of his savings and efforts and as a signifier of adult status in the community. Women developed a more active notion of 'mine', seeing it as a process of her creation: it is 'her home and his haven' (1990, 132-5).

Such considerations of the different and varying uses and meanings of domestic space also apply to questions of age and generation. Again, we may note the frequently voiced parental complaint that their teenage children simply 'treat the house as if it were a hotel'. We also need to consider the position of older generations within the home. For them, home may become identified with past relationships and possessions. The location of older generations in domestic space may be uneasy or problematic where, as is most frequently the case, there is not the symbolic 'west wing' to retire to. The deployment of the imagery of 'home' in collective residences for elderly or retired persons is another way of exploring the multiple meanings of home in a modern society.

The Foucauldian theme of surveillance, discussed in the previous section, also has relevance within the home where we may speak of the operation of a male gaze, a marital gaze or a parental gaze. These gazes may often be linked to professional interventions within domestic life. Linked to a discussion of surveillance and its gendered connotations is the theme of privacy, a term which has, at least since the nineteenth century, been strongly linked to the idea of the home. Yet the distinction between the public and the private is an ambiguous one (Ardener, 1981). Richards's case study shows some of the meanings that can be attached to the idea of 'privacy': there is privacy *for* (a haven, security etc.), privacy *to* (build, for example, a stable family unit in the context of autonomy and independence) and privacy *from* others (Richards, 1990: 100). At a more macro level, there may not be straightforward links between the long historical development of the idea of private property and the more inter-personal notions of private space (Crow and Allen, 1990). Attachment to the value of a 'home of one's own' need not necessarily be associated with wider patterns of privatization (Saunders, 1990). Given these ambiguities and overlapping meanings it would be better to speak of 'privacies', which do not always converge coherently on to the home.

One ambiguity refers to the unit under discussion. Conventionally, the unit of privacy is taken to be the home (household, family); the walls of the house or the flat and the closed door symbolize this sense of a shared privacy. Yet, as studies of domestic violence and abuse have sometimes emphasized, this sense of collective privacy might not be something equally welcomed by all household members. Further, privacies might not be equally distributed throughout the household; children of male authors may learn to tiptoe past their father's study while female authors may, as Virginia Woolf emphasized, have to struggle for a 'room of one's own'. Privacies, within the home as well as in the wider community, are processes rather than fixed and final accomplishments.

Address and Home

There is something artificial about the distinction that I have made between 'address' and 'home' as a way of organizing this material. Here I shall begin to put these pieces back together and to explore interconnections.

(1) The idea of property points both to a location in physical and social space and to an individual or family life project which is increasingly bound up with individual identity. As Perin puts it, the form of tenure can be seen as a 'primary social sign' (Perin, 1977: 32). To have a 'good' address and to be a home-owner is to make certain kinds of status claims, which reflect on one's own sense of personal worth or achievement and, often, upon the identities of those to whom one is associated.

But having an address is an active and an ongoing process. For one thing, as Perin points out, home-ownership is, in most cases, 'home-buying', a process rather than a completed accomplishment (1977: 64). As such, the owning of a home places certain demands upon the 'owner', such as maintaining regular employment or engaging in other strategies in order to maintain or improve one's position in the housing market. This entails making certain choices which have implications for and sometimes involve other members of the household. Further, ownership of a house or dwelling is not a passive act; it entails certain activities or strategies on the part of the owner in order to maintain the property at its current value or, indeed, to improve it. Hence there are close interconnections between the two themes, address and home, around the centrality of private property in many modern societies.

(2) Another way of looking at the same set of issues is in terms of current concerns with risk and danger. Ownership confers identity, a concept which has both its internal and external aspects. Yet ownership also brings with it risks, risks that the mortgage payments may not be kept up, risks that the neighbourhood will deteriorate as a result of unforeseen changes, indeed all the risks associated with the market and market forces. Further, differences between properties and their locations can be understood in terms of the differential allocation of risks: environmental, threats of crime or violence or the risks associated with stigma. Risks, in other words, are not simply in terms of threats to status and identity; they may also be much more directly physical and material.

(3) As was emphasized in chapter 6, there are intimate and complex links between time and space in social life and this is true when we consider address and home. Addresses and dwellings remain relatively fixed in terms of time and space; over time, however, their composition may change. When we talk of 'short-term' accommodation we are, of course, not usually referring to the accommodation as such but to the life course of the individuals involved. The idea of the life course serves as a useful bridge between ideas of address and location and ideas of home. Leaving home is often a complex business and often does not entail a complete and once-and-for-all break; for young people in modern Britain there may be complex patterns of leaving and returning home (Jones, 1995). A death may change the character of a home, its composition, or it may mark the actual 'end' of a home even where the house or flat remains. Finch and Hayes point out that the 'home' can be said to die with its

creator; the often painful business of 'clearing out' a home and handling issues of inheritance has features of a symbolic burial (Finch and Hayes, 1994).

The idea of the home links past and future. Home-ownership is frequently spoken of as 'investing in the future' and while there may be some debate about the economic significance of this argument there is no doubt that the whole idea of creating a home entails some kind of modelling for the future. To 'put down roots' is to have some kind of expectation of relative stability. Even the most humble of purchases 'for the home' have some kind of expectation of future use rather than immediate consumption; this is most dramatically expressed in the display of wedding presents. Setting up a home, the locating of oneself in social and physical space, is also often linked with other projects such as having children or beginning a 'new life' with another partner.

Home also looks backward. Home is often associated with ideas of nostalgia, a return, real or imagined, to a point of origin or departure. Homes may become the repository of memories of the past or sites for the re-creations of semi-imagined pasts (Samuel, 1994).

Drawing these different themes together we can see that the home, both as an address and as a site for domesticity, is a key element in the construction of a self. The way in which weekly magazines or Sunday newspapers invite readers to share in the rooms or homes of celebrated individuals highlights some of the ways in which homes are bound up with autobiographies. Homes, these living spaces defined as such by their inhabitants, may develop a sense of personal identity in even some of the least favourable settings where 'home' is represented by little more than a poster stuck to the wall or a few objects on the mantelpiece. While this sense of a construction of self is often presented in terms of the design and decor and the objects housed within the home, locality is also an important consideration.

It might also be noted that this sense of self is often bound up with public moralities. Pickvance and Pickvance, in their study of housing strategies, note the importance of the theme of 'sacrifice' in the accounts of their informants (C. Pickvance and K. Pickvance, 1995). Taking out a mortgage is a serious undertaking not simply in terms of the amount of money involved and the nature of the commitments being undertaken, but also because it represents some sort of sign of a serious person, one who is prepared to defer some gratifications and to consider others, or anticipated others, in one's calculations. 'Putting the family first' is a major, and generally positive, mode of legitimation in contemporary society (Jordan, Redley and James, 1994) and the serious pursuit of family projects is, at least in Britain, closely linked to notions of home, property and investing for the future.

There is another side to this discussion of self and morality, namely that these selfsame themes may become oppressive and threatening to the idea of self. Those who live in accommodation which is deemed inappropriate (especially where children are involved) may be subject to processes of stigmatization. The other side of a 'good address' is a 'poor address', one on the wrong side of town, and ill-provided privately rented accommodation may present a threat to the self rather than a sense of self-fulfilment. The links between homelessness and constructions of the 'underclass' and marginality are familiar themes in the analysis of modern urban societies.

Conclusion

The home, writes Rakoff (1977), is a 'multivocal symbol' and Gullestad (1992: 79) writes: 'The home is a rich, flexible and ambiguous symbol . . .'. It is this flexibility and ambiguity that makes it a particularly attractive and fascinating area for sociological investigation. Speculation about the home not only informs family sociology but may have implications for much wider sociological inquiry.

The idea of the home serves as a link between many areas of discourse and inquiry. This is not just a matter for intellectual interest; it would also seem to reflect the way in which the world is structured and perceived for many individuals. For example, Saunders outlines the complex patterns of motivation behind the desire to have a home of one's own. These include economic rationality, ideas of autonomy or personal identity and wider cultural values (Saunders, 1990: 39). These are all important, and much discussed, current sociological themes.

This muti-layered significance of the home and home-ownership did not just happen. There is a history of the idea of the home and its changing significance which interacts with other historical themes. It is possible to argue that not only are there histories of housing and of the idea of the home but that the development of the idea of the home represents a major theme in any account of modern history. As private lives take more and more of a central position in historical analysis so too will we find discussions of living space and home as part of that refocusing of historical accounts.

Urban sociology, for example, is woven around themes of domestic spaces, their shifting character and changing significance. A recent example is Zukin's analysis of loft living, which: '. . . started as a trend, turned into a "movement" and finally transformed the market' (Zukin, 1988: 12). Class and social differentiation, woven around individual and household-based life courses, play a major role in the shaping of modern cities.

It is also important to see themes to do with home as having a national and a global significance. The links between two senses of home, as a site for domestic or family life and as a wider locality or region, have often been commented upon. It is possible that these two senses were once closer than they are now: 'The home and local community, once quite similar, have changed in different directions' (Gullestad, 1992: 51).

The home in the narrow sense is intensified as a site for intimacy while the neighbourhood becomes more fragmented and part time. Gullestad is writing about Norway and her generalizations need not necessarily apply straightforwardly in other areas. Nevertheless, there are increasing problems in holding together the domestic and the local.

While these divisions may be opening up, ideologically the links often remain quite strong. Historically, Nash considers the role of the symbol of the cottage in the landscape and the development of Irish nationalism (Nash, 1993: 47). The rural cottage equals traditional rural life and this is identified with women and the values of motherhood, all powerful themes in the development of nationalist symbols. Saunders considers the importance of home-ownership in contemporary British culture and in developing a sense of British identity (Saunders, 1990: 2). Similarly, Gullestad argues for links between ideas of home and modern Scandinavian culture (Gullestad, 1992: 48).

Such ideological and symbolic linkages between home and nation have been a matter of concern as well as celebration. Strong images of the home are bound up with strong images of 'them and us' and have, often, clear implications for the development and rhetorics of racism. It is certainly the case that right-wing politicians can readily call upon images of home in order to reinforce notions of a people, a race or a nation. However, it is also worth noting that most cultures also develop notions of hospitality, of opening up doors and of welcoming strangers. The idea of home need not be a narrow or an inward-looking concept.

Once again we see a theme with strong links to ideas of the family and the household, the home, as drawing upon wider debates within sociological inquiry. These include notions of the self and identity, notions of rational choice, constructions of national and ethnic boundaries and debates about gender and class divisions. This is to name but a few of the wider sociological themes that may converge in the analysis of the home. But again, the influence is two way. The growing interest in the home and domesticity may help to illuminate these other areas of sociological inquiry.

Conclusion

There are two ways in which family studies might develop. The first is to mark out a discrete topic area, identify the distinguishing features of that topic area, and develop research and theorizing within these specialized boundaries. The second, and the one stressed in the course of this book, is to see a family dimension in all or most other areas of social inquiry. 'Family' here represents a quality rather than a thing. In each of the particular topics considered in the this book I argue for a two-way relationship. Developments in the studies of these specialized topics could contribute to our understanding of family processes while, conversely, studies of the family and the household have something to contribute to these other specialized topics. This is relatively clear in the case of some of the more established areas of social inquiry – work, stratification and gender, for example – but could also be argued in the case of some newer areas such as the more theoretical studies of the body or time and space.

This overall argument has been influenced by three sets of related considerations. The first is to do with continuing political and theoretical debates about the family. More specifically, the question is one of whether it is misleading, or possibly even dangerous, to talk of 'the family' in the face of an observable diversity of modern family practices and domestic living arrangements and in the context of a vigorous ideological debate about the importance of family life in the context of society as a whole. To talk about 'the family', something that is at least implied in the phrase 'sociology of the family', might not only obscure the rich diversity of practices to be found in a modern society but might also lend support to right-wing political agendas.

Yet to abandon the word 'family' altogether might also seem to present problems. For one thing, there seem to be few attractive or immediately persuasive alternatives. For another, since the word 'family' is widely used and understood, by lay persons as well as by professionals, it would seem to be counter-productive to place an embargo on its use. One strategy, as has already been noted, is to use the word as a topic rather than a resource, to explore the ways in which and the occasions on which social actors use the word. Here it might be noted that many people use the word flexibly and situationally, with reference to particular, although not necessarily fixed, sets of others. Thus when people use the term 'the family' they are more likely to refer to specific others whose identities are likely to be understood in the context (as, for example, when someone says they will be spending Christmas with the family) rather than an abstract and fixed political entity. A further everyday usage, and one which will be explored at greater length here, is as an adjective rather than as a noun, as when we talk about 'family obligations', for example.

The second set of considerations is to do with a growing sense of fluidity in the way in which sociologists and others understand the categories that they routinely deploy. The headings which identify the chapters of many texts (including this one) are not to be taken as referring to fixed entities or boxes labelled 'work', 'family', 'leisure', 'stratification' and so on but as different ways of looking at similar or overlapping areas of sociological inquiry. In the British context this was perhaps most readily identified with the concept of 'work' but similar principles apply whatever point of departure is taken. The frequently used metaphor of the kaleidoscope, with the emphasis on shifting patterns of relationships, is increasingly used to express this sense of fluidity. Some modes of feminist theorizing together with the 'postmodern turn' provided further theoretical support for a set of understandings that were already in place.

A third set of considerations is perhaps more down-to-earth. The growing interest in auto/biography shifts the attention away from the categories used to describe collectivities, structures or social institutions and towards a processual understanding of a social actor following a variety of careers or trajectories. This is not, straight-forwardly, a switch from society to the individual, since the emphasis is always upon social actors in all their complexity. In terms of the present discussion, the 'auto/biographical turn' entails a recognition of a sense of fluidity and multi-facetedness and a realization that individuals are rarely, if ever, enclosed within the categories chosen by sociologists. Thus even the most dedicated workaholic is never fully enclosed within an occupational title; similarly, family titles such as 'mother', 'son' or 'sibling' only exist as part of a much wider array of potential or actual modes of self-identification. Add to this a sense of where an actor has been and where she or he hopes or expects to go and we have a fluid sense of a movement through and across a variety of statuses and identities.

It would be wrong to suppose that insights or understandings are necessarily novelties within sociological analysis. Role theory, for all its weaknesses, presented an elaborated framework for understanding the multiple roles and sets of role-others (the others with whom a person interacts in carrying out a role) that might cumulatively describe a social actor. Discussions of 'latent social identities' conveyed the idea of a set of potentialities, which might or might not be relevant in particular contexts, rather than a set of fixed characteristics in terms of class, gender, occupation, family status or whatever. This is not to repeat the facile conclusion that sociologists are constantly reinventing the wheel. New terminology does often provide new insights rather than simply recycling old ideas in novel, and possibly obscure, language.

Practices

It is in the context of these few brief observations that I want to develop ideas associated with the use of the term 'family practices', a usage which has already appeared on some of the preceding pages. The ideas developed here are not necessarily particularly new; there will be some overlaps with Bourdieu's usage for example (Bourdieu, 1990). Certainly the word 'practices' is no novelty, although I give it a specific slant in the following discussion. It seems to be the most appropriate term for the argument that I wish to present and I leave it to others to explore the differences between my usage and more established versions.

Thus, when I use the term 'practices' in the following discussion, I seek to convey the following.

(1) I seek to combine, in ways which may not necessarily be harmonious or completely congruent, the perspectives of the actor

and the observer. Claims that we should always adopt the actor's frame of reference seem to me to be both admirable and Utopian. They are admirable in that they stake out a humanistic claim against the worst excesses of sociologizing or reification. They are Utopian since they fail to recognize that the projects of the observer and the observed can never be wholly congruent. It seems better to recognize that the perspectives of observer and observed are necessarily different, although possibly overlapping, and to incorporate this recognition into the subsequent analysis.

Thus the use of the term 'practices' deliberately plays on this sense of difference. Most obviously, social actors do not routinely use the word 'practices' to describe whatever they happen to be doing; they will either use some more concrete term ('mowing the lawn', 'feeding the children') or simply get on with the task to hand. More complexly, the qualifying term used by the analyst may or may not correspond with the actor's own understanding of what is going on. Thus, I may describe 'mowing the lawn' or 'feeding the children' as 'gendered social practices' and my warrant for doing so would be based upon statements derived largely from feminist theory and research, which introduced the question of gender in the first place and which contributed to a mapping of various activities according to the gender of the practitioner. This is not to say that my description is necessarily correct or that it will be met with agreement on the part of the practitioner. However, a rejection of a particular description should not necessarily lead to the abandonment of the idea of gendered practices as applied to these or similar activities. In using the term 'practices', therefore, I am hoping to convey a sense of flow between the perspectives of the observer and the observed.

(2) I intend to convey a sense of the active. If we compare the terms 'family structures' and 'family practices' this point should become clear. The former is static and carries a sense of something thing-like and concrete. Even if the idea of social structure need not have these characteristics there does appear to be a built-in tendency to conceive of it in this way. The latter carries with it a sense of doing and action. Structures of parent–child relations are one thing; practices of feeding children are another.

(3) The term 'practices' is also designed to carry with it some sense of the everyday. The practices observed are usually everyday to the participants themselves, however odd they might appear to the observer. Practices are often little fragments of daily life which are

part of the normal taken-for-granted existence of the practitioners. Their significance derives from their location in wider systems of meaning. Feeding children derives significance from the location of these practices within systems of parenting, of consumption and possible others such as gender or stratification.

(4) The term 'practices' conveys some kind of sense of regularity. We do not usually deploy the word for one-off events. In the English language, indeed, the term conveys a sense of being rehearsed or repeated; practice makes perfect. The meaning and character of feeding the children in part derives from the fact that the same children were fed, usually by the same person, yesterday and at about the same time and it is expected that the same event will take place tomorrow.

(5) Use of the word also conveys a sense of fluidity. This is getting close to the aims of this chapter and this book as a whole. Thus, while practices have a degree of fixity and solidity rooted in their everyday character and the fact that they are repeated with some degree of regularity, they also have an open-ended character. This open-endedness derives from the fact that any set of practices may, often, be described in two or more ways. Thus, as has already been hinted, feeding the children may be described as 'family practices', as 'gendered practices', as 'consumption practices', as 'ethnic prac- tices' and so on. To chose to describe practices one way does not preclude the possibility of these other modes of description. The fact that the practitioner describes the practices in one way does not necessarily invalidate other descriptions. The fact that two or more descriptions are possible of the same set of practices does not preclude the possibility of tension or conflict between them. Thus feeding the children may be located within the domain of family practices but there may be tension here with a simultaneous location within, say, consumption practices, as where children vocally express a preference for some widely advertised breakfast cereal.

(6) Finally, practices constitute major links between history and biography (Mills, 1959). Practices are historically constituted and the linkages and tensions or contradictions between practices are historically shaped. At the same time practices are woven into and constituted from elements of individual biographies. Feeding the children may be shaped by a whole host of factors, often felt as limitations or constraints. Expert notions on nutrition, previous feeding experiences, commercial and advertising pressures, gendered

expectations, expectations located within particular classes, status groups or ethnic groups and external timetables all meet around the breakfast table. At the same time these influences and constraints are also resources which may provide legitimations for the adoption of one set of feeding practices rather than another.

Nothing that has been said in this section will seem especially new. The linking of these concerns under the general heading of 'practices' might provide some measure of novelty and may give emphasis to these or issues that might otherwise be forgotten. In the next section I focus more specifically upon 'family practices'.

What Are Family Practices?

It follows from the argument above that family practices do not have a thing-like existence; the use of the term denotes a particular way of viewing sets of practices which could be described in other ways. 'Family practices' have a theoretical status and part of this status includes a recognition that things could be viewed otherwise, through different sets of lenses.

It might be thought that 'family practices' were those practices which were recognized and defined as such by the practitioners or agents concerned. Otherwise, it might be argued, there is always the danger of imposing an alien definition of the situation. However, there are limitations in taking the 'actors' definition of the situation' as the sole criterion for deciding whether a set of practices could be described as family practices or not. Most trivially, it is unlikely that people routinely talk about 'practices' at all; the very word, un-qualified, stands for a theoretical project which is different from the projects engaged upon by the social actors concerned. More importantly, social actors' definitions of the situation are not always available to the observer. This is often the case with historical analysis, analysis based upon demographic data or many social surveys. In these cases, the test of the validity or otherwise of this particular label cannot rest upon the understandings of the actors themselves.

Nevertheless, the recognition that social actors may understand situations differently remains an important one. In some cases we may be able to test, by direct or indirect means, whether an actor really does regard a particular set of practices as having something to do with 'family' or not. In the absence of such information, we must remain aware of the potentiality that the use of the label 'family' may be inappropriate and may not accord with the actor's view of the social world. Where the researcher uses the word 'family' to describe a set of practices, good reasons must be provided for such a usage.

A slight reformulation might bring us closer to understanding the character of family practices. We may say that family practices are to do with those relationships and activities that are constructed as being to do with family matters. The use of the word 'constructed' here takes in two meanings. At one level there are the perceptions and interpretative work of the actors involved, as discussed in the previous paragraphs. But at another level there are also processes of historical construction. Understandings around the use of the word 'family' are themselves shaped by complex historical processes; most historical accounts of the development of the family are also accounts of the development and shifts in the usages and meanings of the word 'family' and associated terms. What is being argued here is that the word 'family' is a word that is historically available and is used by social actors as they go about their daily business of interpreting and shaping their worlds. When we say that family practices are practices which are constructed as such we are referring to these two levels and their interaction over time.

Family practices are not simply cognitively constructed. They also have some kind of emotional dimension, some sense of personal or moral significance. Part of the process of constructing family practices, historically and individually, is not simply in terms of being able to identify such practices but also the recognition that such practices are significant in some way. The twin aspects of the word 'meaning' in the English language captures this very well; to say that family practices are meaningful is to say that such practices can be identified as such and that they have some degree of significance for the parties involved. Family practices are not just any old practices. In many cases they appear to have a natural or given character, something which is recognized in many folk expressions about family relations and obligations. Part of the complex process of the construction of family practices is that such practices often seem natural, inevitable and significant to the parties involved.

To say that family practices are recognized as being significant in some way is not the same as saying that they are always positively evaluated. Family practices may often seem oppressive, constraining, threatening or dangerous. Understandings of the pluses and minuses of family life may be from the point of view of the participants themselves, from the perspectives of the observers or from the perspective (itself another complex construction) of the wider society. To say that practices are defined as being significant is to state that such practices are difficult to ignore, not that they are necessarily benevolent or agreeable.

Finally, we should stress that family practices do seem to provide particularly strong links between self and society. Again the operative word is perhaps 'seem'. In one sense it could be argued that the linking of self and society was a feature of all recognized sites – work, leisure, education, politics and so on. However, the Janus-faced character of everyday life – looking to both self and society at the same time – is seen or constructed in its clearest form in the case of family practices. Autobiographical accounts, for example, may provide vivid portraits of the routines and the pleasures and terrors of everyday domestic life while also describing the wider society in which these domestic events took place. Some accounts may lean more in one direction than another but most will present some kind of mixture of the immediate and the domestic with the societal or the historical.

To conclude this section on a slightly more concrete note, most observers would agree that family practices had 'something' to do with relationships based upon marriage, parenthood or kinship, whether these relationships be formally or informally recognized. It is, in part, these connotations that give family practices their particular significances and their links between self and society. But to describe family practices in these ways immediately opens up the possibility that they may be described in some other way. Relationships between husbands and wives may also be seen as gendered practices, those between parents and children as age-specific practices and so on.

On the Centrality of Family Practices

The claim that the family is central or basic to society has often been made in sociology textbooks as well as from pulpits. The claim has also been subjected to denials and refutations. Arguments about the supposed universality of the family have been countered with supposed exceptions. The essentialism or biologism on which many claims for the basic character of family life appear to depend has also been subjected to critical denial. There have been more complex critiques of the use of the word 'family', attacking its implication of an unchanging 'thing-like' status. It is likely that these claims and counter-claims will continue, especially at a time when many fear, or hope, that the family is in terminal decline.

The use of the term 'family practices' was partially intended to sidestep these debates. The various claims or counter-claims on behalf of the family and its centrality could themselves be seen as family practices, albeit at a somewhat higher level of elaboration. They could be treated as topics for investigation in their own right, as claims which have their own sociological roots and social consequences. Whether or not such claims correspond to reality may be one part of such an investigation but a necessary preliminary stage must be to emphasize that they are claims and not unproblematic statements about nature or society.

Thus claims about the centrality of family practices have particular histories. They are socially constructed, which is not the same as stating that they are unimportant or trivial. The supposed centrality of family practices focuses upon three interrelated sets of concerns, each set also representing matters for serious consideration: nature, morality and religion, and the state.

(1) It has been noted at several points throughout this book that the claimed special character of family life derives from its closeness to what appear to be universal, biological and unchanging experiences: sexuality, birth, ageing and death. Woven into and through these concerns are themes of care, the body and gender. The point is not that these biological experiences cause family practices since there are all kinds of other ways in which they can be, and have been, handled. Nor is it the case that family practices are exclusively associated with these experiences. Again, a little reflection shows us this is not the case. The point is more that, more often than not, discussion of the family, in the last analysis, gets back to these themes.

As an illustration, let us take the occasion of a reported death. On such occasions we are frequently called upon to remember the deceased's loved ones, often those connected through family ties. We can easily think of exceptions but it remains the case that the occasion of a death, together with the subsequent funeral and disposal of property, routinely and effortlessly brings to the fore questions of family. Even accounts of the deaths of public figures, statespersons or movie stars give some emphasis to the spouses or children left behind.

(2) Another aspect of the previous point, that is the association of family practices with nature, is the links that are made between family, morality and religion. In modern societies these links seem, in one sense, to be especially strong as morality has come to be largely equated with sexual morality and religion is increasingly identified with the more private spheres of individual conscience and the family. The clergy are called upon to give a 'clear lead' in matters to do with sex and the family; they become more controversial when they speak on matters to do with economics or politics. There seem to be particularly intimate links between morality, religion, sexuality and the family.

It would be wrong to see these linkages as being solely a product of modernity, associated with the rationalization of public life, secularization and general privatization. This is part of the story, just as the strategies and rhetorics of public leaders are also part of the story. But the links between these practices have deeper roots. The links which politicians regularly make between morality and the family are echoed in everyday discourses about family obligations and the place of these within individual scales of values. It is not that individuals automatically or unthinkingly 'put the family first'; it is, rather, that family members and family obligations are seen as being an important part of an individual's moral horizons, something that they need to take into account. The strategies associated with these obligations and their consequences may be extremely various; what matters is that they are so often part of the reckoning whatever the final outcome.

To go over some of the same ground we may say that matters to do with morality and religion are serious matters and that their seriousness in part derives from their associations with birth, sexuality and death. To return to our earlier example, the death of an individual is also a time for a kind of moral bookkeeping, an assessment of the overall significance of a life. To caution against speaking ill of the dead is to bear witness to the seriousness of the occasion. Again it must be stressed that religion and morality have concerned themselves with matters other than birth, sex and death or marriage and the family. Nevertheless, there is a sense in which we can say that family practices are moral practices in that they deal with matters that so often appear to be shared, part of the common currency of human experience.

(3) The third element in considering the central character of family practices is also, historically speaking, the most recent. This is to do

with the state and politics and debates associated with the state. Links between politics and the family have been given detailed examination elsewhere (Morgan, 1985). There has been detailed investigation of the ways in which legislation, even where this does not explicitly refer to family matters, draws upon common assumptions about family life and has consequences for the ways in which people understand or construct their domestic lives. There are discussions of the complex and strong linkages between ideology, state practices, gender and family and of the ways in which these may be challenged or broken. There have also been discussions of more specific family rhetorics such as those associated with the 'New Right' in Britain and the United States. There are links to be made between issues to do with marriage and the family and more recent discussions of citizenship (Bjornberg, 1995; Vogel, 1994).

The apparent re-emergence of family matters in recent political debates should be understood in a wider context. First, the fact that there has been more overt discussion of family practices in recent years does not mean that there were no linkages between family and politics prior to these debates. The links between state and family have a long and complex history and, as has been stressed often, state practices have consequences for family practices even where such practices are not instantly to the fore. One need only think of the multiple impacts of a declaration of war on all aspects of family and domestic practices. Second, if family practices seem to be moving more to the fore in political debate, this is partly due to the perception of particular challenges to the family (from feminism, from 'the sixties generation' and so on) and the way in which these challenges, both real and imagined, have been woven into political rhetoric. Finally, it may be suggested that a political focus on family practices – whether that focus comes from the right or the left – may reflect a general decline of politics elsewhere. If global issues and economic forces increasingly seem to evade the rational control of national governments, a concentration on domestic matters and moralities may seem to be an attractive option for contending parties who wish to retain their credibility. Put simply, if the long-term close links between religion and family morality is a reflection of secularization then the increasing political focus on family matters may reflect a similar process of political secularization.

To conclude this section, if family practices continue to seem central to society and to individual lives this is largely a consequence of a complex but overdetermined convergence of these three areas of discourse and their historical roots: nature, morality and religion and the state. What needs to be repeated is that this is a complex unity, composed of conflicting and sometimes contradictory elements. Thus if, to put matters crudely, nature dictates that women have babies and men impregnate women, economics and politics dictate that mothers and fathers should stay together. Further, it is a unity which is subject to challenge and change.

On the Declining Significance of Family Practices

Part of the debate and challenge has been to call into question the continuing significance of family practices in a modern society. The point of departure for this assessment is frequently a demographic analysis of the society under consideration. Thus, in many or most western societies the statistical indicators all seem, with some variation, to be pointing in the same direction. In the field of marriage, people are marrying later in life and getting divorced with greater frequency. More people are choosing to remain outside marriage, whether in a cohabitation relationship or in some other arrangement. People are having fewer children and are increasingly likely to have children outside wedlock. The single-person household is one of the most rapidly growing household types.

These trends are frequently associated with key features of modernity or high modernity. Chief among these would be the reordering of relationships between the sexes. While few would accept the label 'post-patriarchal' or 'post-feminist', the general point would seem to be that considerable change in gender relationships have already taken place and, perhaps more importantly, the wider framework of expectations around gender have shifted. This applies especially to the expectations of women. The expectations and responses of men have been somewhat more confused, although the need for change here is something that is increasingly recognized if less frequently practised. The other set of modern features have been variously described as individualism, the development of the project of the self or the pursuit of personal autonomy. These both lead to and derive from a weakening of traditional or institutional controls, especially those associated with family and domestic ties and gendered expectations. The pursuit of individualism and the shifts in the gender order converge in discussions of gendered life styles and multiple sexualities.

At this point a note of caution should be struck. In the last two paragraphs I have highlighted some broad demographic findings and some broad narratives about social change in the twentieth century. It is all too easy to read the second set of ideas off from the first. These may be persuasive readings but, in many cases, the links have yet to be established. Any one of the categories established through demographic analysis – single parents, reconstituted households, single-person households, childless couples, cohabitees and so on – contain varieties of persons, experiences and expectations. They have arrived at these statuses by various routes and expect to leave them in equally various ways.

What may be said, therefore, is that the demographic trends and the more speculative accounts of high modernity do not necessarily neatly combine to form a package labelled 'decline of family practices'. What is perhaps more significant is that these statistics and debates are more generally available, more widely discussed and are part of a wider process of societal monitoring and evaluation. In Britain, the annual publication of *Social Trends* is now something of a media event, as are the results of other regular or less regular surveys. These publications become the occasion for the deployment of various claims and counter-claims concerning the decline of the family and family values. Is it decline or is it change? Are these changes to be welcomed or deplored? If deplored, are such changes reversible?

It should be noted that these debates are themselves family practices. They derive, in part, from individuals' experiences of and hopes for families and have consequences for the ways in which people live their domestic lives. The meaning of this increasing statistical and political monitoring is not straightforward. To some it may reflect the last gasp of societies which have lost any real sense of wider solidarity or ties that bind; even 'community' seems too remote or too much of an abstraction. 'The family' in this model represents the last bastion against wholly atomized individuals. To others, these debates may provide the occasion for the nostalgic reassertion of integrated values of family, community and nation. To yet others, the debate may represent a call for the reassertion of new values which may or may not derive from models of family obligations and ethics of care.

The contribution of this present discussion to these debates may not seem immediately obvious. I have dealt largely with debates within the social sciences rather than in the wider community. Yet there is no doubt that there are exchanges, direct and indirect, between the social science and research communities and political debates that have more immediate consequences for individuals' lives. One need only think of the work of the Institute of Economic Affairs, the Family Policy Studies Centre and the Policy Studies Institute in the UK or the work of Amitai Etzioni in the USA. My central concern in this present volume has been to argue that there is a family dimension in many areas of social inquiry and not simply in those areas which might be formally labelled as 'family studies'. The notion of 'family practices' was elaborated to convey a sense of flow and movement between a whole set of overlapping social practices, practices which were both constructed by the observer and lived by the actual practitioners. Thus 'family', in this account, is not a thing but a way of looking at, and describing, practices which might also be described in a variety of other ways.

The implications of this approach are possibly twofold. In the first place, in as much as family life remains an important strand in the lives of individuals and a term which they continue to use to convey matters of some importance, family practices continue themselves to be important. Such importance may not correspond to the categories or constructions of statisticians, sociologists or politicians. It may rarely be an unconditional importance. But while there may be good grounds for talking about the decline of any one particular model of 'the family' we can be less confident in talking about the decline of family practices. Second, in policy terms, the implication would seem to be against the establishment of any ministry for the family or specifically labelled family policy. But it would seem to entail a recognition that all legislation and social change has consequences for the significant relationships that link individuals rather than just the individuals themselves. This is true not simply for legislation (such as, in the UK, the Child Support Act 1991) which might be explicitly designed with family relationships in mind but also for issues to do with transport, the environment and crime and punishment. It would entail, further, a recognition that significant relationships are partly organized around gender and generation, that they deal with the relationships of adults and children and women and men. And finally, it is implied that these significant relationships are not fixed, are the product of complex and ongoing negotiations and are subject to constant reflexive monitoring.

I have one final observation to make. This book has, necessarily, focused upon family and domestic practices and their relationship with other practices. But this is not done in some spirit of academic imperialism, of seeking to stake out claims for family territory. In principle there is no reason why the analysis could not have begun with stratification, gender, work, the body or any of the other points highlighted in the preceding chapters. Many of these – especially work and class – are themselves undergoing thorough re-evaluation and concerns about their alleged decline. In beginning at any of these other points, the researcher will arrive at or pass through many other areas of inquiry, some of which have been considered here. This sense of flow and fluidity is probably part of a postmodernist understanding; it is certainly implied in the deliberate use of the term 'practices'.

References

Abbott, P. and Sapsford, R. 1987: *Women and Social Class*. London: Tavistock.

Abbott, P. and Wallace, C. 1990a: *An Introduction to Sociology: Feminist Perspectives*. London: Routledge.

Abbott, P. and Wallace, C. (eds) 1990b: *The Sociology of the Caring Professions*. London: Falmer Press.

Abercrombie, N., Hill, S. and Turner, B.S. 1986: *The Sovereign Individuals of Capitalism*. London: Allen and Unwin.

Abercrombie, N. and Urry, J. 1983: *Capitalism, Labour and the Middle Classes*. London: Allen and Unwin.

Abrams, P., Deem, R., Finch, J. and Rock, P. (eds) 1981: *Practice and Progress: British Sociology, 1950–1980*. Basingstoke: Macmillan.

Abrams, P. and Lewthwaite, P. (eds) 1980: *Transactions of the Annual Conference of the British Sociological Association Held at the University of Lancaster, April 8–11, 1980*. London: BSA Publications.

Adam, B. 1990: *Time and Social Theory*. Cambridge: Polity Press.

Adam, B. 1994: *Timewatch: The Social Analysis of Time*. Cambridge: Polity Press.

Allatt, P., Keil, T., Bryman, A. and Bytheway, B. (eds) 1987: *Women and the Life Cycle: Transitions and Turning Points*. Basingstoke: Macmillan.

Allen, I. and Perkins, E. (eds) 1995: *The Future of Family Care for Older People*. London: HMSO.

Allen, S., Waton, A., Purcell, K. and Wood, S. (eds) 1986: *The Experience of Unemployment*. Basingstoke: Macmillan.

Allen, S. and Wolkowitz, C. 1987: *Homemaking: Myth and Reality*. Basingstoke: Macmillan.

Althusser, L. 1971: *Lenin and Philosophy and Other Essays*. London: New Left Books.

Anderson, M., Bechofer, F. and Gershuny, J. (eds) 1994: *The Social and Political Economy of the Household*. Oxford: Oxford University Press.

Applegate, J.S. and Kaye, L. W. 1993: Male elder caregivers. In C.L. Williams (ed.), *Doing 'Women's Work': Men in Non-Traditional Occupations*, Newbury Park, Ca.: Sage, 152–67.

Arber, S. and Gilbert, N. 1989: Men: the forgotten carers. *Sociology*, 23 (1), 111–18.

Arber, S. and Ginn, J. 1992: In sickness and in health: care-giving, gender and the independence of elderly people. In C. Marsh and S. Arber (eds), 86–105.

Ardener, S. (ed.) 1981: *Women and Space*. London: Croom Helm.

Askham, J. 1984: *Identity and Stability in Marriage*. Cambridge: Cambridge University Press.

Backett, K.C. 1982: *Mothers and Fathers*. Basingstoke: Macmillan.

Bagguley, P. and Mann, K. 1992: Idle thieving bastards? Scholarly representation of the 'underclass'. *Work, Employment and Society*, 6 (1), 113–26.

Balbo, L. 1987: Crazy quilts: rethinking the welfare state debate from a womans point of view. In A. S. Sassoon (ed.), 45–71.

Barrett, M. 1980: *Womens Oppression Today*. London: Verso.

Barrett, M. and McIntosh, M. 1985. Ethnocentricism and socialist–feminist theory. *Feminist Review*, 20, 23–48.

Beardsworth, A. and Keil, T. 1992: The vegetarian option: varieties, conversions, motives and careers. *Sociological Review*, 40 (2), 253–93.

Beck, U. 1992: *Risk Society: Towards A New Modernity*. London: Sage.

Bell, C. 1968: *Middle-Class Families*. London: Routledge and Kegan Paul.

Bernardes, J. 1988: Founding the *New* 'Family Studies'. *Sociological Review*, 36 (i), 57–86.

Bernstein, B. 1971: *Classes, Codes and Controls*, vol. 1. London: Routledge and Kegan Paul.

Bertaux, D. and Thompson, P. (eds) 1994: *Between Generations: Family Models, Myths and Memories*. Oxford: Oxford University Press.

Bjornberg, U. 1995: Family policies in Europe: a feminist perspective. In L. Hantrais and M.-T. Letablier (eds), *The Family in Social Policy and Family Policy*, Loughborough: The Cross-National Research Group, Loughborough University of Technology, 57–68.

Blaxter, M. 1992: Inequality in health and the problem of time. *Medical Sociology News*, 18 (1), 12–24.

Blumberg, R.L. 1991a: Income under female versus male control: hypotheses from a theory of gender stratification and data from the Third World. In R.L. Blumberg (ed.), 97–127.

Blumberg, R.L. (ed.) 1991b: *Gender, Family and Economy: The Triple Overlap*. Newbury Park, Ca.: Sage.

Blumberg, R.L. and Coleman, M.T. 1989: A theory guided look at the gender balance of power in the American couple. *Journal of Family Issues*, 10 (2) 225–50.

Blumin, S.M. 1989: *The Emergence of the Middle Class: Social Experience in the American City*. Cambridge: Cambridge University Press.

Bocock, R. 1980: British sociologists and Freud: a sociological analysis of the absence of a relationship. In P. Abrams and P. Lewthwaite (eds), 479–505.

Bologh, R.W. 1990: *Love or Greatness: Max Weber and Masculine Thinking – A Feminist Inquiry*. London: Unwin Hyman.

Bornat, J., Pereira, C., Pilgrim, D. and Williams, S. (eds) 1993: *Community Care: A Reader*. Basingstoke: Open University/Macmillan.

Bott, E. 1971 (2nd edn): *Family and Social Network*. London: Tavistock.

Boulton, M.G. 1983: *On Being A Mother*. London: Tavistock.

Bourdieu, P. 1984: *Distinction: A Social Critique of the Judgement of Taste*. London: Routledge and Kegan Paul.

Bourdieu, P. 1990: *The Logic of Practice*. Cambridge: Polity Press.

Brannen, J., Dodd, K., Oakley, A. and Storey, P. (eds) 1994: *Young People, Health and Family Life*. Buckingham and Philadelphia: Open University Press.

Brannen, J. and Wilson, G. (eds) 1987: *Give and Take in Families*. London: Allen and Unwin.

Britten, N. and Heath, A. 1983: Women, men and social class. In E. Gamarnikow et al. (eds), *Gender, Class and Work*, London: Heinemann, 46–60.

Brown, G. and Harris, T. 1978: *Social Origins of Depression*. London: Tavistock.

Bryman, A., Bytheway, B., Allatt, P. and Keil, T. (eds) 1987: *Rethinking the Life Cycle*. Basingstoke: Macmillan.

Burgess, R.G. (ed.) 1986: *Key Variables in Social Investigation*. London: Routledge and Kegan Paul.

Bytheway, B. and Johnson, J. 1990: On defining ageism. *Critical Social Policy*, 29, 27–39.

Chafetz, J.S. 1991: The gender division of labor and the reproduction of female disadvantage: toward an integrated theory. In R.L. Blumberg (ed.), 74–95.

Chandler, J. 1991: *Women Without Husbands: An Exploration of the Margins of Marriage*. Basingstoke: Macmillan.

Chapman, D. 1955: *The Home and Social Status*. London: Routledge and Kegan Paul.

Charles, N. 1990: Women and class – a problematic relationship?. *Sociological Review*, 38 (1), 43–89.

Charles, N. and Kerr, M. 1988: *Women, Food and Families*. Manchester: Manchester University Press.

Cheal, D. 1988a: *The Gift Economy*. London: Routledge.

Cheal, D. 1988b: Relationships in time: ritual, social structure and the life course. In N. Denzin (ed.), *Studies in Symbolic Interaction*, vol. 9, New York: JAI Press Inc., 83–109.

Clark, D. 1993: 'With my body I thee worship' : the social construction of marital sex problems. In S. Scott and D. Morgan (eds), 22–34.

Clark. J., Modgil, C. and Modgil, J. (eds) 1990: *John H. Goldthorpe: Consensus and Controversy*. London: Falmer Press.

Clarke, L. 1995: Family care and changing family structure: bad news for the elderly? In I. Allen and E. Perkins (eds), 19–50.

Cohen, T.F. 1987: Remaking men: mens experiences becoming and being husbands and fathers and their implications for reconconceptualizing mens lives. *Journal of Family Issues*, 8, 57–77.

Collier, R. 1995: *Masculinity, Law and the Family*. London: Routledge.

Collins, R. 1991: Women and men in the class structure. In R.L. Blumberg (ed.), 52–73.

Connell, R.W. 1987: *Gender and Power*. Cambridge: Polity Press.

Connerton, P. 1989: *How Societies Remember*. Cambridge: Cambridge University Press.

Conway, M. 1990: *Autobiographical Memory: An Introduction*. Milton Keynes: Open University Press.

Cooley, C.H. 1909: *Social Organization*. New York: Scribner.

Cornwell, J. 1984: *Hard-Earned Lives*. London: Tavistock.

Cottle, T.J. 1976: *Perceiving Time: A Psychological Investigation with Men and Women*. New York: John Wiley.

Coward, N. 1986: *Autobiography*. London: Methuen.

Coxon, A.P.M., Davies, P.M. with Jones, C.L. 1986: *Images of Social Stratification: Occupational Structures and Class*. London: Sage.

Craib, I. 1995: Some comments on the sociology of emotions. *Sociology*, 29 (1), 151–58.

Crompton, R. 1986: Women and the service class. In R. Crompton and M. Mann (eds), 119–36.

Crompton, R. 1989: Class theory and gender. *British Journal of Sociology*, 40 (4), 565–87.

Crompton, R. 1993: *Class and Stratification: An Introduction to Current Debates*. Cambridge: Polity Press.

Crompton, R. and Mann, M. (eds) 1986: *Gender and Stratification*. Cambridge: Polity Press.

Crow, G. 1989: The use of the concept of 'strategy' in recent sociological literature. *Sociology*, 23 (1), 1–24.

Crow, G. and Allen, G. 1990: Constructing the domestic sphere: the emergence of the modern home in post-war Britain. In H. Corr and L. Jamieson (eds), *Politics of Everyday Life*, Basingstoke: Macmillan, 11–36.

Curthoys, A. 1993: Identity crisis: colonialism, nation and gender in Australian history. *Gender and History*, 5 (2), 165–76.

Dale, A. and Marsh, C. (eds) 1993: *The 1991 Census Users Guide*. London: HMSO.

Dalley, G. 1988: *Ideologies of Caring: Rethinking Community and Collectivism*. Basingstoke: Macmillan.

Davidoff, L and Hall, C. 1987: *Family Fortunes*. London: Hutchinson.

Davies, K. 1990: *Women, Time and the Weaving of the Strands of Everyday Life*. Aldershot: Avebury.

Davis, K. 1991: Critical sociology and gender relations. In K. Davis, M. Leijenaar and J. Oldersma (eds), 65–86.

Davis, K., Leijenaar, M. and Oldersma, J. (eds) 1991: *The Gender of Power*. London: Sage.

Deem, R. 1986: *All Work and No Play*. Milton Keynes: Open University Press.

Delphy, C. and Leonard, D. 1992: *Familiar Exploitation*. Cambridge: Polity Press.

Dennis, N., Henriques, F. and Slaughter, C. 1956: *Coal Is Our Life*. London: Tavistock.

Dickinson, J. and Russell, B. (ed.) 1986: *Family, Economy and State: The Social Reproduction Process Under Capitalism*. London: Croom Helm.

Dobash, R.E. and Dobash, R. 1979: *Violence Against Wives: A Case Against The Patriarchy*. London: Open Books.

Dobson, B., Beardsworth, A., Keil, T. and Walker, R. 1994: *Diet, Choice and Poverty*. London: Family Policy Studies Centre.

Duncombe, J. and Marsden, D. 1993: Love and intimacy: the gender division of emotions and 'emotion work'. Sociology, 27 (2), 221–42.

Dyhouse, C. 1986: Mothers and daughters in the middle-class home, c.1870–1914. In J. Lewis (ed.), 27–48.

Edgell, S. 1980: *Middle-Class Couples*. London: Allen and Unwin.

Edwards, R. and Ribbens, J. 1991: Meandering around 'strategy': A research note on strategic discourse in the lives of women. *Sociology*, 25 (3), 477–89.

Elder, G.H. 1978: Approaches to social change and the family. In J. Demos and S.S. Boocock (eds), *Turning Points: Historical and Sociological Essays on the Family*, Chicago: University of Chicago Press, 1–39.

Eldridge, J. 1980: *Recent British Sociology*. Basingstoke: Macmillan Reference Books.

Elliott, B. 1994: Biography, family history and the analysis of social change. In M. Drake (ed.), *Time, Family and Community: Perspectives on Family and Community History*. Oxford: Blackwell/Open University, 44–63.

England, P. and Farkas, G. 1986: *Households, Employment and Gender*. New York: Aldine.

Everingham, C. 1994: *Motherhood and Modernity*. Buckingham: Open University Press.

Evetts, J. 1988: Managing childcare and work responsibilities: the strategies of married women primary and infant headteachers. *Sociological Review*, 36 (3), 503–31.

Fenstermaker, S., West, C. and Zimmerman, D.H. 1991: Gender inequality: new conceptual terrain. In R.L. Blumberg (ed.), 289–307.

Finch, J. 1986: Age. In R.G. Burgess (ed.), 12–30.

Finch, J. 1989: *Family Obligations and Social Change*. Cambridge: Polity Press.

Finch, J. and Groves, D. 1980: Community care and the family: a case for equal opportunities?. *Journal of Social Policy*, 9 (4), 487–514.

Finch, J. and Hayes, L. 1994: Inheritance, death and the concept of the home. *Sociology*, 28 (2), 417–33.

Finch, J. and Mason, J. 1993: *Negotiating Family Responsibilities*. London: Routledge.

Fisher, M.F.K. 1991: *The Art of Eating*. Basingstoke: Macmillan.

Frankenberg, R. 1966: *Communities in Britain*. Harmondsworth: Penguin.

Gallie, D. (ed.) 1988: *Employment in Britain*. Oxford: Blackwell.

Gallie, D., Marsh, C. and Vogler, C. (eds) 1994: *Social Change and the Experience of Unemployment*. Oxford: Oxford University Press.

Gallie, D. and Vogler, C. 1994: Labour market deprivation, welfare and collectivism. In D. Gallie, C. Marsh and C. Vogler (eds), 299–366.

Gell, A. 1992: *The Anthropology of Time*. Oxford: Berg.

Ginn, J. 1993: Grey power: age-based organisations response to structured inequalities. *Critical Social Policy*, 38, 23–47.

Gittings, D. 1993 (2nd edn): *The Family in Question*. Basingstoke: Macmillan.

Glucksmann, M. 1986: In a class of their own? Women workers in the new industries in inter-war Britain. *Feminist Review*, 24, 7–39.

Goldthorpe, J.H. 1983: Women and class analysis: in defence of the conventional view. *Sociology*, 17 (4), 466–88.

Goldthorpe, J.H., Llewellyn, C. and Payne, C. 1980: *Social Mobility and Class Structure in Modern Britain*. Oxford: Oxford University Press.

Goldthorpe, J.H. and Marshall, G. 1992: The promising future of class analysis: a response to recent critiques. *Sociology*, 26 (3), 381–400.

Gould, J. 1977: *The Attack on Higher Education: Marxism and Radical Penetration*. London: Institute for the Study of Conflict.

Graetz, B. 1991: The class location of families: a refined classification of analysis. *Sociology*, 25 (1), 101–18.

Graham, H. 1983: Caring: a labour of love. In J. Finch and D. Groves (eds), *A Labour of Love: Women, Work and Caring*, London: Routledge and Kegan Paul, 13–50.

Graham, H. 1985: *Caring for the Family*. Milton Keynes: Open University Press.

Graham, H. 1987: Being poor: perceptions and coping strategies of lone mothers. In J. Brannen and G. Wilson (eds), 56–74.

Graham, H. 1993a: *Hardship and Health in Womens Lives*. New York and London: Harvester/Wheatsheaf.

Graham, H. 1993b: Feminist perspectives on caring. In J. Bornat et al. (eds), 124–33.

Gregson, N. and Lowe, M. 1994: *Serving the Middle Classes: Waged Domestic Labour in Britain in the 1980s and 1990s*. London: Routledge.

Grundy, E. 1995: Demographic influences on the future of family care. In I. Allen and E. Perkins (eds), 1–18.

Gullestad, M. 1984: *Kitchen Table Society*. Cambridge: Cambridge University Press.

Gullestad, M. 1992: *The Art of Social Relations: Essays on Culture, Social Action and Everyday Life in Modern Norway*. Oslo: Scandinavian University Press.

Gunaratnum, Y. 1993: Breaking the silence: Asian carers in Britain. In J. Bornat et al. (eds), 114–23.

Haas, L. 1990: Gender equality and social policy: implications of a study of parental leave in Sweden. *Journal of Family Issues*, 11 (4), 401–23.

Halle, D. 1984: *America's Working Man: Work, Home and Politics Among Blue-Collar Property Owners*. Chicago: University of Chicago Press.

Handy, C. 1984: *The Future of Work*. Oxford: Blackwell.

Hareven, T.K. (ed.) 1978: *Transitions: The Family and Life Course in Historical Retrospect*. New York: Academic Press.

Harris, C. 1987: The individual and society: a processual view. In A. Bryman et al. (eds), 17–29.

Harris, C. and Morris, L. 1986: Households, labour markets and the position of women. In R. Crompton and M. Mann (eds), 86–96.

Hartmann, H. 1983: Capitalism, patriarchy and job segregation by sex. In E. Abel and E.K. Abel (eds), *The 'Signs' Reader: Women, Gender and Scholarship*, Chicago: University of Chicago Press, 193–228.

Haskey, J. 1984: Social class and socio-economic differentials in divorce in England and Wales. *Population Studies*, 38, 419–38.

Henshall, C. and McGuire, J. 1986: Gender development. In M. Richards and M. Light (eds), 135–66.

Hernes, H. M. 1988: *Welfare State and Woman Power: Essays in State Feminism*. Oxford: Oxford University Press.

Hewitt, P. 1993: *About Time: The Revolution in Work and Family Life*. London: Rivers Oram Press.

Hochschild, A.R. 1983: *The Managed Heart: Commercialization of Human Feeling*. Berkeley: University of California Press.

Hoggart, R. 1958: *The Uses of Literacy*. Harmondsworth: Penguin.

Holmilla, M., Mustonen, H. and Rannik, E. 1990: Alcohol use and its control in Finnish and Soviet Marriages. *British Journal of Addiction*, 85 (4), 509–20.

Huber, J. and Spitze, G. 1983: *Sex Stratification: Children, Housework and Jobs*. New York: Academic Press.

Hughes, C. 1991: *Stepparents: Wicked or Wonderful?* Aldershot: Avebury.

Humphries, J. 1982: The working-class family: a Marxist perspective. In

J.B. Elshtain (ed.), *The Family in Political Thought*, Brighton: Harvester Press.

Hutson, S. and Cheung, W.-Y. 1992: Saturday jobs: sixth-formers in the labour market and family. In C. Marsh and S. Arber (eds), 45–62.

Illich, I. 1983: *Gender*. London: Boyers.

Jackson, B. and Marsden, D. 1966 (1962): *Education and the Working Class*. Harmondsworth: Penguin.

Jackson, S. 1993: Even sociologists fall in love: an exploration in the sociology of emotions. *Sociology*, 27, 201–20.

James, A. 1990: The good, the bad and the delicious: the role of confectionery in British society. *Sociological Review*, 38 (4), 666–88.

James, A. and Prout, A. (eds) 1990: *Constructing and Reconstructing Childhood*. London: Falmer Press.

James, N. 1989: Emotional labour: skill and work in the social regulation of feelings. *Sociological Review*, 37 (1), 15–42.

Jamieson, L. 1986: Limited resources and limiting conventions: working-class mothers and daughters in urban Scotland, *c.* 1890–1925. In J. Lewis (ed.), 49–71.

Johnson, P., Coward, C. and Thomson, D. 1989: *Workers Versus Pensioners: Intergenerational Conflict in an Ageing World*. Manchester: Manchester University Press.

Jones, G. 1988: Integrating process and structure in the concept of youth: a case for secondary analysis. *Sociological Review*, 36 (4), 706–32.

Jones, G. 1992: Short-term reciprocity in parent–child economic exchanges. In C. Marsh and S. Arber (eds), 26–44.

Jones, G. 1995: *Family Support for Young People*, London: Family Policy Studies Centre.

Jordan, B., James, S., Kay, H. and Redley, M. 1992: *Trapped in Poverty? Labour-Market Decisions in Low Income Households*. London: Routledge.

Jordan, B., Redley, M. and James, S. 1994: *Putting the Family First: Identities, Decisions and Citizenship*. London: UCL Press.

Kantor, D. and Lehr, W. 1973: *Inside the Family*. San Francisco: Jossey Bass Inc.

Knights, D. and Morgan, G. 1990: The concept of strategy in sociology: a note of dissent. *Sociology*, 24, 475–84.

Korbin, J.E. (ed.) 1981: *Child Abuse and Neglect: Cross-Cultural Perspectives*. Berkeley: University of California Press.

Kranichfeld, M. L. 1987: Rethinking family power. *Journal of Family Issues*, 8 (1), 42–56.

La Fontaine, J. 1986: An anthropological perspective on children in social worlds. In M. Richards and P. Light (eds), 10–30.

Land, H. and Rose, H. 1985: Compulsory altruism for some or an altruistic society for all?. In P. Bean, J. Ferris and D. Whynes (eds), *In Defence of Welfare*, London: Tavistock, 74–98.

Lawson, A. 1988: *Adultery: An Analysis of Love and Betrayal*. Oxford: Oxford University Press.

Leira, A. 1992: *Welfare States and Working Mothers*. Cambridge: Cambridge University Press.

Leiulfsrud, H. and Woodward, A.E. 1988: 'Women at class crossroads': a critical reply to Erikson and Goldthorpe's note. *Sociology*, 22 (4), 555–62.

Levine, D. 1977: *Family Formation in the Age of Nascent Capitalism*. New York: Academic Press.

Lewis, J. (ed.) 1986: *Labour and Love: Women's Experiences of Work and Family, 1850–1940*. Oxford: Blackwell.

Lewis, J., Clark, D. and Morgan, D. 1992: *'Whom God Hath Joined Together': The Work of Marriage Guidance*. London: Routledge.

Lockwood, D. 1958: *The Black-Coated Worker*. London: Allen and Unwin.

Lopata, H.Z. 1971: *Occupation Housewife*. New York: Oxford University Press.

Loudon, J.B. 1977: On body products. In J. Blacking (ed.), *The Anthropology of the Body*, London: Academic Press, 161–78.

Lynch, K. 1989: Solidary labour: its nature and marginalization. *Sociological Review*, 37 (1), 1–14.

Mannheim, K. 1952: The problem of generations. In P. Kecskemeti (ed.), *Essays on the Sociology of Knowledge by Karl Mannheim*, London: Routledge and Kegan Paul.

Margolin, L. 1992: Beyond maternal blame: physical child abuse as a phenomenon of gender. *Journal of Family Issues*, 13 (3), 410–23.

Marsh, C. and Arber, S. (eds) 1992: *Families and Households: Divisions and Change*. Basingstoke: Macmillan.

Marshall, G. 1990a: *In Praise of Sociology*. London: Unwin Hyman.

Marshall, G. 1990b: John Goldthorpe and class analysis. In J. Clark, C. Modgil and J. Modgil (eds), 51–64.

Marshall, G., Rose, D., Newby, H. and Vogler, C. 1990: *Social Class in Modern Britain*. London: Unwin Hyman.

Martin, B. 1984: 'Mother wouldn't like it': housework as magic. *Theory, Culture and Society*, 2 (2), 19–36.

Martin, J. and Roberts, C. 1984: *Working Women in Recession*. Oxford: Oxford University Press.

McCrone, D. 1994: Getting by and making out in Kirkaldy. In M. Anderson, F. Bechofer and J. Gershuny (eds), 68–99.

McKee, L. 1987: Households during unemployment: the resourcefulness of the unemployed. In J. Brannen and G. Wilson (eds), 96–116.

McKee, L. and Bell, C. 1986: His unemployment, her problem: the domestic and marital consequences of male unemployment. In S. Allen et al. (eds), 134–49.

McRae, S. 1986: *Cross-Class Families*. Oxford: Oxford University Press.

McRae, S. 1990: Women and class analysis. In J. Clark, C. Modgil and J. Modgil (eds), 117–34.

Melbin, M. 1987: *Night as Frontier*. New York: Free Press.

Mennell, S. 1985: *All Manners of Food*. Oxford: Blackwell.

Mennell, S., Murcott, A. and Van Otterloo, A. H. 1992: *The Sociology of Food*. London: Sage.

Meyer, J. 1991: Power and love: conflicting conceptual schemata. In K. Davis, M. Leijenaar and J. Oldersma (eds), 21–41.

Mills, C. Wright 1959: *The Sociological Imagination*. Harmondsworth: Penguin.

Morgan, D.H.J. 1975: *Social Theory and the Family*. London: Routledge and Kegan Paul.

Morgan, D.H.J. 1985: *The Family, Politics and Social Theory*. London: Routledge and Kegan Paul.

Morgan, D.H.J. 1986: Gender. In R. Burgess (ed.), 31–53.

Morgan, D.H.J. 1989: Strategies and sociologists: a comment on Crow. *Sociology*, 23 (1), 25–30.

Morgan, D.H.J. 1992: *Discovering Men*. London: Routledge.

Morris, L. 1990: *The Workings of the Household*. Cambridge: Polity Press.

Morrison, B. 1993: *And When Did You Last See Your Father?*. London: Granta.

Munthesius, S. 1982: *The English Terraced House*. New Haven and London: Yale University Press.

Murcott, A. 1983: Cooking and the cooked: a note on the domestic preparation of meals. In A. Murcott (ed.), The Sociology of Food and Eating, Aldershot: Gower, 178–93.

Murcott, A. 1993: Purity and pollution: body management and the social place of infancy. In S. Scott and D. Morgan (eds), 122–34.

Nash, C. 1993: Remapping and renaming: new cartographies of identity, gender and landscape in Ireland. *Feminist Review*, 44, 39–57.

Netting, R.M., Wilk, R.R. and Arnould, E.J. (eds) 1984: *Households: Comparative and Historical Studies of the Domestic Group*. Berkeley: University of California Press.

Newby, H., Vogler, C., Rose, D. and Marshall, G. 1985: From class structure to class action: British working-class politics in the 1980s. In B. Roberts, R. Finnigan and D. Gallie (eds), 86–102.

Newson, J. and Newson, E. 1965 (1963): *Patterns of Infant Care in an Urban Community*. Harmondsworth: Penguin.

Newson, J. and Newson, E. 1970 (1968): Four Years Old in an Urban Community. Harmondsworth: Penguin.

Noddings, N. 1984: *Caring: A Feminist Approach to Ethics and Moral Education*. Berkeley: University of California Press.

Oakley, A. 1974: *The Sociology of Housework*. Oxford: Martin Robertson.

Oakley, A. 1989: Womens studies in British sociology: to end at our beginning?. *British Journal of Sociology*, 40 (3), 442–70.

Oakley, A. and Rajan, L. 1991: Social class and social support: the same or different?. *Sociology*, 25 (1), 31–60.

O'Connor, P. 1991: Women's confidants outside marriage: shared or competing sources of intimacy?. *Sociology*, 25 (2), 241–54.

Oliver, P. 1981: The galleon on the front door. In P. Oliver, I. Davis and I. Bentley (eds), 155–172.

Oliver, P., Davis, I. and Bentley, I. (eds) 1981: *Dunroamin: The Suburban Semi and its Enemies*. London: Barrie and Jenkins.

O'Neill, J. 1985: *Five Bodies: The Human Shape of Modern Society*. Ithica and London: Cornell University Press.

Osborn, A.F. 1987: Assessing the social-economic status of families. *Sociology*, 21 (3), 429–48.

Pahl, J. 1990: Household spending, personal spending and the control of money in marriage. *Sociology*, 24 (1), 119–38.

Pahl, R.E. 1984: *Divisions of Labour*. Oxford: Blackwell.

Pahl, R.E. and Wallace, C. 1985: Forms of work and privatisation on the Isle of Sheppey. In B. Roberts, R. Finnegan and D. Gallie (eds), 368–86.

Parker, G. and Lawton, D. 1994: *Different Types of Care, Different Types of Carer*. London: HMSO.

Parker, R. 1981: Tending and social policy. In E. Goldberg and S. Hatch (eds), *A New Look at the Personal Social Services*, London: Policy Studies Institute, 17–34.

Parkin, F. 1972: *Class Inequality and Political Order: Social Stratification in Capitalist and Communist Societies*. St Albans: Paladin.

Parkin, F. 1974: Strategies of social closure in class formation. In F. Parkin (ed.), *The Social Analysis of Class Structure*, London: Tavistock, 1–18.

Paterson, F.M.S. 1988: Schooling the family. *Sociology*, 22 (1), 65–86.

Payne, J. 1987: Does unemployment run in families? Some findings from the General Household Survey. *Sociology*, 21 (2), 199–214.

Pennington, S. and Westover, B. 1989: *A Hidden Workforce: Homeworkers in England, 1850–1985*. Basingstoke: Macmillan.

Perin, C. 1977: *Everything in its Place: Social Order and Land Use in America*. Princeton: Princeton University Press.

Phillips, R. 1991: *Untying the Knot: A Short History of Divorce*. Cambridge: Canto.

Pickvance, C.G. and Pickvance, K. 1995: The role of family help in the housing decisions of young people. *Sociological Review*, 43 (1), 123–49.

Prout, A. 1988: 'Off school sick': mothers accounts of school sickness absence. *Sociologcial Review*, 36 (4), 765–89.

Purcell, K., Wood, S., Waton, A. and Allen, S. (eds) 1986: *The Changing Experience of Employment: Restructuring and Recession*. Basingstoke: Macmillan.

Rakoff, R.M. 1977: Ideology in everyday life: the meaning of the house. *Politics and Society*, 7, 85–104.

Redclift, N. 1985: The contested domain, gender, accumulation and the labour process. In N. Redclift and E. Mingione (eds), *Beyond Employment: Household, Gender and Subsistence*, Oxford: Blackwell, 92–126.

Reiger, K. 1985: *The Disenchantment of the Home: Modernizing the Australian Family, 1880–1940*. Oxford: Oxford University Press.

Resources Within Households 1985: *Register of Research*. London: Thomas Coram Research Unit.

Rex, J. and Moore, R. 1967: *Race, Community and Conflict: A Study of Sparkbrook*. Oxford: Oxford University Press.

Richards, L. 1990: *Nobody's Home: Dreams and Realities in a New Suburb*. Melbourne: Oxford University Press.

Richards, M. and Light, P. (eds) 1986: *Children of Social Worlds: Development in a Social Context*. Cambridge Mass.: Harvard University Press.

Roberts, B., Finnegan, R. and Gallie, D. (eds) 1985: *New Approaches to Economic Life*. Manchester: Manchester University Press.

Rodger, J.R. 1991: Family structure and the moral politics of caring. *Sociological Review*, 39 (4), 799–822.

Rosenblum, K.E. 1986: Leaving as a wife, leaving as a mother: ways of relinquishing custody. *Journal of Family Issues*, 7 (2), 197–214.

Rubin, G. 1975: The traffic in women: notes on the 'political economy' of sex. In R.R. Reiter (ed.), *Toward an Anthropology of Women*, New York: Monthly Review Press, 157–210.

Rustin, M. 1991: *The Good Society and the Inner World*. London: Verso.

Samuel, R. 1994: *Theatres of Memory*. London: Verso.

Sanday, P.R. 1981: *Female Power and Male Dominance*. Cambridge: Cambridge University Press.

Saradamoni, K. (ed.) 1992: *Finding the Household: Conceptual and Methodological Issues*. New Delhi, Newbury Park and London: Sage.

Sassoon, A.S. (ed.) 1987: *Women and the State*. London: Hutchinson.

Saunders, P. 1990: *A Nation of Home Owners*. London: Unwin Hyman.

Savage, M., Barlow, J., Dickens, P. and Fielding, T. (eds) 1992: *Property, Bureaucracy and Culture: Middle-Class Formations in Contemporary Britain*. London: Routledge.

Schlegel, A. 1977: Toward a theory of sexual stratification. In A. Schlegel (ed.), *Sexual Stratification: A Cross-Cultural View*, New York: Columbia University Press, 1–40.

Schumpeter, J. 1955: *Imperialism and Social Classes*. New York: Meridian Books.

Schutz, A. 1945: The homecomer. *American Journal of Sociology*, vol. L (4), 363–76.

Scott, A.M. (ed.) 1994: *Gender Segregation and Social Change*. Oxford: Oxford University Press.

Scott, A.M. and Burchell, B. 1994: 'And never the twain shall meet?' Gender segregation and work histories. In A. Scott (ed.), 121–56.

Scott, S. and Morgan, D. (eds) 1993: *Body Matters*. London: Taylor and Francis.

Seeley, J.R., Sim, R.A. and Loosley, E.W. 1956: *Crestwood Heights*. Toronto: University of Toronto Press.

Segalen, M. 1986: *Historical Anthropology of the Family*. Cambridge: Cambridge University Press.

Seidler, V.J. 1994: *Unreasonable Men: Masculinity and Social Theory*. London: Routledge.

Shaver, S. 1993/4: Body rights, social rights and the liberal welfare state. *Critical Social Policy*, 39, 66–93.

Shilling, C. 1993: *The Body and Social Theory*. London: Sage.

Sklair, L. 1981: Sociologies and Marxisms: the odd couples. In P. Abrams et al. (eds), 151–71.

Smith, D.J. 1992: Defining the underclass. In D.T. Smith (ed.), *Understanding the Underclass*, London: Policy Studies Institute, 3–8.

Spark, M. 1992: *Curriculum Vitae*. Harmondsworth: Penguin.

Stacey, J. 1991: *Brave New Families*. New York: Basic Books.

Stacey, M. 1981: The division of labour revisited or overcoming the two Adams. In P. Abrams et al., 172–90.

Stanley, L. 1992: *The Auto/Biographical 'I'*. Manchester: Manchester University Press.

Thatcher, M. 1992: Don't undo my work. *Newsweek*, 27. 4. 95, 14–15.

Thomas, C. 1993: De-constructing concepts of care. *Sociology*, 27 (4), 649–69.

Thorne, B. 1993: *Gender Play: Girls and Boys in School*. Buckingham: Open University Press.

Thorogood, N. 1987: Race, class and gender: the politics of housework. In J. Brannen and G. Wilson (eds), 18–41.

Tilly, L. and Scott, J. 1978: *Women, Work and the Family*. New York: Holt, Rinehart and Winston.

Townsend, P. 1979: *Poverty in the United Kingdom*. Harmondsworth: Penguin.

Traustadottir, R. 1991: Mothers who care: gender, disability and family life. *Journal of Family Issues*, 12 (2), 211–28.

Turbin, C. 1989: Beyond dichotomies: interdependence in mid-nineteenth-century working-class families in the United States. *Gender and History*, 1 (3), 293–308.

Turner, B.S. 1984: *The Body and Society*. Oxford: Blackwell.

Turner, B.S. 1992: *Regulating Bodies: Essays in Medical Sociology*. London: Routledge.

Urry, J. 1990: Time and space in Giddens's social theory. In C. Bryant and D. Jary (eds), *Giddens's Theory of Structuration: A Critical Appreciation*, London: Routledge, 160–75.

Vogel, U. 1994: Marriage and the boundaries of citizenship. In B. Van Steenbergen (ed.), *The Condition of Citizenship*, London: Sage, 76–89.

Vogler, C. 1994: Segregation, sexism and labour supply. In A.M. Scott (ed.), 39–79.

Wadsworth, M. 1986: Evidence from three birth cohort studies for long-term and cross-generational effects on the development of children. In M. Richards and P. Light (eds), 116–34.

Waerness, K. 1987: On the rationality of caring. In A.S. Sassoon (ed.), 207–34.

Walby, S. 1986: *Patriarchy at Work*. Cambridge: Polity Press.

Walby, S. 1989: Theorising patriarchy. *Sociology*, 23 (2), 213–34.

Walby, S. 1990: *Theorising Patriarchy*. Oxford: Blackwell.

Walby, S. 1994: Is citizenship gendered? *Sociology*, 28 (2), 379–95.

Wallace, C. 1993: Reflections on the concept of 'strategy'. In D. Morgan and L. Stanley (eds), *Debates in Sociology*, Manchester: Manchester University Press, 94–117.

Wallerstein, I. and Smith, J. 1990: Households as an institution of the world economy. In J. Sprey (ed.), *Fashioning Family Theory: New Approaches*, Newbury Park, Ca.: Sage, 34–50.

Wallman, S. 1984: *Eight London Households*. London: Tavistock.

Warde, A. 1990: Household work strategies and forms of labour: conceptual and empirical issues. *Work, Employment and Society*, 4 (4), 495–516.

Warde, A. and Hetherington, K. 1994: English households and routine food practices. *Sociological Review*, 42 (4), 758–78.

Watson, S. 1984: Definitions of homelessness: a feminist perspective. *Critical Social Policy*, 11, 60–73.

Wenger, G.C. 1984: *The Supportive Network*. London: Allen and Unwin.

Werbner, P. 1993: *The Migration Process: Capital, Gifts and Offerings among British Pakistani*. New York and Oxford: Berg.

Wheelock, J. 1990: *Husbands at Home: The Domestic Economy in Post-Industrial Society*. London: Routledge.

Wilk, R.R. 1989: Decision making and resource flows within the household: beyond the black box. In R.R. Wilk (ed.), *The Household Economy*, Oxford: Westview Press, 23–54.

Wilk, R.R. and Netting, R.M. 1984: Households: changing forms and functions. In R.M. Netting, R.R. Wilk and E.J. Arnould (eds), 1–28.

Wilson, G. 1987: Money: patterns of responsibility and irresponsibility in marriage. In J. Brannen and G. Wilson (eds), 136–154.

Wilson, P. and Pahl, R.E. 1988: The changing social construct of the family. *Sociological Review*, 36 (2), 233–72.

Witz, A. 1992: *Professions and Patriarchy*. London: Routledge.

Worsley, P. 1970: *Introducing Sociology*. Harmondsworth: Penguin.

Wright, E.O. 1993: Explanation and emancipation in Marxism and feminism. *Sociological Theory*, 11 (1), 39–54.

Yeandle, S. 1984: *Women's Working Lives: Patterns and Strategies*. London: Tavistock.

Young, M. and Willmott, P. 1962 (rev. edn): *Family and Kinship in East London*. Harmondsworth: Penguin.

Zaretsky, E. 1982: The place of the family in the origin of the welfare state. In B. Thorne and M. Yalom (eds), *Rethinking the Family: Some Feminist Questions*, New York: Longman, 188–224.

Zukin, S. 1988 (1982): *Loft Living: Culture and Capital in Urban Change*. London: Radius.

Index